ROMAN MARYPORT

AND ITS SETTING

ROMAN MARYPORT
AND ITS SETTING

ESSAYS IN MEMORY OF MICHAEL G. JARRETT

EDITED BY R. J. A. WILSON

PUBLISHED ON BEHALF OF THE

TRUSTEES OF THE SENHOUSE ROMAN MUSEUM, MARYPORT

BY THE CUMBERLAND AND WESTMORLAND
ANTIQUARIAN & ARCHAEOLOGICAL SOCIETY

CUMBERLAND AND WESTMORLAND
ANTIQUARIAN & ARCHAEOLOGICAL SOCIETY
EXTRA SERIES VOLUME XXVIII

The Editor of this volume and the Trustees of the Senhouse Roman Museum acknowledge with gratitude financial assistance received from the following, without which the publication of this volume would not have been possible:

HISTORIC SCOTLAND
THE MOUSWALD TRUST
THE ROMAN RESEARCH TRUST
THE ROYAL COMMISSION ON THE HISTORICAL MONUMENTS OF ENGLAND

First published in Great Britain 1997
© individual authors 1997
ISBN 1-873124-22-8

No part of this volume may be reproduced
or transmitted in any form, or by any means,
electronic or mechanical, including photocopy,
or stored in a retrieval system, without prior
written permission of the publisher

This book is set in Palatino 10/12pt
Designed by Charlotte Westbrook Wilson
Printed in Great Britain by Technical Print Services Ltd, Nottingham

Contents

	Acknowledgements	7
	Abbreviations	9
	Michael Grierson Jarrett (1934-1994)	11
	Bibliography of the published writings of M. G. Jarrett	13

Part 1: Roman Maryport

1	Maryport from the first to the fourth centuries: some current problems *R. J. A. Wilson*	17
2	Maryport and the Flavian conquest of North Britain *I. D. Caruana*	40
3	The earthworks of the Maryport fort: an analytical field survey by the Royal Commission on the Historical Monuments of England *Amy Lax and Keith Blood*	52
4	The regiments stationed at Maryport and their commanders *David J. Breeze*	67
5	A note on the Maryport altars *J. C. Mann*	90
6	The Maryport altars: some first thoughts *P. R. Hill*	92
7	The women of Roman Maryport *Lindsay Allason-Jones*	105
8	The stone sculptures *J. C. N. Coulston*	112
9	Roman coins from Maryport *David Shotter*	132

Part 2: Maryport and the Senhouses

10   Senhouse of Netherhall – 1726 Achievement of Arms: recovery of an eighteenth-century masterwork
Brian Ashmore   141

11   George Senhouse of Maryport 1739-1793
Mary E. Burkett   148

The Senhouse family of Netherhall, Maryport (family tree)   160
List of contributors   161
List of illustrations   162
Index   164

Acknowledgements

The preparation of a multi-author book of this kind always requires the help and co-operation of many people. I am grateful to the Trustees of the Senhouse Roman Museum for entrusting me with the task of editing this book, which has been a labour of love, and for their continued support, both moral and financial: in particular David Breeze, Ian Caruana and Lindsay Allason-Jones have all in their different ways assisted me beyond the call of duty. All the contributors, however, deserve my thanks for their cheerful co-operation and patience. I am also grateful to those scholars who, in addition to the contributors, have provided illustrations, namely Robert Bewley (Swindon), Barri Jones (Manchester), Bill Manning (Cardiff), Timothy Potter (British Museum), and Jutta Ronke (Stuttgart). Charles Benson, Keeper of Early Printed Books at Trinity College, Dublin, kindly answered a query about the copy of Camden's *Britannia* in his care.

The abbreviated Senhouse family tree which appears on page 160 was prepared from a more detailed study by C. L. Randall, secured through the good offices of Mary Burkett, and has been checked and emended by David Breeze and Brian Ashmore. I am also grateful to the Administrators of the Haverfield Bequest (Oxford) and to their chairman, Dr Alan Bowman, for permission to reproduce Figs. 4.10, 4.11, 6.2, 6.3, and the drawing of the Setlocenia altar which appears on the half-title page and at the head of each chapter and elsewhere (such as on this page).

A special word of thanks must be reserved for the Roman Research Trust and for the Mouswald Trust, for their most generous publication grants without which publication of this book at a realistic price would simply not have been possible. The Cumberland and Westmorland Antiquarian & Archaeological Society kindly agreed to accept the volume for their Extra Series. Before they and the Mouswald Trust came to their decisions they commissioned independent refereeing of the book, which Dr Lawrence Keppie and Dr Brian Dobson kindly agreed to undertake; the Editor acknowledges with gratitude the comments of these referees which were passed to him, suggestions for improvement which have been incorporated into the final text. I also gratefully acknowledge the grants made by RCHME and Historic Scotland towards the costs of producing Chapters 3 and 4 respectively.

Compilation of both the bibliography of Mike Jarrett's publications and this book's index was undertaken by myself as editor. Charlotte Westbrook Wilson spent many hours designing the book's layout to her customary high professional standards, and I am grateful to her for her infinite patience and meticulous care. Paul Roper of Technical Print Services, Nottingham, devoted equal attention to detail in seeing the book through the press.

My final words of thanks, however, are reserved for those without whom this book would have never come into being – to Lt Cdr Brian Ashmore, formerly Curator of the Senhouse Collection, who single-handedly saved the Collection for posterity after the death of Roger Senhouse in 1970, and in particular after the Netherhall fire of 1973; and to the present owner of the Collection, Mr Joseph Scott-Plummer, now of Kelso, Roxburghshire, whose generosity has placed the bulk of the Senhouse Collection on loan to the Senhouse Roman Museum at Maryport, so making this important collection of sculptural and epigraphic material available to the public for the first time.

R. J. A. Wilson *July 1997*

Abbreviations

AA	*Archaeologia Aeliana*		3 vols. in 5 [ed. H. Dessau] (Berlin 1892-1916)
AE	*L'Année épigraphique*		
BAR	*British Archaeological Reports*	JRS	*Journal of Roman Studies*
CIL	*Corpus Inscriptionum Latinarum*	LRBC	P. V. Hill, R. A. G. Carson and J. P. C. Kent, *Late Roman Bronze Coinage* (London 1960)
CSIR	*Corpus Signorum Imperii Romani, Great Britain*		
	1.1 E. J. Phillips, *Corbridge, Hadrian's Wall East of the North Tyne* (London 1977)	LS	J. C. Bruce, *Lapidarium Septentrionale* (Newcastle upon Tyne 1875)
	1.4 L. J. F. Keppie and B. Arnold, *Scotland* (London 1984)	PSAS	*Proceedings of the Society of Antiquaries of Scotland*
	1.5 R. J. Brewer, *Wales* (London 1986)	RCHME	*Royal Commission on the Historical Monuments of England*
	1.6 J. C. Coulston and E. J. Phillips, *Hadrian's Wall West of the North Tyne, and Carlisle* (London 1988)	RE	A. Pauly and G. Wissowa (eds.), *Real-Encyclopädie der klassischen Altertumswissenschaft*
		RIB	R. G. Collingwood and R. P. Wright, *Roman Inscriptions in Britain* I (Oxford 1965; 2nd. ed. Stroud 1995)
CW	*Transactions of the Cumberland and Westmorland Antiquarian & Archaeological Society* (CW^1 for 1st series, CW^2 for second series)	RIC	*Roman Imperial Coinage*
		RRC	M. H. Crawford, *Roman Republican Coinage* (Cambridge 1974)
ILS	*Inscriptiones Latinae selectae,*		

Michael Grierson Jarrett (1934-1994)

Michael Grierson Jarrett
1934-1994

This book is a collection of essays by his friends and colleagues in memory of the late Mike Jarrett, whose premature death in November 1994 at the age of 60 has robbed Romano-British studies of a distinguished practitioner. A Lancastrian by birth, he went on from Manchester Grammar School to the University of Durham, where as a history student he fell under the spell of Eric Birley, who fired him with an interest in Roman epigraphy and the Roman army which were to stay with him all his life. It was also due to Birley that Mike's associations with Maryport began, for it was at his mentor's prompting that he took the site as the subject of his undergraduate dissertation. Finds from Maryport also formed the subject of his earliest articles, published in 1954 when the precocious young scholar was still only twenty. Other problems of the northern frontier were soon to occupy him, with excavations at Haltonchesters on Hadrian's Wall, at Ebchester in its hinterland, and elsewhere; but the geographical focus of his work, although not its principal themes, changed with his appointment in 1960 to a teaching post in what was then University College Cardiff. For the next eight years he threw himself into tackling the problems of the Roman army in Wales, aided by a series of carefully planned small-scale research excavations designed to find answers to specific queries. This work culminated in the publication in 1969 of his extensively revised and rewritten edition of V. E. Nash-Williams' *The Roman Frontier in Wales*, a book which, although now in need of further revision, remains fundamental to the study of Roman Wales. But Maryport was not forgotten during all this energetic activity, and when the opportunity arose to excavate in the Roman fort, in 1966, he seized it eagerly. The publication of these excavations and his other thoughts on Maryport, in *Maryport: a Roman fort and its garrison* (1976), remains a definitive statement about the site. The present volume, in presenting further research on Maryport in the context of current scholarship, is intended as a supplement to, not a replacement for, Mike's 1976 book.

But Mike's involvement with Maryport did not end with his 1976 publication. In 1970, the owner of the fort site Roger Senhouse, whose encouragement had been instrumental to the success of the 1966 excavations, died. He was the last in a distinguished line of Senhouses whose continued interest in the fort and its antiquities over successive generations had resulted in the careful preservation of the Roman inscribed and sculptured stones from the site, and it is wholly appropriate that two of the contributions to this volume concern new research on different aspects of the history of the Senhouse family. On discovery, each of the Roman stones had been transferred to the Senhouse family home at Netherhall, on the eastern outskirts of Maryport. In 1965 the stones had been removed from the house to a coachhouse in the grounds, pending a decision on their future. Eight years later, and three years after Roger Senhouse's death, a disastrous fire swept through Netherhall. The house, already in poor condition before the fire, was now beyond repair, and a decision was taken to demolish it. The role played throughout this time by Lt Cdr Brian Ashmore, a Maryport resident and a contributor to this volume, was crucial in saving the stones for posterity. The coachhouse remained as an increasingly unsatisfactory and vulnerable temporary shelter for the Senhouse Collection: a new and permanent home for the stones had to be found urgently.

The best way forward, it was decided, was the establishment of the Senhouse Museum Trust, which was eventually created in 1985 under the Chairmanship of the late Professor Jocelyn Toynbee. Along with Professor Sir Ian Richmond (whose untimely death in 1965 had robbed Maryport archaeology of another major champion – he had intended to lead the 1966 excavations in the fort), Professor Toynbee had for many years been active in raising the awareness of the plight of the Collection. Ill health forced her to relinquish the Chairmanship soon afterwards (she became the Trust's first and only Patron), and Mike was the obvious choice to succeed her. With characteristic energy and foresight he drove the project forward, surmounting considerable financial and practical obstacles along the way. With the help of Cdr Ashmore, a nineteenth-century coastal battery alongside the Roman fort was secured as an eminently suitable home for the museum, and through the generosity of the present owner of the collection, Roger Senhouse's heir Mr J. Scott Plummer, the Collection was made available on loan. Eventually in 1990 the Senhouse Roman Museum opened its doors to the public. That the project was crowned with success was due in no small way to Mike's boundless enthusiasm and sheer determination.

This is not the place to dwell on Mike Jarrett's many other achievements – his influential role, as Lecturer and later as Professor, in teaching and administration at University College Cardiff; his important excavations of an Iron Age and Roman farmstead at Whitton in South Glamorgan; his no less important excavations of a deserted medieval village at West Whelpington in Northumberland; his many contributions to learned journals. The list of his principal publications given below reflects something of the range and variety of his interests. Maryport, however, occupied a special place in his affections, and is therefore a very apposite subject for a book dedicated to his memory. With Mike Jarrett's passing Romano-British studies have lost a rigorous and productive scholar, and those who knew him have lost a perceptive, witty and genial friend.

R. J. A. Wilson

Bibliography of the published writings of M. G. Jarrett

1954
'A Christian monogram from Maryport', CW^2 54 (1954), 268-70
'A Roman mortar from Maryport', ibid. 270-1
'The coin', in R. L. Bellhouse, 'Roman sites on the Cumberland coast', ibid. 28-55, at 49-50

1958
'Excavations at Maiden Castle, Durham, in 1956', *Transactions of the Durham Architectural and Archaeological Society* 11.1-2 (1958), 124-7
'The pre-Hadrianic occupation of Roman Maryport', CW^2 58 (1958), 63-7
(with B. Dobson) 'Excavations at Binchester, 1955', ibid. 115-24

1959
'The defences of the Roman fort at Halton Chesters', AA^4 37 (1959), 177-90
'Excavations at High Brunton turret, 1957', ibid. 349-50
'A medieval coin from Heddon-on-the-Wall', ibid. 350
'Two Roman coins from Sunderland', ibid. 351

1960
'Roman coins and potters' stamps from Halton Chesters (with a contribution by K. F. Hartley)', AA^4 38 (1960), 153-60
'The Roman fort at Ebchester, County Durham (with a note by K. Hartley)', ibid. 193-229
'Makers of clay pipes recorded in North-Eastern England', ibid. 238-9
'An inscription relating to Kirkby Thore', CW^2 60 (1960), 32-6
'Coins', in J. J. Wilkes, 'Excavations at Housesteads in 1959', AA^4 38 (1960), 61-71, at 70-1

1961
(with B. J. N. Edwards) 'Medieval and other pottery from Finchale Priory, County Durham', AA^4 39 (1961), 229-78
'Appendix' in W. G. Putnam, 'Excavations at Pen-y-Crocbren', *Montgomeryshire Collections* 57.1 (1961), 33-41

1962
'The African contribution to the imperial equestrian service', *Historia* 12 (1962), 209-26
'The career of L. Titinius Clodianus', *Latomus* 21 (1962), 853-9
'The deserted village of West Whelpington, Northumberland', AA^4 40 (1962), 189-225
'Excavations at Tomen-y-Mur, 1962', *Journal of the Merioneth Historical and Record Society* 4.2 (1962), 171
'Excavations at Llys Brychan, Llangadog 1961', *Carmarthen Antiquary* 4.1-2 (1962), 2-8

(with B. J. N. Edwards) 'Medieval and other pottery from Hartlepool, County Durham', *AA*⁴ 40 (1962), 241-51
'Mediaeval pottery in County Durham' in B. Dobson, 'Some current archaeological problems of medieval Durham', *Transactions of the Durham Architectural and Archaeological Society* 11.3-4 (1962), 177-88, at 184-5

1963

'The military occupation of Roman Wales', *Bulletin of Board of Celtic Studies* 20.2 (1963), 206-20
(with B. J. N. Edwards) 'Medieval pottery in the possession of the Society of Antiquaries of Newcastle-upon-Tyne', *AA*⁴ 41 (1963), 85-106

1964

'Early Roman campaigns in Wales', *Archaeological Journal* 121 (1964), 23-39
'Excavations at Gelligaer, Glamorgan, 1963', *Morgannwg. Transactions of the Glamorgan local history society* 8 (1964), 66-9
'Legio II Augusta in Britain', *Archaeologia Cambrensis* 113 (1964), 47-63
'Makers of clay pipes recorded in North-Eastern England II', *AA*⁴ 42 (1964), 255-60
(with B. J. N. Edwards) 'The medieval pottery', in R. Hogg, 'Excavations at Tullie House, Carlisle 1954-56', *CW*² 64 (1964), 14-62, at 41-57

1965

'Roman officers at Maryport', *CW*² 65 (1965), 115-32
'Town defences in Roman Britain', *Antiquity* 39 (1965), 57-9
'Recent archaeological excavaton and discovery in Glamorgan: II. The Roman villa at Whitton, Glamorgan, excavations of 1965', *Morgannwg. Transactions of the Glamorgan local history society* 9 (1965), 91-5
'Septimius Severus and the defences of York', *Yorkshire Archaeological Journal* 41 (1965), 516-23

1966

(with B. Dobson) Editor, *Britain and Rome: essays presented to Eric Birley on his sixtieth birthday* (Titus Wilson: Kendal 1966), pp. 208
'The garrison of Maryport and the Roman army in Britain', ibid. 27-40
'Recent archaeological excavation and discovery in Glamorgan: II, 2. The Roman villa at Whitton, Glamorgan: 2nd interim report', *Morgannwg. Transactions of the Glamorgan local history society* 10 (1966), 59-63
'A polished stone axe of the Great Langdale group from Clyro, Radnorshire', *Bullletin of the Board of Celtic Studies* 22 (1967), 271-2

1967

'Aktuelle Probleme der Hadriansmauer', *Germania* 45 (1967), 96-105
'The Roman villa at Whitton, Glamorgan', *Morgannwg. Transactions of the Glamorgan local history society* 11 (1967), 78-81
'The Roman frontier in Wales', in *Studien zu den Militärgrenzen Roms: Vorträge des 6 internationalen Kongresses in Süddeutschland* [*Bonner Jarhbücher* Beihefte XIX] (Cologne and Graz 1967), 21-31
(with J. C. Mann) 'The division of Britain', *JRS* 57 (1967), 61-4

1968

'The Roman fort at Brecon Gaer: some problems', *Bulletin of the Board of Celtic Studies* 22 (1968), 426-32
'Archaeological excavations and discovery in Glamorgan: II, 2. The Roman villa at Whitton, Glamorgan: excavations of 1968', *Morgannwg. Transactions of the*

Glamorgan local history society 12 (1968), 101-4
'Legio XX Valeria in Britain', *Archaeologia Cambrensis* 117 (1968), 77-91
'Coarse pottery', in A. H. A. Hogg, 'Pen Llystyn: a Roman fort and other remains', *Archaeological Journal* 125 (1968), 101-92, at 173-8

1969
Editor, V. E. Nash-Williams, *The Roman Frontier in Wales*, 2nd. ed. (University of Wales Press: Cardiff), pp. xv + 206
'Thracian units in the Roman army', *Israel exploration journal* 19 (1969), 215-24

1970
'The deserted village of West Whelpington, Northumberland. Second Report', with sections by others, *AA*[4] 48 (1970), 183-302
'Recent archaeological excavation and discovery in Glamorgan: II. Late Iron Age and Roman periods', *Morgannwg. Transactions of the Glamorgan local history society* 14 (1970), 84-8
(with J. C. Mann) 'Britain from Agricola to Gallienus', *Bonner Jahrbücher* 170 (1970), 178-210

1971
'Decurions and priests', *American Journal of Philology* 92 (1971), 513-38
'Some current problems of Hadrian's Wall', in *Roman Frontier Studies 1967* [Proceedings of the Seventh International Congress held at Tel Aviv] (Tel Aviv University: Tel Aviv 1971), 55-8
(with J. Belcher) 'Stem-bore diameters of English clay-pipes: some northern evidence', *Post-medieval archaeology* 5 (1971), 191-3

1972
'An album of the equestrians from North Africa in the Emperor's service', *Epigraphische Studien* IX (Dusseldorf 1972), 146-232
'The changing face of Roman Britain', *Proceedings of the Classical Association* 69 (1972), 28

1973
'A revolution in British archaeology?', *Antiquity* 47 (1973), 193-6

1974
(with Eric Birley and Brian Dobson) Editor, *Roman frontier studies 1969: eighth international congress of Limesforschung* (University of Wales Press: Cardiff 1974), pp. xii + 262

1975
'Rescue archaeology and research', *Antiquity* 49 (1975), 137-9

1976
Maryport: a Roman fort and its garrison [Cumberland and Westmorland Antiquarian & Archaeological Society, Extra Series 22] (Titus Wilson: Kendal 1976), pp. 96
'An unneccessary war', *Britannia* 7 (1976), 145-51
'The civitas Silurum inscription – a reply', *Bulletin of the Board of Celtic Studies* 26 (1976), 513-5

1977
(with Stuart Wrathmell) 'Sixteenth- and seventeenth-century farmsteads: West Whelpington, Northumberland', *Agricultural History Review* 25 (1977), 108-19

1978
'The case of the redundant official', *Britannia* 9 (1978), 289-92

1980

'Introduction: setting the scene', in P. A. Clayton (ed.), *A Companion to Roman Britain* (Phaidon: London 1980), 9-36

1981

(with Stuart Wrathmell) *Whitton: an Iron Age and Roman farmstead in south Glamorgan* (University of Wales Press: Cardiff 1981), pp. xv + 262

1983

'Magnus Maximus and the end of Roman Britain', *Transactions of the Honourable Society of Cymmrodorion 1983*, 22-35

1985

'History, archaeology and Roman Scotland', *Proceedings of the Society of Antiquaries of Scotland* 115 (1985), 59-66

'Early Glamorgan: a review article', *Morgannwg. Transactions of the Glamorgan local history society* 29 (1985), 10-19

(with G. R. Stephens) 'Two altars of Cohors IV Gallorum from Castlesteads', *CW*² 85 (1985), 77-80

1987

(with D. H. Evans) 'The deserted village of West Whelpington, Northumberland: third report, part one', *AA*⁵ 15 (1987), 199-308

(with G. R. Stephens) 'The Roman garrisons of Maryport', *CW*² 87 (1987), 61-6

1988

(with D. H. Evans and S. Wrathmell) 'The deserted village of West Whelpington, Northumberland: third report, part two', *AA*⁵ 16 (1988), 139-92

1989

(with D. H. Evans) 'Excavation of two palisaded enclosures at West Whelpington, Northumberland', *AA*⁵ 17 (1989), 117-39

1994

Early Roman campaigns in Wales [Seventh Annual Caerleon Lecture] (National Museum of Wales: Cardiff 1994), pp. 36

'Non-legionary troops in Roman Britain: part one, the units', *Britannia* 25 (1994), 35-77

Book reviews are not included

1 Maryport from the first to the fourth centuries: some current problems

R. J. A. Wilson

The first part of this book presents the results of some recent research which has centred on the Roman fort at Maryport in Cumbria. The impetus for this work has been the creation of the Senhouse Roman Museum, a private museum run by Trustees, which since 1990 has provided a permanent home for the artefacts and epigraphic and sculptured material collected at the site since the sixteenth century by successive members of the Senhouse family. The purpose of this introduction is to draw attention to some of the results of the research presented later in this book, and also to highlight a few of the many current deficiencies in our knowledge of Roman Maryport.

The Roman fort at Maryport (Fig. 1.1 for its overall setting) lies on a bluff 55 m above sea level 750 m north of the mouth of the river Ellen.[1] In Roman times both fort and river were almost certainly called ALAVNA, a name still reflected in the modern name of the river. This was a common appellation in Roman Britain, where at least half a dozen rivers and/or places are known by this name; its precise meaning is disputed.[2] Memory of the Roman site has never been entirely lost: even today its earthworks are still a prominent landmark (Fig. 1.2), and much more was clearly visible when Camden, the first to record the site, visited it in 1599. Indeed that remained the case until the beginning of the eighteenth century, when the major despoliation of stonework from both fort and attendant civilian settlement (*vicus*), to build the burgeoning town of Maryport, began in earnest.[3] Yet despite the splendid series of inscribed and sculptured stones which have come from the site, the latest found *circa* 1970,[4] our knowledge about Maryport is still very deficient, not least because, apart from a single excavation season in 1966, there has been no modern exploration of either the fort or *vicus*.

Maryport and its relation to the Cumbrian coastal defences in the early second century

The first unresolved matter concerns the precise foundation date of the site. It has long been known that the fort at Maryport was a key element in the Cumberland coastal defences which formed an integral part of the Hadrianic frontier system, and the nature of these coastal defences has become better understood over the past two decades, thanks to the work in particular of Barri Jones and Richard Bellhouse.[5] At 2.58 ha (6.5 acres) measured over the ramparts, Maryport was one of the biggest forts on the entire Wall system, and was directly linked by road to Carlisle[6] and the fort at Stanwix, the nerve-centre for the whole frontier command (Fig. 1.1). Maryport from its size and central position in the line of western coastal forts has, there-

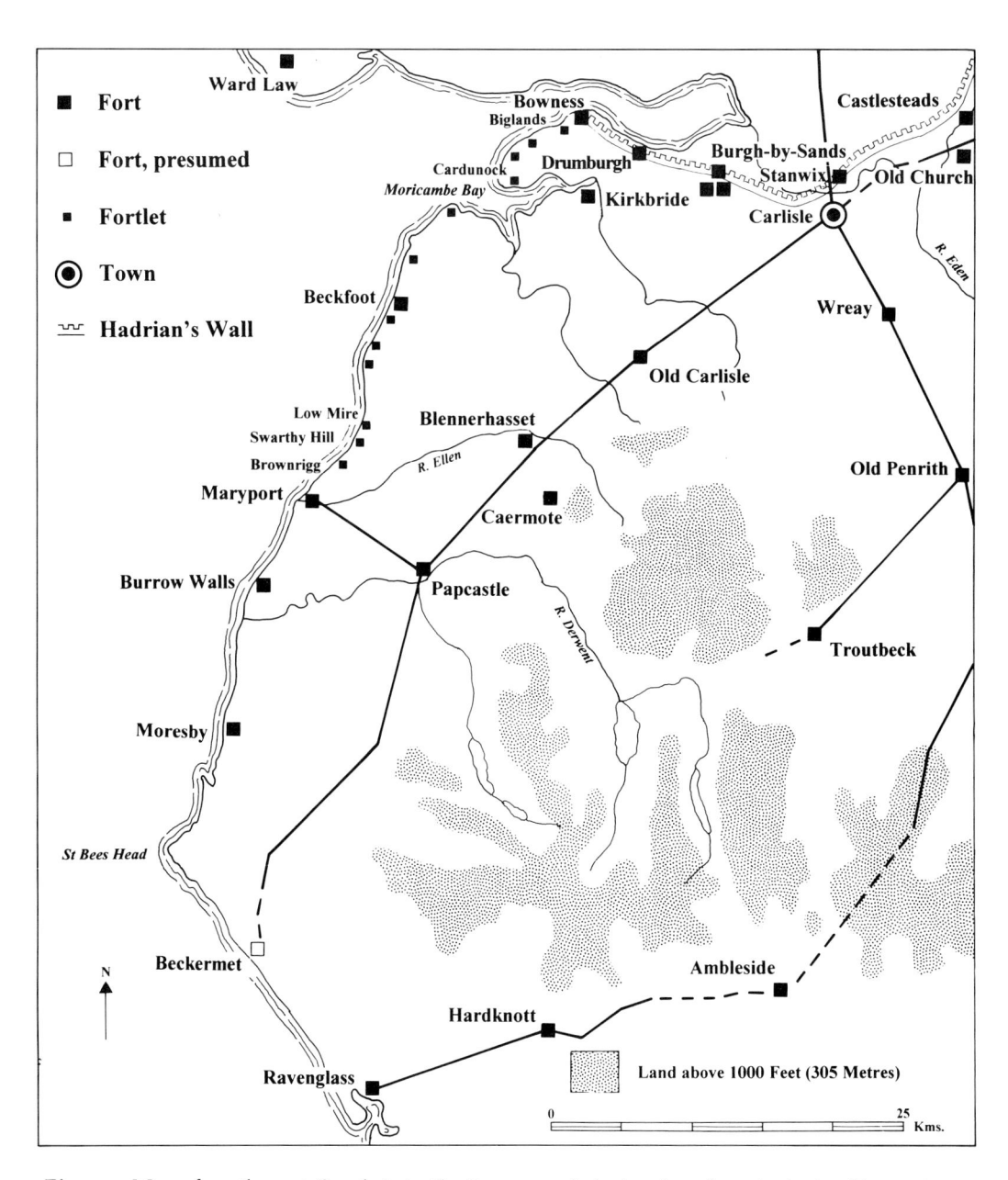

Fig. 1.1 Map of north-west Cumbria in the Roman period, showing the principal military sites (all periods) and the road system which connected them. Of the Cumbrian coastal defences only certainly identified milefortlets are marked; of these, only those mentioned in the text of this book are also named. Towers between these milefortlets, and the turrets and milecastles of Hadrian's Wall, are not shown.

Fig. 1.2 Aerial photograph of the Roman fort at Maryport, seen from the south-west in the early morning sun. The Senhouse Roman Museum occupies the former Naval Battery (built in 1885) which is prominently visible as the isolated building on the cliff edge (left).

fore, good claim to be reckoned as the principal station in the Cumbrian coastal defences.[7]

The chronology of the evolution of these western coastal defences is, however, still poorly understood. It is logical to assume, by analogy with Hadrian's Wall, that the original Hadrianic plan was to have a system of milefortlets with two towers between each at 540 yard (495 m) intervals running down the Cumberland coast to somewhere beyond Maryport (its extension as far as St Bees Head has been assumed but is not proven).[8] Although elements of a ditch and palisade system of more than one phase have been identified at the northern end of the Cumberland system, west of the Wall's terminal fort at Bowness, it is far from clear that this was ever completed for more than a few miles; but the intention may have been to provide a continuous timber palisade running close by the milefortlets and towers, as was certainly the case on the Taunus *limes* in upper Germany, where the palisade is not only of Hadrianic date but almost exactly contemporary.[9]

The milefortlets had turf ramparts with timber gates and internal buildings, as did the milecastles on Hadrian's Turf Wall, but it has been assumed until recently that the towers, again by analogy with the Hadrianic Turf Wall, were built of stone from the start.[10] Recent excavation by Professor Barri Jones, however, has shown that the whole development of the system

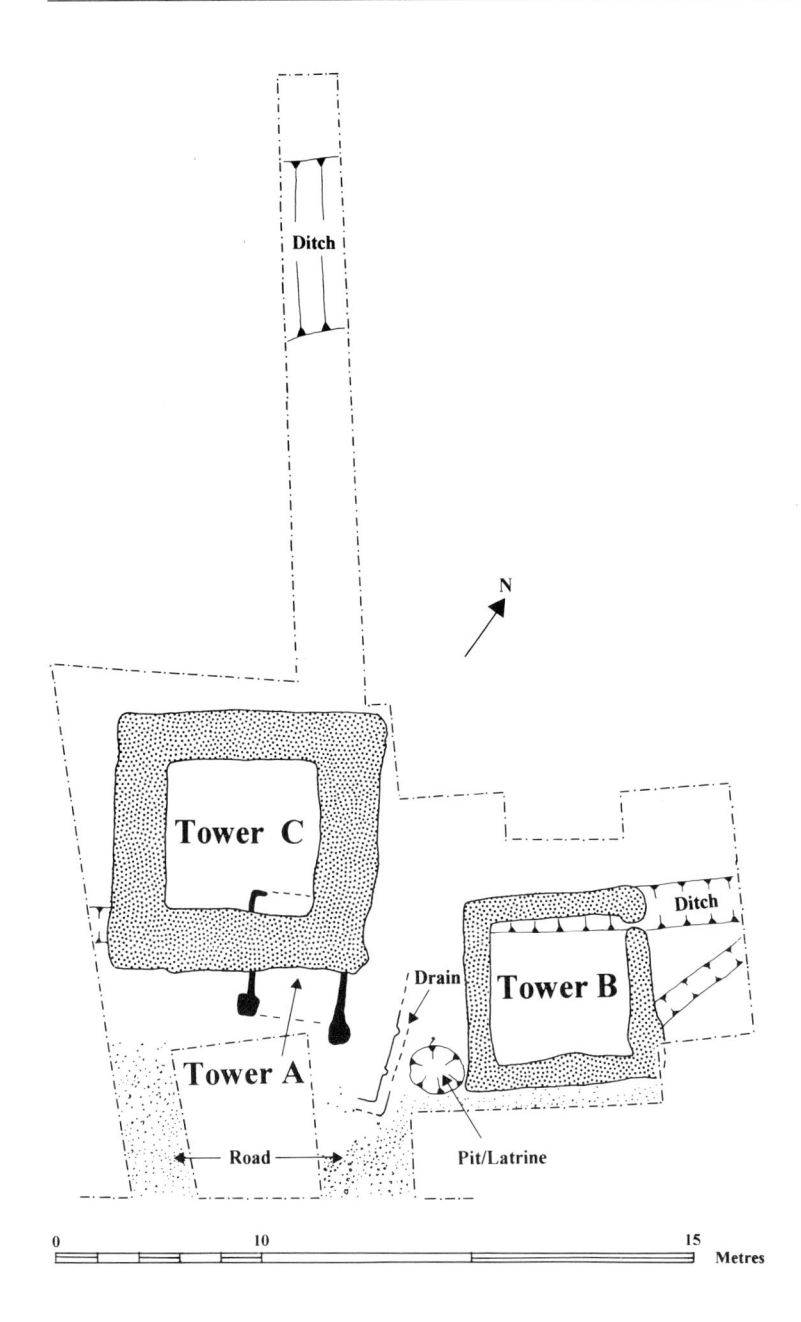

Fig. 1.3 Tower 2B (Campfield) on the Cumbrian coastal defences west of Bowness-on-Solway: plan of excavated structures, showing parts of a defensive ditch, a road, and three successive towers, two (A and B) of timber, and the latest (C) of stone

is likely to be considerably more complex than is at present thought. In particular, his excavations at Campfield (Tower 2b) have clearly revealed that at least one, and possibly two, timber towers preceded the stone tower. The first, largely destroyed by the later stone tower, is interpreted as a structure c. 2.7 metres square, which is much smaller than the norm for timber towers on the German frontier (about 4 m square), and no doubt correspondingly less high. This was replaced by a timber tower 4 m by 3.6 m, in turn later replaced by a stone tower even bigger (respectively marked Tower B and Tower C on Fig. 1.3). The chronology is still uncertain, but it was thought that the stone tower was still occupied in the third century before being demolished towards the end of that century.[11] It now seems a distinct possibility, therefore, that the primary Hadrianic series of watchtowers along the Cumbrian coast was built of timber, and that these were replaced after an unknown interval by the stone towers whose sequence has been established by Richard Bellhouse and others.[12]

How does the fort at Maryport relate to this system? Our knowledge of the arrangement of the towers and milefortlets in the stretch to the north of Maryport has been significantly improved in recent years, first by the discovery and total excavation of MF 21 (Swarthy Hill), which was found to be 77 yards (70 m) to the north of the position predicted for it by Bellhouse,[13] and also by the discovery through aerial photography that the true position of MF 23, the first milefortlet to the north of Maryport fort, lay at least 50 yards (45 m) to the south of its previously calculated position.[14] In order to allow room for two distances of 540 yards between this milefortlet and the north-west corner of Maryport fort via an intervening tower (23A), Richard Bellhouse has assumed that the latter lay on a bluff now removed by quarrying. This is certainly possible, but such a degree of precision is only necessary if we accept Bellhouse's theory,[15] which has been widely adopted, that the Cumbrian coastal defences in the stretches north and south of Maryport were laid out from Maryport fort, which is seen as integral to the original Hadrianic system. This, however, is far from certain; indeed the incorporation of a newly-built fort as part of the primary Hadrianic scheme would in that case be unique, for on the line of the Wall itself, although the barrier ran close to existing forts (such as at Carvoran), nowhere in the original conception (as far as we know) was a fort planned to lie actually on the Wall line *sensu stricto*. If, on the other hand, the presence of forts on the Cumbrian coast represents a secondary addition to the Hadrianic system in modification of the original plan, as on Hadrian's Wall itself (as seems logical), Tower 23B may have been started or indeed already completed on or very close to the site later occupied by the fort at Maryport, when the decision to add the forts to the system was made.

Bellhouse draws attention to the 'dislocation' of his proposed system south of Maryport, and the 'unexpected' discovery of a tower at Rise How, which casts doubt on the hypothesis that the milefortlet/ watchtower system in this sector was in fact laid out based on Maryport fort.[16] The alternative is to suppose that Tower 23B more or less underlies the fort, and that Milefortlet 24 lies some 400 yards to the south of the fort (Fig. 1.4). Charles Daniels has already demonstrated that such a system accommodates perfectly well the two known towers located south of Maryport, without the need to claim 'dislocation';[17] and this is surely more likely to have been the system as it was originally planned. If the first fort on the clifftop at Maryport was indeed of Hadrianic date, then either it was primary and formed part of the original plan, which I think unlikely (in which case either Tower 23B was suppressed or it lay south of the fort, the latter therefore interrupting the usual sequence of spacing), or the fort was added to the original system perhaps *c.* AD 124, in line with the traditional chronology for the placing of the forts on Hadrian's Wall. At least one of the Cumbrian coastal forts, Moresby, however, was probably not

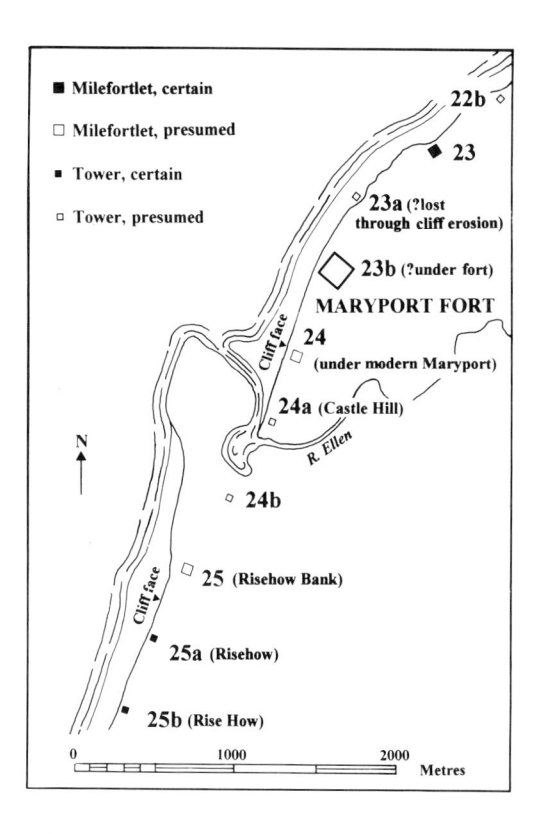

Fig. 1.4 Map showing the known and conjectured locations of milefortlets and towers near Maryport, with a proposed numbering system south of Maryport different from that of Richard Bellhouse (who numbers the towers at Risehow and Rise How 26A and B, not 25A and B)

completed before AD 128, because an inscription from there names Hadrian as *pater patriae*, a title he took in that year.[18]

But was the site a Hadrianic foundation, or was there an earlier fort, either underneath the present site or elsewhere in the immediate vicinity? The 1966 excavations concluded that the visible fort at Maryport was indeed Hadrianic, and Jarrett then gave up the thoughts he had earlier entertained about an Agricolan foundation,[19] although he did not exclude the possibility that an earlier fort existed somewhere else at Maryport.[20] Others too have raised the suggestion of pre-Hadrianic occupation at Maryport. Eric Birley in 1961 first proposed a Trajanic foundation for the visible fort, and then Dr Timothy Potter, in a review of the 1976 publication of the Maryport excavations, also questioned whether the pottery from the site (including the pre-1966 finds) did not point to a date in the 90s AD rather than later, in line with the foundation dates of other forts in the Lake District, such as Watercrook and Ambleside.[21] Now David Shotter, in his review below of the coin evidence from Maryport (p. 136), has also cautiously concluded that the numismatic information is consistent with a foundation date for the fort at Maryport in the 90s, after the abandonment of Scotland and the establishment of the Stanegate as the *limes*. The sample of both coins and pottery of Flavio-Trajanic date from the 1966 excavations is small, and of the pre-1966 material the exact provenance of much of it is unknown (the bulk of it, however, is likely to come from in and around Maryport); but although more evidence is needed for conclusive proof, what there is suggests the likelihood of military occupation at Maryport before the Hadrianic period.

Other early material from the site is reviewed below by Ian Caruana (pp. 41-2), in the light of the important discovery that the foundation of Carlisle can be dated precisely by dendrochronology to AD 72 or 73 and also, more significantly for Maryport, that the date of the fort of Blennerhasset, discovered in 1984, looks from the surface material likewise to belong to the governorship of Petillius Cerialis (71-73/4). The siting of a fort at Blennerhasset, only 10 miles (16.5 km) from Maryport, very probably points to the use of harbour facilities on the coast at that time; and the nearest suitable location is a probable port installation at the mouth of the Ellen, the river on which Blennerhasset lies. Whether the river mouth was guarded by another fort of the same period remains an open question, but Caruana makes a plausible case for one. If there was, it is likely to have been short-lived, because we would otherwise expect early Flavian material to be better represented among the admittedly ill-recorded casual finds coming from Maryport. Could an earlier fort, possibly closer to the river Ellen than its successor, perhaps lie underneath the heart of modern Maryport,[22] or else await detection through aerial photography just outside the modern town? Was it then this putative alternative fort-site which was re-occupied in the 90s, if the ceramic and numismatic evidence has been correctly interpreted to suggest a military presence at Maryport at that time? The alternative is to suggest that there is in fact a pre-Hadrianic fort on the bluff at Maryport: with commendable frankness Jarrett and his colleagues were not absolutely certain that the level taken to be natural subsoil was indeed the natural,[23] leaving open the possibility that renewed excavation might reveal a late Flavian or Trajanic fort below the Hadrianic one.[24] If there was one, it need not have affected the systematic placing of milefortlets and towers in the primary Hadrianic system proposed above: Tower 23B may have been placed beside a Trajanic fort underlying the Hadrianic one without interrupting the sequence, and if a palisade was ever planned to accompany the milefortlets and towers (unproven for this sector, and in any case surely omitted here where cliffs provided a natural obstacle), there was sufficient room between the line of the west ditches and the cliff edge to accommodate it. In any case a hypothetical Flavio-Trajanic fort need not have lain on exactly the same site on the hill-top as its Hadrianic successor.

To sum up, then: a Cerialan fort at Maryport remains a tentative hypothesis which requires more evidence to substantiate; if there was one, it may have been elsewhere than on the cliff top. A fort in the 90s is a stronger possibility, but whether that too was sited elsewhere at Maryport or under the known Hadrianic fort (whether exactly or approximately) requires verification. Even if there was, the primary Hadrianic series of regular watchtowers and milefortlets could still have been laid out ignoring it, especially if a hypothetical Trajanic fort lay on a slightly different site. Then, later, a Hadrianic fort was built, probably c. 124 when the decision was taken to make forts an integral part of the system; and that is the fort whose earthworks, with later modifications and additions, survive impressively to this day.

The fort from Hadrian to the late fourth century

Very little is known in detail of the second-century fort. The excavated rampart section appeared to show that both the rampart and the stone wall fronting it were contemporary. Overall the primary defences were 7.95 m wide including the foundations of the stone wall about 2 m wide; there was a triple ditch system. The fort is believed to have faced west, i.e. north-west,[25] towards the sea, but very little is known of its layout. The position of all four gates is clear, and the stonework of both the north and east gates was uncovered in the eighteenth century and subsequently robbed. The headquarters building was also investigated in both the seventeenth and the eighteenth centuries, when the arch of the strong room vault was uncovered, as well as the well in the adjacent *principia* courtyard; this well may have been located on the ground by the RCHME survey (p. 60). The dimensions of the vaulted strong room were recorded as measuring 10.5 feet by 12 feet (3.20 m by 3.65 m). If the size is accurately reported, this strong room is the second largest in Roman Britain after the massive third-century example at South Shields (3.80 m by 4.40 m).[26] The size of the Maryport strong room strengthens the notion that the fort had a special importance in the western coastal defences, perhaps implying that the pay chests for more than one garrison, or bullion in transit, were stored there. It is also plausible that its importance was enhanced by the presence of a harbour, and that in addition to Maryport's normal role as an auxiliary fort it served in part at least as a stores base. Whether the strong room of Hadrianic date at Maryport is likely to have been as large as the one uncovered is doubtful; as at South Shields, the excavated structure at Maryport may well belong to a later rebuilding. The internal bath located in 1788 presumably belonged to the *praetorium* (commander's residence): bath-houses inside forts are rare in Britain until the fourth century except on the Antonine Wall, and if the Maryport bath did not belong to the *praetorium* it too is likely to be late Roman.[27]

The only other structures known within the fort are those incompletely excavated in 1966 in its north-east corner. The remains were found to be very robbed, but appear to belong to a barracks with centurion's quarters at the north end in the Hadrianic period, later rebuilt; this was replaced by what was interpreted as a stores-cum-stable-block in the second quarter of the third century; and there was further reorganisation in the fourth century, but structures were fragmentary. The excavators were, however, uncertain whether they had encountered three periods or four, and called for 'further excavation in a less disturbed area of the fort'.[28] Clearly a wider area-excavation in the interior of the fort is a *desideratum* at some stage in the future, for our present knowledge of the layout and development of the fort over its 270-year existence is at present extremely paltry.

Nor do we know for sure if the fort was continuously occupied from the Hadrianic period through to the late fourth century. The clearest evidence for occupation, at any rate for the second century, comes from the epigraphic and numismatic material rather than archaeological finds. We can be certain from the inscriptions that Maryport was continuously occupied during the reign of Hadrian, because the group of altars found in 1870, discussed in detail below by David Breeze, shows that we are very likely to have the names of all or virtually all the Hadrianic commanders of the garrison at that period, the *cohors I Hispanorum*, if, as seems likely, a tour of duty for each lasted a little less than three years (p. 85): no less than six commanding officers are attested between c. 123/4 and 136/8. We know that *cohors I Hispanorum* was part-mounted (*equitata*) from the altars of one of these men, Cammius Maximus (*RIB* 827-9), and it is usually assumed from the title tribune that the unit was *milliaria*, 1000 strong, when it was first stationed at Maryport. This makes sense for a fort which is as big as 2.58 ha (6.5 acres) in size, because the part-mounted auxiliary unit 1000 strong in theory needs the largest accommodation of all the six different types of auxiliary regiment, apart from that for the full cavalry equivalent (*ala milliaria*); and there was only one of those regiments stationed in each province (in Britain it was from the Hadrianic period onwards stationed at Stanwix, a fort of 3.96 ha [9.79 acres]).[29]

Maryport, however, is unlikely to have been home to a *cohors equitata milliaria* for long. Professor Jarrett came to the conclusion,[30] accepted in this volume by David Breeze (pp. 74-5), that a sizeable proportion of the regiment must have been detached from the parent unit for service elsewhere (initially no doubt on a temporary basis, but in fact never to return), to explain the change in the commander's title from that of tribune (appropriate to a milliary unit) to that of prefect (the commanding officer of a quingenary unit). If, as seems likely, the *cohors I Hispanorum* was expecting a return to full milliary strength, we would not expect drastic alterations to the fort at Maryport during the Hadrianic period; but a reduction in size might have been expected when the next regiment arrived, the *cohors I Delmatarum*, probably in 138 or 139, a 500-strong unit (pp. 79-80). In fact, since prefect is the title of all the remaining commanding officers known for the second century, it looks as though a 500-strong *cohors* was the favoured size of unit at Maryport in the Antonine period and later. But there is no evidence at present that the 2.58 ha (6.5 acre) fort was ever reduced in size by the building of an inner rampart to curtail the size of the fort interior, as frequently happened elsewhere when the size of garrison changed, and the RCHME survey did not find any traces of such a reduction in size. It remains a puzzling feature of the Maryport fort that a unit 500-strong occupied a fort so much larger than was customary throughout much of the second, and probably for much of the third, century.[31]

But to return to the question of continuity of occupation. The *cohors I Delmatarum* was at Maryport by 139, because the title *pater patriae* is missing from Antoninus Pius' titulature in one of the two stones which records this unit (p. 79). How long it stayed is uncertain. Jarrett thought on the basis of the 1966 excavations that the fort was continuously occupied from Hadrian through to the late fourth century.[32] Dr Potter, however, in his review of Jarrett's book, suggested that there might have been breaks in the occupation,[33] and this is also supported by the coin evidence discussed in detail below by Dr Shotter (pp. 136-7). Shotter's tentative conclusion is that the coin evidence points to Maryport's being given up, like many of the forts on Hadrian's Wall, when the Antonine advance into Scotland took place, and only regarrisoned after the abandonment of Scotland in the 160s. If that is right, *cohors I Delmatarum* is likely to have had only a brief stay at Maryport before being withdrawn for service in Scotland. Since two prefects of this unit are known, the unit may have returned to Maryport after the withdrawal from Scotland and a recommissioning of Maryport in the 160s.[34] This may be the context also for a fort rebuilding with the help of legionary detachments, if the two undated stones (*RIB* 852-3) attesting legionaries at Maryport do indeed belong to the second century, as has been suggested on stylistic grounds for one of them (p. 71). A little later in the second century we find the *cohors I Baetasiorum* stationed at Maryport; but it must have left there sometime in the first half of the third century, if not before the end of the second century, for the newly-constructed fort at Reculver.[35]

Although the epigraphic evidence alone is not full enough to postulate continuous occupation of Maryport from the 160s to the end of the second century, the numismatic evidence does not suggest a significant diminution of activity then. The only period in that century when Maryport might have been vacated, therefore, was during the Antonine occupation of Scotland, in which case the site may have shared a similar occupation history to that of many of the Hadrian's Wall forts, with evacuation *c.* 139/40 (or in 142?), reoccupation *c.* 155, and renewed abandonment from *c.* 158 to 163, if the current orthodoxy for the occupation of the Antonine Wall is correct.[36] But such an evacuation at this time is hypothetical for Maryport, and needs to be tested in future excavation; the alternative is to assume that occupation was unbroken at our site throughout the second century.

It was probably before the end of the second century that the system of watchtowers and milefortlets along the Cumbrian coast – of which the Hadrianic fort at Maryport was an integral part – was largely given up. Not many of the milefortlets of the Cumbrian defences have been adequately investigated, but the Biglands milefortlet (MF 1), while showing evidence of two re-occupations, seems to have been abandoned c. AD 180, and recent re-investigation of milefortlet 20 (Low Mire) has also revealed three phases; the pottery sequence there also suggests that there was Antonine occupation or re-occupation. There are hints of the same at Milefortlets 16 and 22.[37] On the other hand, recent total excavation at Milefortlet 21 (Swarthy Hill) revealed only a single period of use, in the Hadrianic period (Fig. 1.5). This is now the most completely investigated milefortlet on the Cumbrian defences, and its full publication is awaited with interest.[38] There were two entrances, but only the west one was furnished with a gate tower. The ditch was omitted on the sea side, and inside were three mud-walled buildings on one side of the central roadway and a long aisled building on the other. Ovens and hearths were also uncovered. The defences and interior buildings have now been partly reconstituted and laid out for permanent view, the only place on the Cumbrian defences where any Roman monument (the forts apart) has been made permanently accessible in this way. As for the stone towers between each milefortlet, the evidence for the length of their occupation is more equivocal: Jones[39] thought that Tower 2B was still in use in the third century before its demolition in the late third century, but elsewhere there is very little evidence that the system of milefortlets and towers was maintained after the end of the second century. In some cases, as at Swarthy Hill, occupation lasted less than two decades. Only the milefortlet at Cardurnock, where the Hadrianic fortlet was twice the size of the other milefortlets, shows clear signs of fourth-century rebuilding, with new defences provided within the line of the Hadrianic ramparts. Although a little fourth-century pottery has been picked up at other milefortlet sites, it is premature to talk of widespread refortification at that period: the Solway coastal defences, the major forts apart, had largely outlived their usefulness by the end of the second century.[40]

Much less is known about the fort at Maryport in the third century. The epigraphic evidence is much less full than for the second century (see pp. 81-3), and apart from one fragmentary stone which may attest some rebuilding under Gordian III (238-44) (*RIB* 854: Fig. 8.2 on p. 113), there is little direct evidence of major activity. The 1966 excavators suggested that one of the fresh starts made within the fort could be associated with the rebuilding indicated by this inscription, but there was little independent archaeological dating evidence to confirm this.[41] The numismatic evidence discussed by Dr Shotter below (p. 138), on the other hand, does tentatively suggest a period of unbroken activity at Maryport down into the mid-fourth century at least. The troubled times of the late Empire are harder to reconstruct, but it is significant that the *Notitia Dignitatum* still records a garrison at Maryport (the 3rd cohort of Nervii, assuming that Maryport is indeed to be identified with ALAVNA, as seems very probable), and the site was probably therefore still occupied towards the close of the fourth century; the latest

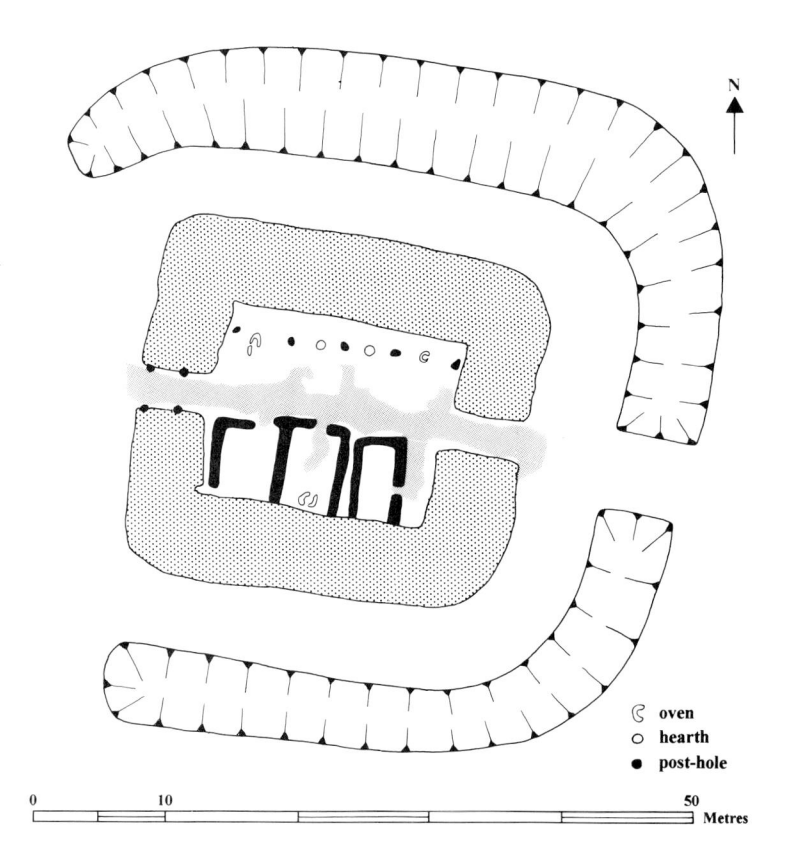

Fig. 1.5 Plan of Milefortlet 21 (Swarthy Hill) on the Cumbrian coastal defences, 4 miles north of Maryport, excavated in 1990-91. The earth rampart (which was revetted with turves) is shown by stippling; the ditch was left undug on the sea side (where there is a cliff edge). The central roadway (grey tone) was flanked by three earth-walled buildings on the south, and a long building on the north with five post-holes supporting the roof, all backing onto the rampart. The front of the north building (resting on timber sill-beams?) did not leave traces, nor the did the internal partitions assumed to have divided it into four separate cubicles, postulated by the presence of an oven or hearth in each, and the straying of the roadway pebbling into the presumed entrance area of three of the cubicles.

coins from the 1966 excavations were issues of Valentinian (364-78) and Theodosius (388-402).[42] The unit recorded in the Notitia is the third cohort of Nervii, and it is just possible that a fragmentary stone found about 1970 records that garrison.[43] Very little is known about the buildings of the fourth-century fort, but one of the structures reused a tombstone robbed from a cemetery outside the fort walls.[44] In this connection it is also worth noting that the altar dedicated to the 'Genius of the Place, Fortune the Home-bringer, Eternal Rome and Good Fate' (RIB 812) was found immediately inside the north-west corner of the defences (see Fig. 1.6), where a shrine is not to be expected;[45] it too may have been re-used as a building slab in a late Roman structure inside the fort. This stone was the great altar, the largest to

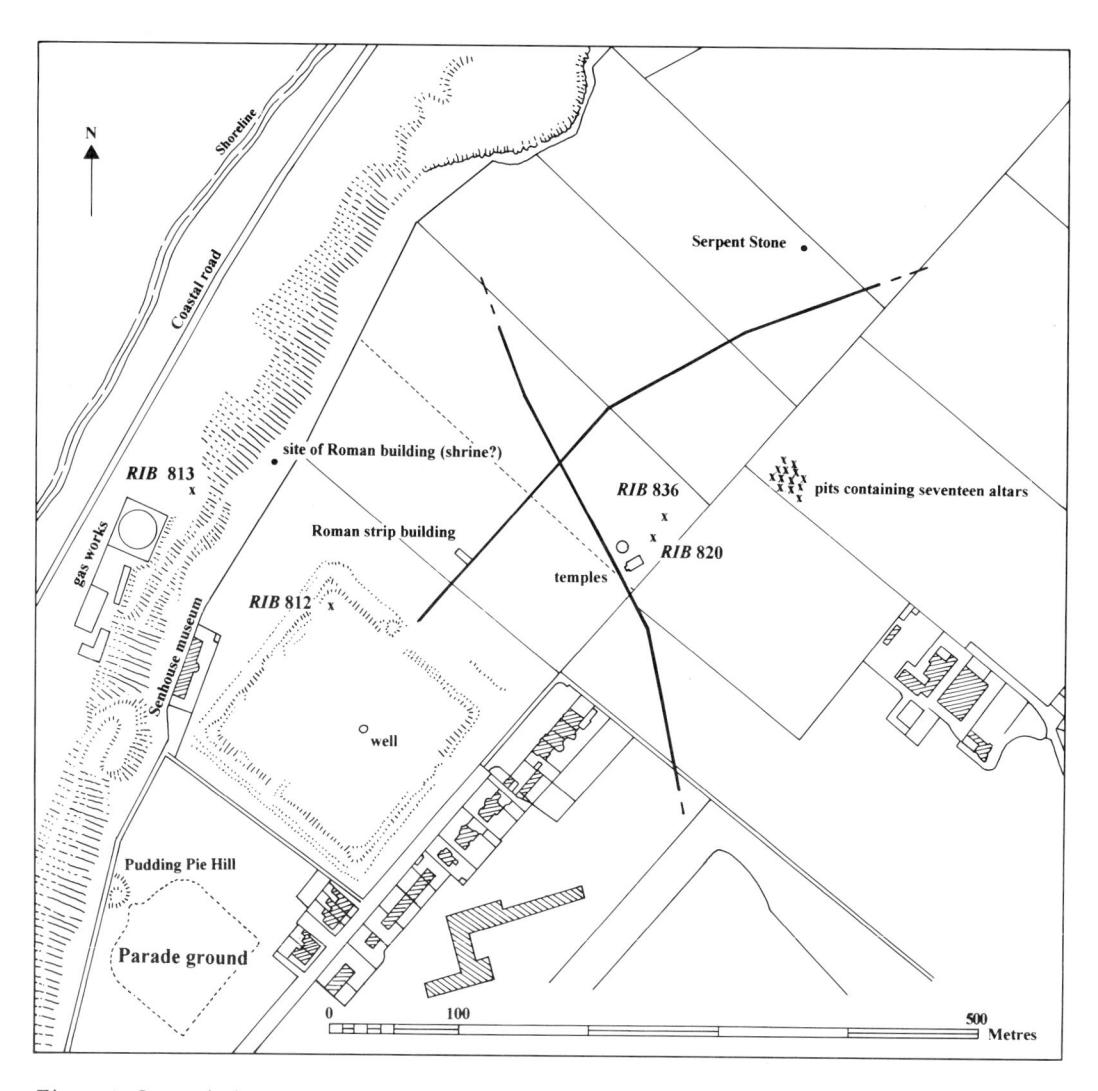

Fig. 1.6 General plan of the Roman fort at Maryport in its setting, with modern roads, field boundaries and buildings indicated; the area of the parade ground to the south of the Roman fort, however, is shown in its pre-1920s state before it was covered by modern houses. Also indicated are the positions of the buildings in the vicus *excavated in 1880 and the find-spots of some of the inscribed and sculptured stones. Solid black lines show the known course of Roman roads, on the evidence of aerial photography (cf. Fig. 3.2).*

have come from Maryport, which was seen by Camden in 1599 and given away by John Senhouse in 1683 to his friend Sir John Lowther of Lowther Castle (see p. 145), whence it passed by sale in 1969 to the British Museum (Fig. 4.13, p. 83).[46]

Particularly intriguing in the context of late Roman Maryport is the possibility of a further military fortification near the river mouth, based on observations made in 1886 and 1920, and plotted with a degree of approximation onto an overall map of

Maryport by Jarrett: he wondered whether there was a late Roman *burgus* here with walls open to the river, such as are known on the Rhine and Danube frontier, a type of fortification probably represented in Britain by the fortlet at Caer Gybi, Holyhead.[47] Alternatively, this might have been a fortified supplies compound, comparable with the situation at Caernarfon where the powerfully walled late Roman enclosure known as Hen Waliau was probably built to supplement the traditional auxiliary fort there, which remained occupied, like Maryport, until near the close of the fourth century.[48] If so, the importance of Maryport as a key strong-point in the frontier defence of north-west Britain down to the very end of the Roman occupation would be further underlined. But all this is pure speculation: recent work at the harbour has doubted whether what was recorded in this area in the late nineteenth and early twentieth century was anything more than natural bedrock.[49] Nevertheless, there must have been some harbour installations along the river Ellen in Roman times, accompanied by at least a scatter of storehouses and other buildings, and it would not be surprising if a fortified strong-point was considered a necessary addition in the insecure times of the late Empire; but for the present it is safest to admit that we know nothing of substance about them.

The *vicus*

Outside the fort lay an extensive civilian settlement, especially to the north. Very substantial remains of it were still visible in the eighteenth century, when it aroused the enthusiasm of Stukeley; from him we learn, for example, that the 'streets' were paved in flagstones, 'visibly worn with use'.[50] The only excavations, however, of which some degree of detail was recorded, were those of Joseph Robinson in 1880, which were reported in the Cumberland and Westmorland *Transactions* the following year; his account has recently been reprinted together with several examples of Robinson's hitherto unpublished photographs.[51] Robinson's account is the basis for Salway's summary of the *vicus* published in 1965,[52] and there has been little to add to his observations in the intervening thirty years; fresh discoveries have been minimal. Nevertheless the research presented below in this book has considerably advanced our knowledge in certain important respects, and a brief re-appraisal of the *vicus* is appropriate here.

No overall site plan was made of the 1880 excavations, although a sketch of some key features was published with Robinson's account; some of the information from it was transcribed, none too accurately, by Bailey onto a new map which accompanied his catalogue of the Senhouse collection in 1915.[53] Since then, some of the late Kenneth St Joseph's aerial photographs of the *vicus* have been published,[54] showing clearly strip buildings along the main road leaving the north gate of the fort; but these and other details which could be gleaned from aerial photographs had never been plotted onto a map.[55] Now, thanks to Ms Lax and Mr Blood's RCHME survey of the site reported in detail below, this has been achieved for the first time. The reader is referred to their detailed analysis on pp. 63-4, but a glance at their plan (Fig. 3.2, p. 56) shows clearly the course of the Roman road for Old Carlisle (A-A), at first straight and then swinging away north-eastwards, bisecting the settlement in the second, third and fourth fields north of the fort; and also – and this represents a particularly valuable addition to our knowledge of the *vicus*' topography – a north-south road (B-B) crossing the main road obliquely. Its northward extension no doubt joined the coast road for Beckfoot, and in the southward direction it soon reached the road for Papcastle issuing from the east gate of the fort. These roads are also indicated on Fig. 1.6. The new survey has also discounted a Roman date for an earthwork outside the fort, which Bailey took to be the defences of an annexe, and which after Collingwood's discovery of a third-century building beneath the bank has been tentatively interpreted as earthen defences for the *vicus*: it is shown, for example, on the plan of Maryport in the thirteenth edition of Collingwood Bruce's *Handbook*.[56]

The fresh RCHME work has not, however, revealed further details of the structures excavated in the 1880s, and for convenience of reference their location has been indicated here on the simplified plan, Fig. 1.6, which should be compared with Fig. 3.2 on p. 56. The first field to the north of that containing the fort has not produced any crop marks; here Robinson excavated a simple strip-building 40 feet 6 inches by 17 feet (12.35 m by 5.20 m).[57] The stone inscribed SIG(*nifer*?) with an incised human figure 'doodled' on it, mentioned below by Professor Breeze (p. 84) and by Dr Coulston (p. 126), was found in this building. In the second field, the new work has shown that the two principal structures recorded by Robinson can now be seen to have been aligned with the north-south road referred to above. These structures are of considerable interest in their own right (Fig. 1.7). The more southerly was rectangular, 46 feet by 25 feet (14 m by 7.60 m) with an eastern porch, a flagged floor in the main *cella*, and a rectangular apse at the west end (Fig. 1.8; for its location, see Fig. 1.6; the building is also marked by a cross at the centre of Fig. 3.2). Remarkably, its rear wall had lain as it had fallen, indicating an original height for the building of at least 18 feet (5.50 m). Adjacent to the north was a circular structure 34 feet in diameter (10.35 m), with

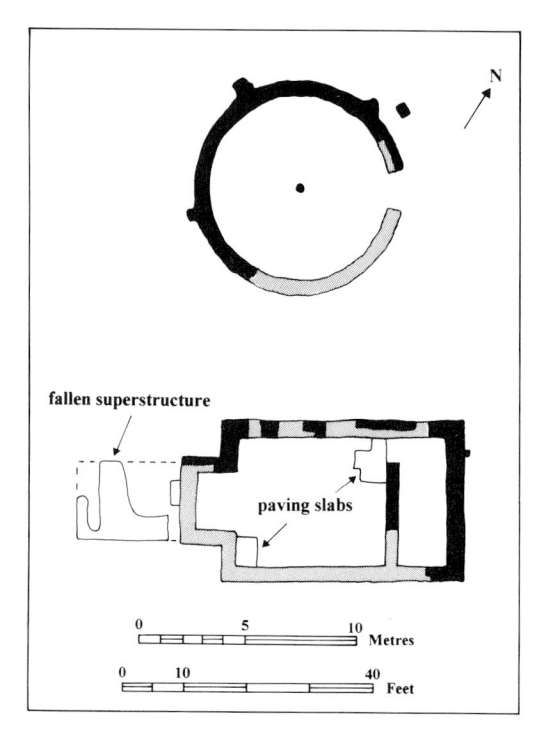

Fig. 1.7 Plan of the two temples first uncovered by Robinson in 1880 in the vicus, and re-excavated in 1885; solid black indicates recorded footings or superstructure, grey tone indicates foundations. The entrance to the rectangular temple must have been in its south-east wall, but the masonry was not sufficiently well preserved at this point to indicate the precise position or width of the doorway.

three (originally five) external buttresses or pilasters, and a central support for the roof. Both buildings faced east.[58] Although burials were found in the same general area, they probably ante-date the two buildings, which are surely both temples as Robinson proposed, even though Salway followed Collingwood in interpreting the circular one as a mausoleum.[59] By contrast, interpretation of the rectangular building as a temple has not been challenged. Furthermore Lewis, in his monograph on Romano-British temples published in 1966, was convinced that the rectangular structure could be identified as a temple of Mithras, in view of the plan's similarity to the period-2 *mithraeum* at Carrawburgh.[60] But not all temples in Roman Britain with rectangular recesses at the rear can be claimed as *mithraea*, any more than every temple with a semicircular apse is necessarily to be interpreted as a Christian church.[61] Furthermore, the presence of flagging at a single (floor) level the full width of the *cella* does not suggest that provision was made for raised benches at the sides, such as we would expect in a normal *mithraeum*; nor was there a single artefact or inscribed fragment that might hint at mithraic use. The interpretation of this building as a mithraic temple seems to me very improbable. Nevertheless the identification of two temples facing east, with their backs turned to the street running behind them, is clearly of considerable interest.

Immediately east of this pair of temples, two altars were found in the 1880 excavations, and the position of their find-spots, reported as 20 yards (18.25 m) apart, is indicated on Fig. 1.6. One (*RIB* 820) was an altar dedicated to Jupiter by C. Caballius Priscus, tribune of the *cohors I Hispanorum*; the other (*RIB* 836) was so badly damaged that only two letters of the inscribed face survived. Nevertheless the wheel decoration along the top of this altar is sufficiently similar to others in the altar series from Maryport for us to be certain that it too forms one of the series of altars dedicated under Hadrian by the same regiment (see below p. 86, note 3). The precise archaeological context of the two altars is not completely clear, but the first is reported as having been found on a 'pavement of free-

Fig. 1.8 Joseph Robinson's photograph of the excavation of the rectangular temple in 1880

stone blocks', the extent of which is not indicated. The closeness of the relationship between a possible paved open area with at least two altars, and the two temples immediately to the west which face towards the altars, cannot be established with any certainty on the evidence presently available; but it is intriguing to speculate that all formed part of the same temple precinct. A head of a mother goddess, the sculptured 'wheel' from the bolster of another altar, and a small (uninscribed) household altar are also reported from the same excavation.[62]

About 80 m to the east of where the second of the two altars was found in 1880, Humphrey Pocklington Senhouse had discovered ten years earlier the extraordinary cache of seventeen altars buried in 57 pits.[63] It is this discovery which makes Maryport unique in Roman Britain, and the altars are rightly the focus of detailed study in three of the chapters of this book (Chapters 4, 5 and 6 below). Until this latest research, it has been assumed that the altars, the majority of them vowed to Jupiter Optimus Maximus, 'Jupiter Best and Greatest', were part of a series of annual dedications made by the unit or its commander, either on January 3rd each year or on the anniversary of the emperor's accession, by solemn vow on the parade ground. This view, put forward by Wenham in 1939,[64] has held sway ever since, and entailed the further theory that alongside the pits must have been an 'early' parade ground later covered by the expansion of the *vicus*. At some stage in the third century, therefore, according to this theory, the original parade ground was abandoned and a new parade ground was laid out immediately south of the fort. Re-examination of this hypothesis, in particular by David Breeze and Peter Hill below, in the light of new discoveries at Osterburken in Germany (Fig. 6.1, p. 93)

and Sirmium in what is now Serbia, where large caches of altars have also been found in the past twenty years (although dedicated by *beneficiarii* rather than regiment commanders), have led to the conclusion that the altars might just as easily have stood in a conventional sanctuary, and the need to postulate the existence of a parade ground in this area is unwarranted.[65] In view of the fact that two of the altars in this series (and a possible fragment of a third) were not found buried with the rest but were apparently discovered at or near their original position in a religious precinct a short distance away, it is reasonable to conclude that all the altars originally stood in the same area; at some stage, presumably, a group of them was disposed of, perhaps to make way for new dedications. If this precinct can also be linked to the two temples immediately to the west, then is it just possible that the rectangular temple described above was none other than the shrine to Jupiter Optimus Maximus who was the focus of all this devotion? The original building here in the Hadrianic period[66] need not have been the one excavated by Robinson (it may well have been of timber), but the stone building that we do have was clearly in the context of the Maryport *vicus* a substantial one: it stood to an impressive height of more than five metres, no doubt towering above the other buildings in the settlement.

No other temples in the *vicus* can be securely located in the light of current knowledge: a range of deities appears on the sculptured material from the site, many with a decorative purpose rather than strictly as objects of cult (pp. 114-21 below); the whereabouts of the (epigraphically attested) shrines to Belatucadrus and the otherwise unknown deity Setlocenia (see half-title page and chapter-opening pages), are unknown.[67] The dedication to Juno, however, by Hermione (*RIB* 813: see below, pp. 107 and 109)⁶⁸ was found during quarrying of the cliff on the west side of the fort (see Fig. 1.6), and may have once stood in a shrine to that goddess near the cliff edge here. Indeed the Roman building located above the quarry in 1880 (its position is indicated on Fig. 1.6) may conceivably have been it or another shrine: a small altar with a representation of a horned god came from it.⁶⁹ Perhaps also fallen from a hill-top shrine is a dedication set up in honour of Neptune (*RIB* 839), found during extension to the gas works (marked on Fig. 1.6), just to the south of where the Juno inscription was found. A major lacuna in our knowledge of the settlement is the location of the fort's bath-house; indeed, beyond the customary well in the *principia* courtyard inside the fort, nothing is known of Roman Maryport's water supply.⁷⁰

Nor is the extent of the village as a whole easy to ascertain. The fourth field away from the fort contained many burials,⁷¹ including the remarkable Serpent Stone (pp. 121-3 and Fig. 8.15), and probably marks the limits of the inhabited area on the north: the expansion of the village over the former cemetery area mentioned above (at a point which lies approximately 250 yards [230 m] to the south of the findspot of the Serpent Stone) is itself an indication of the economic prosperity of this frontier settlement. If that is right, it is probably correct to view the Serpent Stone and its accompanying burials as late Roman, belonging to the third or, perhaps more likely, the fourth century. The extent of the *vicus* on the east and south sides of the fort cannot now be established because of modern building which has encroached on the site: the loss of the parade ground south of the fort, complete with its earth mound, the *tribunal* (known locally as Pudding Pie Hill), from which officers could shout orders or address the troops, is particularly regrettable, as it gave way to housing only in the 1920s.⁷² Had it been preserved, it would have ranked with that on Hardknott Pass as the best surviving example of such a parade ground in Britain.⁷³

There is much still to learn, therefore, about both the layout and the chronological development of Roman Maryport. In particular fresh excavation is required before many points of contention are likely to be clarified, although geophysical survey, not so far undertaken at Maryport, may also be able to resolve some questions. In the meantime, the new research presented below in this book has cast abundant fresh light on many current problems about the site and its antiquities, and opened up stimulating new lines of enquiry for the future.

Acknowledgements

I am grateful to David Breeze for kindly reading an earlier draft of this essay and making helpful suggestions. David Taylor drew with his customary skill the final versions of the maps and plans which appear here as Figs. 1.1 and 1.3-7.

Notes

1 Jarrett 1976, 7, fig. 1, for the relationship between the fort, the Ellen and modern Maryport.
2 Rivet and Smith 1979, 243-6: the name means essentially 'rocky place' or (of a river) 'the rocky one', but other possible senses are 'mighty' and 'shining'. For the Roman name of Maryport, see also Jarrett 1976, 15-16 and Shotter 1993, 107-8, who prefers Axelodunum, where the *Notitia Dignitatum* (Occ. 40.49) places a *coh. I Hispanorum*. Opinion is divided, however, as to whether this is a straight error for Uxellodunum [Stanwix] (so Rivet and Smith 1979, 220-1 and 483, who suggest that *coh. I Hispanorum* should be placed instead at Maia [Bowness-on-Solway], a fort otherwise inexplicably omitted from

the *Notitia*, and which comes at the correct place for Maia, after Congavata [Burgh-by-Sands]); or else, alternatively, whether it is a separate place-name altogether (in which case there are several candidates among the Cumbrian forts). The problem is incapable of strict resolution without further evidence, but on a balance of probabilities I prefer to follow Rivet and Smith 1979. See also note 42 below.
3   For a full synthesis of what the antiquarian reports tells us about Maryport, see Birley 1961, 216-23.
4   Frere and Tomlin 1991, 295-6, no. 2.
5   Jones 1982; Higham and Jones 1985, 30-4; Bellhouse 1989.
6   Margary 1967, 398-9 (Maryport to Old Carlisle, his road 754) and 395-6 (Carlisle-Old Carlisle-Papcastle-Egremont, his road 75: Egremont lies just to the north of the suspected fort at Beckermet). See Fig. 1.1.
7   Jarrett 1976, 88.
8   Cf. Bellhouse 1989, 3: 'nothing has been found beyond Risehow and the case for extending it further south become weaker with every mile from Maryport'; but for more recent discussions of where the system is likely to have ended, see Daniels 1990 and Woolliscroft 1994. Potter's suggestion (1979, 14-18, 48 and 359), that the Hadrianic fortlet preceding the fort at Ravenglass might indicate a possible extension of the system to south Cumbria, has not been supported by new discoveries on the ground, although the cropmark near Harrington (dismissed by Bellhouse 1989, 57-8) deserves archaeological investigation.
9   Baatz 1993, 46-9. The palisade has been located at Silloth south of Moricambe Bay, but the ditch system is only known north of the Bay (Jones 1982).
10 E.g. Daniels 1978, 33-4. For an up-to-date summary of what is known about the Cumbrian defences, see Shotter 1996, chapter 6.
11 Jones 1993; in brief, Burnham et al. 1994, 261-3. At Cardurnock (Tower 4B) a clay-and-turf platform on the line of the palisade preceded a stone tower (Jones 1982, 290-1), but there was no evidence of a timber tower as such. A timber tower 4 m square associated with another palisade has been located by Jones at Farnhill (Jones 1994-95), but this lies between Burgh-by-Sands and Kirkbride and belongs not to the Cumbrian coastal defences but to the preceding Stanegate system; another is known west of the fort at Old Carlisle, at Raise Howe, Aldoth (Burnham et al. 1993, 286), but this too lies inland and is not part of the coastal defences.
12 Bellhouse 1989.
13 Frere, Hassall and Tomlin 1992, 270.
14 So Bellhouse 1989, 49; measured from his plan (51, fig. 13; reproduced also in Daniels 1989, 16, fig. 3), it appears rather more (nearer 100 yards?).
15 Bellhouse 1970, 40-7; accepted by (e.g.) Jarrett 1976, 88 and Daniels 1978, 273.
16 See Bellhouse in Daniels 1989, 91.
17 The numbering system adopted by Bellhouse makes Tower 23b the same as the fort's north-west corner tower, and Tower 24a that at the south-west corner of the fort (Bellhouse 1989, 49 and 56), about 170 yards (rather than the standard 540 yards) apart; milefortlet 24 is therefore suppressed.
18 *RIB* 801.
19 Jarrett 1958.
20 Jarrett 1976, 87.
21 Birley 1961, 222; Potter 1978; cf. also Breeze and Dobson 1987, 82: 'Maryport was probably occupied [*sc.* in the early Hadrianic period] and continued to be held'. For a survey of the evidence for the foundation dates of the Lake District forts, see Potter 1979, 358.
22 Its earthworks, if they survived on the surface at all, were probably too slight to have attracted the attention of the early antiquaries. The objection to the siting of a fort under modern Maryport (perhaps to be sought on the south rather than the north bank of the river) is the presence of the hill to the north which blocks out a view in that direction; but a harbour installation worth protecting may have been considered a more vital consideration which outweighed this drawback. In any case, not all

23 Jarrett 1976, 29.
24 Bellhouse 1989, 50-2, who takes a fort at Maryport to be integral to the first Hadrianic coastal system, is convinced that the fort is a Trajanic foundation and points to its almost square shape, like Trajanic Kirkbride, as opposed to the normal rectangular Hadrianic fort-plan. But this is not invariably so: Hardknott, Wallsend, Stanwix and probably Castlesteads (to mention only some British examples) are examples of Hadrianic forts of squarish plan. Examples of forts in northern Britain shifting position slightly in successive rebuildings but remaining more or less on the same site are too numerous to list here (examples include Carlisle, South Shields, Vindolanda, Ambleside, etc.). On the irrelevance of the existence or otherwise of a Trajanic fort on the hilltop to the regular layout of the milefortlet/watchtower system, see Daniels 1990, 405 (comparing pre-existing Carvoran fort's relationship to Hadrian's Wall).

forts enjoyed panoramas in all directions (e.g. Flavian Fendoch).

25 In keeping with convention (cf. also pp. 64-5, note 2 below), I refer to the rampart running parallel to the cliff as the west rampart (rather than the north-west one), and so on.
26 Bidwell and Speak 1994, 80-2.
27 Rooke 1792, 141, recording (without indicating its precise location within the fort) an immersion-bath 16 feet (4.88 m) long and 2 feet 10 inches (0.85 m) deep. Internal baths on Antonine Wall: Johnson 1983, 193-4. Elsewhere in Britain they are known at Brecon Gaer, of uncertain date (third century?) (Nash-Williams 1969, 51), Caernarfon (Hadrianic/Antonine and late third/early fourth century: Casey and Davies 1993, 47-50 and 62-5), and in Saxon Shore forts of Reculver, Richborough and Lympne (Johnson 1976; Maxfield 1989).
28 Jarrett 1976, 41.
29 On the thorny problem of relating fort-size to garrison type, see Hassall 1983 with earlier literature; cf. also Austen and Breeze 1979, 124 for a specific correlation between certain fort sizes and garrison types assigned to them where known: 500 infantry: 3.36 acres/1.34 ha (Greatchesters); 500 *equitata*: 4.3 acres/1.72 ha (Haltonchesters); 1000 infantry: 5 acres/2 ha (Housesteads); 1000 *equitata*: 6.5 acres/2.64 ha (Maryport); 500 cavalry: 5.75 acres/2.35 ha (Chesters); 1000 cavalry: 9.79 acres/3.96 ha. On Stanwix, Daniels 1978, 236-9; later work is summarised in Daniels 1989, 31-2.
30 Jarrett 1976, 21.
31 Only one tribune is recorded in the third century, but by then the title did not necessarily carry implications for the size of the unit he commanded: see below, p. 82. Indeed one of the Vindolanda tablets (Bowman and Thomas 1994, no. 154) appears to show that already by the 90s AD the commander officer of a *cohors milliaria* could be styled a prefect rather than a tribune, and the strict assumption that we can know the size of the unit from the title of its commander even for the second century is therefore called into question. The Tungrians, however, appear to have been a special case, and to have adopted titles for its commanders out of line with other auxiliary units (pers. comm. David Breeze). The same Vindolanda document also shows that at any one time more than 50% of the troops might be stationed elsewhere, challenging the neat assignment to an individual fort of a whole unit as a relatively permanent and undivided garrison. It is just possible that the fort at Maryport as it appears today is the result of later enlargement (as, for example, happened at South Shields: Bidwell and Speak 1994), and that the second-century defences enclosed a rather smaller perimeter. There was no hint of this in the single section cut through the defences in 1966, but that may not tell the whole story (Jarrett 1976, 29-32). The likely importance of Maryport as a supply depot, alluded to above (on p. 24; cf. also Bidwell and Speak 1994, 31), provides a possible explanation for the large size of the fort: does it contain, for example, more than the standard two granaries (as Jarrett apparently first suggested, according to Birley

1961, 223, although the notion is not expressed in Jarrett 1976)? Or even a detachment of the *classis Britannica*?

32 Jarrett 1976, 19.

33 Potter 1978.

34 If a regiment commander served for nearly three years, there is unlikely to have been time for a *cohors I Delmatarum* to have had two separate commanders (Paulus Postumius Acilianus and L. Caecilius Vegetus) in the brief period between its arrival in 139 and its hypothetical withdrawal to Scotland (perhaps in 142?), unless one of the two commanders was already in post at the time of the unit's transfer to Maryport and was replaced soon after its arrival; hence the suggestion here that the unit returned to Maryport later in Antoninus' reign. The alternative (and simpler) solution is that Maryport was garrisoned throughout the period of advance into Scotland (so Breeze, below, pp. 80-1).

35 The date of the foundation of the fort at Reculver, and with it the likely transfer of *cohors I Baetasiorum* from Maryport, is disputed, because the identity of the Rufinus in the inscription recording the building of the *principia* there is uncertain, and the archaeological evidence for the foundation date is equivocal: Birley 1981, 173-6; Johnson 1976, 47; Maxfield 1989, 136-9. It might have been founded as early as the late second century or as late as the second quarter of the third century.

36 For an alternative view, that there was single period of Antonine occupation in Scotland, with a single withdrawal beginning c. 158, see Hodgson 1995.

37 See the discussion in Potter 1977, 178-83 with more recent work summarised in Bellhouse 1989 and Daniels 1989, 15-19 and 89-91 with further bibliography.

38 Turnbull 1991; Frere, Hassall and Tomlin 1992, 270-1.

39 Jones 1993.

40 For a rather different emphasis, see Shotter 1993, 94, who thinks on coin evidence that there might possibly have been refortification of this coast under Theodosius, 'possibly in the form of towers'; but Cardurnock apart (Daniels 1978, 264-5) there is no *structural* evidence for fourth-century occupation except in the forts, and the 'small amount of ceramic evidence' from MF 12 and 20 (Breeze and Dobson 1987, 220) does not necessarily attest military re-occupation of these sites in the fourth century.

41 Jarrett 1976, 39-41.

42 *Notitia Dignitatum* Occ. 40.53: *pace* Jarrett 1976, 25-6 who believed that Maryport was omitted by the *Notitia* and that the Alione listed as the home of the Third Cohort of Nervii is not to be identified with Alauna. Rivet and Smith, on the other hand (1979, 244-5), maintain that Alione, otherwise unattested, is a corruption of Alauna. Cf. Shotter 1993, 107, who also rejects the Alauna=Alione identification, and suggests that Alione is to be placed at Burrow-in-Lonsdale, in keeping with its position in the *Notitia* list between Glannibanta (Ravenglass) and Bremetenraco (Ribchester). He suggests instead that Maryport is the Axellodunum of the *Notitia* (see note 2 above). I prefer, with Rivet and Smith, to identify Axellodunum with Uxellodunum (Stanwix) and Alauna with Alione, even though the order in which Alione, if indeed Maryport, is placed in the often chaotic *Notitia* is very odd. The problem is incapable of strict resolution without further evidence. For the late-fourth-century coins found in the Maryport excavations of 1966, see J. Casey in Jarrett 1976, 47; and for the overall Maryport coin lists in the late Roman period, see Shotter below, p. 135. The finds of metalwork at Maryport attest occupation at least until the mid-fourth century: D. Brown in Jarrett, 76-82, re-assessed by Webster 1986.

43 Frere and Tomlin 1991, 295-6, no. 2.

44 Jarrett 1976, 42-5.

45 The personal nature of this dedication makes it likely that it originally stood in an extramural shrine, such as the precinct of the *Genius loci* discovered outside the fort at Carrawburgh: Smith 1962.

46 Wilson and Wright 1970, 315.

47 Jarrett 1976, 6-8 with fig. 1 on p. 7. Caer

Gybi: Nash-Williams 1969, 135-7.
48 Nash-Williams 1969, 63; Casey and Davies 1993, 6-7.
49 Turnbull 1996.
50 Stukeley 1725, 50.
51 Robinson 1881; Bellhouse 1992, 35-53 with pl. X-XVI.
52 Salway 1965, 102-6; cf. also Jarrett 1976, 5-8 and Sommer 1984, 89 (references).
53 Robinson 1881, plan between 236 and 237; Bailey 1915, plan facing p. 135. Both are reproduced in Bellhouse 1992. Bailey omitted the strip building in the first field north of the fort and changed the orientation of the temples to be parallel with the field boundaries; their orientation as shown on Robinson's plan has been restored on my Fig. 1.6.
54 E.g. Salway 1965, pl. VIII; Jarrett 1976, pl. III; Sommer 1984, pl. 22.
55 A point made in criticism of Jarrett 1976 by Potter 1978, 494.
56 Daniels 1978, 276-7 with plan on 274; also discussed by Salway 1965, 106 and Jarrett 1976, 5-6. See below, p. 63.
57 Robinson 1881, 250-3; Salway 1965, 103; Bellhouse 1992, 49-51 with fig. 10.
58 Robinson 1881, 244-7; Bellhouse 1992, 43-5, with fig. 9 and plates X-XII.
59 Collingwood 1936, 91; Salway 1965, 104. Burials antedating the structures: Jarrett 1976, 5, and see n. 66 below.
60 Lewis 1966, 106: 'it is difficult to believe it is not a Mithraeum'; accepted by Jarrett 1976, 5. Salway 1965, 104 also noted the similarity in plan to the Carrawburgh *mithraeum*, but without claiming the Maryport building as one.
61 Rectangular temples with projecting rectangular recesses at the rear include Thistleton, two at Verulamium (Lewis 1966, figs. 66, 95 and 99), and one at Silchester, in insula XIX. Boon 1973, 112, accepting the Maryport example as a *mithraeum*, was also tempted to interpret the Silchester temple as the site of a 'mystery' cult. Rectangular buildings with semicircular apses in Roman Britain which are definitely not churches include the temple of Antenociticus at Benwell, the London *mithraeum* and another temple at Silchester (Lewis 1966, figs. 71, 75 and 100).
62 Robinson 1881, 248; Bellhouse 1992, 48.
63 For the number of pits, Daniels 1978, 276, information which probably derives from the unpublished plan of them made by Humphrey Pocklington Senhouse and preserved until recently (now lost?) in the Netherhall Collection. Bruce 1874 does not mention the total number of pits discovered, but indicates that the 17 altars came from 9 pits (see p. 101 below). One wonders why there were so many pits: were there once many more altars buried here, disturbed by earlier ploughing and broken up for building stone? Cf. Bruce 1874, 179: 'the appearances presented by these barren pits led the excavators to suppose that they too had originally been occupied by altars, but that at some period anterior to the present they had been noticed and removed'. The notion of the ritual burial of votive offerings which had become 'surplus to requirement' (no doubt because of the need to provide more room in the sanctuary for new votives) is a commonplace in ancient religion (as 'holy' objects, they could not simply be destroyed); for an excellent example from a different period (the fourth century BC), cf. the thousands of terracotta figurines ritually buried in the precinct of the sanctuary of Demeter at Syracuse, Sicily, because they had become 'surplus to requirement' and had to make way for new dedications (*Archaeological Reports* 1976-77, 65, fig. 31).
64 Wenham 1939; for subsequent bibliography, see especially Breeze, below p. 86, works cited in his note 1.
65 The location of the 'third-century' parade ground immediately south of the fort rather than further away might presuppose that some earlier *vicus* buildings on the south side of the fort were demolished to make way for it (for which there is no evidence); rather it is more logical to assume that this area was reserved for the parade ground from the period of the fort's foundation.
66 The relationship between the burials and

the temple precinct remains problematic. Robinson reported burials immediately adjacent to the circular temple, which induced Collingwood to interpret it as a mausoleum (see n. 59 above). Either the Hadrianic sanctuary lay on the edge of the earliest *vicus* at the beginning of the cemetery area, or else the Hadrianic altars originally stood on a slightly different site (perhaps associated with a timber temple, as at Osterburken: Fig. 6.1), and were moved here when a new precinct was paved and the stone temples built.

67 *RIB* 809 and 841.
68 Cf. also Salway 1965, 239-40, who speculates that she was the daughter or wife of the fort's commandant.
69 Robinson 1881; Bellhouse 1992, 39. The altar is probably that shown in the centre of the top row of objects in one of Robinson's photographs published by Bellhouse (1992, 55, pl. XIV); it is apparently now lost.
70 Jarrett 1976, 6.
71 Robinson 1881; Bellhouse 1992, 40-2. The Serpent Stone was apparently matched by a similar, more fragmentary example, of which two parts of the shaft, with a snake carved in relief 'somewhat broader than the other', were found.
72 Daniels 1978, 277.
73 On parade grounds in general, see Johnson 1983, 215-9; Holder 1982, 86 and 90; and especially Davies 1989, 93-123, at 98. The Maryport parade ground measured 285 feet by 279 feet (86.9 m by 85 m), while the *tribunal* mound, of boulder clay on a cobble foundation, measured about 35/40 yards by 12 yards (31/36 m by 11 m).

References

AUSTEN, P. S. and BREEZE, D. J. 1979 'A new inscription from Chesters on Hadrian's Wall', *AA*[5] 7, 115-26
BAATZ, D. 1993 *Der römische Limes*, 3rd. ed. (Berlin)
BAILEY, J. B. 1915 'Catalogue of Roman inscribed and sculptured stones, coins, earthenware, etc., discovered in and near the Roman fort at Maryport, and preserved at Netherhall', *CW*[2] 15, 135-72
BELLHOUSE, R. L. 1970 'Roman sites on the Cumberland coast 1968-1969', *CW*[2] 70, 9-47
BELLHOUSE, R. L. 1989 *Roman sites on the Cumberland coast. A new schedule of coastal sites* [CW Research Series No. 3] (Kendal)
BELLHOUSE, R. L. 1992 *Joseph Robinson of Maryport: archaeologist extraordinary* (privately published)
BIDWELL, P. and SPEAK, S. 1994 *Excavations at South Shields Roman fort. Volume I* [Society of Antiquaries of Newcastle upon Tyne Monograph Series No. 4] (Newcastle upon Tyne)
BIRLEY, E. B. 1961 *Research on Hadrian's Wall* (Kendal)
BIRLEY, A. R. 1981 *The Fasti of Roman Britain* (Oxford)
BOON, G. C. 1973 'Sarapis and tutela: a Silchester coincidence', *Britannia* 4, 107-14
BOWMAN, A. K. and THOMAS, J. D. 1994 *The Vindolanda writing-tablets (Tabulae Vindolandenses II)* (London)
BREEZE, D. J. and DOBSON, B. 1987 *Hadrian's Wall*, 3rd. ed. (Harmondsworth)
BRUCE, J. C. 1874 'Altars recently found in the Roman camp at Maryport', *CW*[1] 1, 175-88
BURNHAM, B. C., KEPPIE, L. J. F., ESMONDE CLEARY, A. S., HASSALL, M. W. C. and TOMLIN, R. S. O. 1993 'Roman Britain in 1992', *Britannia* 24, 267-322
BURNHAM, B. C., KEPPIE, L. J. F., ESMONDE CLEARY, A. S., HASSALL, M. W. C. and TOMLIN, R. S. O. 1994 'Roman Britain in 1993', *Britannia* 25, 245-314
CASEY, P. J. and DAVIES, J. L. 1993 *Excavations at Caernarfon (Segontium)* [Council for British Archaeology Research Report No. 90] (London)
COLLINGWOOD, R. G. 1936 'The Roman fort and settlement at Maryport', *CW*[2] 36, 85-99
DANIELS, C. M. 1978 *Handbook to the Roman Wall with the Cumbrian coast and outpost forts*, 13th. ed. (Newcastle upon Tyne)
DANIELS, C. M. 1989 *The Eleventh Pilgrimage of Hadrian's Wall, 26 August – 1 September 1989* (Newcastle upon Tyne)
DANIELS, C. M. 1990 'How many miles on the Cumberland coast?', *Britannia* 21, 401-6
DAVIES, R. W. 1989 *Service in the Roman army*

[edited by D. Breeze and V. A. Maxfield] (Edinburgh)
FRERE, S. S., HASSALL, M. W. C. and TOMLIN, R. S. O. 1992 'Roman Britain in 1991', *Britannia* 23, 256-323
FRERE, S. S. and TOMLIN, R. S. O. 1991 'Roman Britain in 1990', *Britannia* 22, 221-311
HARTLEY, B. R. and WACHER, J. S. (eds.) 1983 *Rome and her northern provinces. Papers presented to Sheppard Frere* (Gloucester)
HASSALL, M. W. C. 1983 'The internal planning of Roman auxiliary forts', in Hartley and Wacher 1983, 96-131
HIGHAM, N. and JONES, G. D. B. 1985 *The Carvetii* [Peoples of Roman Britain] (Gloucester)
HODGSON, N. 1995 'Were there two Antonine occupations of Scotland?', *Britannia* 26, 29-49
HOLDER, P. A. 1982 *The Roman army in Britain* (London)
JARRETT, M. G. 1958 'The pre-Hadrianic occupation of Roman Maryport', CW^2 58, 63-7
JARRETT, M. G. 1976 *Maryport, Cumbria: a Roman fort and its garrison* (Kendal)
JOHNSON, A. 1983 *Roman forts of the 1st and 2nd centuries AD in Britain and the German provinces* (London)
JOHNSON, J. S. 1976 *The Roman forts of the Saxon Shore* (London)
JONES, G. D. B. 1982 'The Solway frontier: interim report 1976-81', *Britannia* 13, 283-97
JONES, G. D. B. 1993 'Excavations of a coastal tower, Hadrian's Wall. Campfield Tower 2B, Bowness on Solway', *Manchester Archaeological Bulletin* 8, 31-9
JONES, G. D. B. 1994-95 'Farnhill. Excavations on the Solway frontier, 1994', *Manchester Archaeological Bulletin* 9, 23-7
LEWIS, M. J. T. 1966 *Temples in Roman Britain* (Cambridge)
MARGARY, I. D. 1967 *Roman roads in Britain*, rev. ed. (London)
MAXFIELD, V. A. (ed.) 1989 *The Saxon Shore. A handbook* (Exeter)
NASH-WILLIAMS, V. E. 1969 *The Roman frontier in Wales*, second edition revised by M. G. Jarrett (Cardiff)
POTTER, T. W. 1977 'The Biglands milefortlet and the Cumberland coast defences', *Britannia* 8, 149-83
POTTER, T. W. 1978 Review of JARRETT 1976 in *Britannia* 9, 493-5
POTTER, T. W. 1979 *Romans in North-west England* [CW Research Series Volume 1] (Kendal)
ROBINSON, J. 1881 'Notes on the excavations near the Roman camp, Maryport, during the year 1880', CW^1 5, 237-55
ROOKE, H. 1792 'An account of some Roman antiquities in Cumberland hitherto unnoticed', *Archaeologia* 10, 137-42
RIVET, A. L. F. and SMITH, C. 1979 *The place-names of Roman Britain* (London)
SALWAY, P. 1965 *The frontier people of Roman Britain* (Cambridge)
SHOTTER, D. 1993 *Romans and Britons in north-west England* (Lancaster)
SHOTTER, D. 1996 *The Roman frontier in Britain* (Lancaster)
SMITH, D. J. 1962 'The shrine of the Nymphs and the Genius Loci at Carrawburgh', AA^4 50, 59-81
SOMMER, S. 1984 *The military vici of Roman Britain* [BAR British Series No. 129] (Oxford)
STUKELEY, W. 1725 *Iter Boreale* (London)
TURNBULL, P. 1991 'Excavation of milefortlet 21 in 1990 (part of the 'The coastal defences of Hadrian's Wall' project): interim summary', *Archaeology North* 1, 21-7
TURNBULL, P. 1996 'The supposed Roman harbour at Maryport', CW^2 96, 233-5
WEBSTER, J. 1986 'Roman bronzes from Maryport in the Netherhall Collection', CW^2 86, 49-70
WENHAM, L. P. 1939 'Notes on the garrisoning of Maryport', CW^2 39, 19-30
WILSON, D. R. and WRIGHT, R. P. 1970 'Roman Britain in 1969', *Britannia* 1, 269-315
WOOLLISCROFT, D. J. 1994 'Signalling and the design of the Cumberland coast system', CW^2 94, 55-64

2 Maryport and the Flavian conquest of North Britain

I. D. Caruana

Introduction

The possibility of Flavian, and specifically Agricolan, occupation at Maryport has been canvassed in the past (Jarrett 1958, 64-5). It was based in part on the literary testimony of the *Agricola* but also on the presence of a small number of supposedly Flavian samian sherds in the collection at Netherhall. At least one of the Neronian/early Flavian samian sherds cited can now be discounted (Jarrett 1976, 14), and the artefactual evidence has been thought too slight to sustain the original conclusion.

Jarrett belonged in a tradition, particularly strong among excavators, which dated the foundation of all forts in north Britain to the governorship of Agricola, taking at face value the claims of Tacitus, his biographer and son-in-law. At the same time, running alongside this archaeological tradition, there have been strong dissenting voices coming from classicists and historians who have warned that the *Agricola* cannot be taken too literally, and that there are other historical fragments which point to different conclusions about the pace of Roman conquest in the north (e.g. E. Birley 1952, A. Birley 1973, Mann 1985).

Discoveries from the excavations in Carlisle during the 1970s and 1980s and from Blennerhasset, only discovered in 1984, have given independent dating to two forts. Both appear to be earlier than the governorship of Agricola, thus confirming the historians in their doubts about the *Agricola* as a source. Intriguingly, the firm date provided by dendrochronology for Carlisle carries implications for all aspects of the conquest period in the north of England and southern Scotland, which can only be explored as new work is undertaken and new dating evidence is recovered. More specifically, the dating of these two sites also carries interesting implications for the origins of Maryport.

The date of Carlisle

The earliest phase of occupation of the fort at Carlisle has been successfully and unequivocally dated by dendrochronology. The dated timbers from the lowest levels of the rampart, cross-matched with other, less precisely dated timbers without bark, and with firmly dated timbers from primary construction deposits, leave little doubt that the first fort was founded either in the second half of AD 72 or early in AD 73, with a strong preference for AD 72 (Groves 1990; Caruana forthcoming). The first fort dates, therefore, to the governorship of Petillius Cerialis (AD 71-73: A. Birley 1981, 66).

Other lines of evidence corroborate this absolute date. Many late Neronian or early Flavian samian forms and stamps gives strong indications of pre-Agricolan occupation, a point already made at the beginning of this century. (It is worth acknowledging, in passing, how samian specialists, alone among archaeologists to depart from Agricolan orthodoxy, have assigned Cerialan dates to Carlisle [Bushe-Fox 1913], and pre-Agricolan dates to forts on the Stainmore route, including Carlisle [Hartley 1971, 58]). Certain mid-first-century brooch types (Snape 1993, 97-100) and shoe forms also point in the same direction. The different pattern of coin loss between a Cerialan and an Agricolan occupation is now recognizable (Shotter 1993a, 4-7).

Blennerhasset

The Roman fort at Blennerhasset was discovered by aerial photography in 1984 by the RCHME (Frere et al. 1985, 273-4). It lies on the south bank of the river Ellen facing north-east. Its overall area is estimated at 3.4 ha (8.4 acres) and is apparently of a single period. Subsequent field walking of the site has produced abundant Flavian samian, including a strong presence of late Neronian/early Flavian pieces (Evans and Scull 1990). The authors are cautious in their dating, but chronological parallels to the assemblage from Carlisle make a Cerialan date very probable.

The publishers of the finds from Blennerhasset discuss the fort in terms of control of the Solway Plain and of the Cumbrian massif to the rear (Evans and Scull 1990, 136). However, the strategic importance of this fort is in reality quite different. The need for control of the Cumbrian massif is highly debatable (Higham 1986, 173-4). Blennerhasset is surely part of a primary road link between Carlisle and the coast; it lies 16 miles (26 km) from Carlisle and 10 miles (16.5 km) from Maryport.

Its role can be seen as the predecessor of Old Carlisle, just under six miles away, or Papcastle, 7.5 miles to the south-west. In the later years of the Roman occupation, this road was garrisoned by a line of the most important forts in Cumbria. Old Carlisle, Papcastle, and, at least in the second century, Maryport, were garrisoned by high-status units (*alae* and milliary cohorts), reflected in the richness of the finds from these sites.

Evidence from Maryport

When Jarrett considered the evidence for first-century occupation at Maryport, he concentrated on the surviving pottery from the site. Several other pieces of evidence should also be considered.

1. A Langton Down derivative bow brooch (Webster 1986, no. 1 = Bailey 1915, pl. XIp). The type had died out by the time of the Flavian period (Collingwood and Richmond 1969, 292-3; Hattatt 1982, 80-2) and is not represented at all in the recently published corpus of brooches from Stanegate and Hadrian's Wall sites (Snape 1993: Maryport does not form part of this corpus). It is common at Claudian/Neronian sites such as Colchester (Hawkes and Hull 1947, 317-9), the King Harry Lane cemetery at Verulamium (Stead et al. 1989, 91-3) and Hod Hill (Brailsford 1962, 8). A single derivative type is recorded from an early Flavian level at The Lunt (Mackreth 1969, 108-9, no. 4).

2. A gable fragment from the tombstone of Vireius Pau[(RIB 859), found in 1870 in a field north of the fort. The full form of the dedication (*Dis Manibus*) is generally regarded as characteristic of a relatively early period, i.e. Neronian or Flavian (Anderson 1984, 36). It stands apart from the other tombstones from Maryport which have D M (*RIB* 860-1, 866-8, *JRS* 58 [1968] 214), D M S (*RIB* 857) and DIS MA[(*RIB* 858). The lettering on this tombstone is also of high quality, another feature of early tombstones (Anderson ibid.). Unfortunately, nothing is known about the deceased or his origins.

3. A building stone of Legio XX (*RIB* 853) is unusual in omitting the letters VV of the cognomina. A recent study of the legion's titles concluded that 'stone-cutters were punctilious in giving the Twentieth Legion its cognomina' (Tomlin 1992, 155). Tomlin discounts *RIB* 853 as an 'informal building stone' (which it is) and discusses the other stones omitting the cognomina. He concludes that the cognomina are well attested after *c.* AD 86, but not before, and suggests the possibility that they might have been awarded about AD 84 rather than, as traditionally believed, in AD 61 (ibid. 158). If this is so, it creates the possibility that *RIB* 853 should also date to the early Flavian period, say *c.* AD 72/85, something recognized at the time of its discovery (Ferguson 1880, 393), but since overlooked.

4. There is a significant presence of pre-Flavian coinage from Maryport (Casey 1976, 48; Shotter 1980; Shotter, this volume), including three *aes* of Nero, as well as less diagnostic Republican issues. Casey thought that there was a Flavian presence at Maryport (ibid. 47), although this was not originally accepted by Shotter because of the proportions of Trajanic to Flavian coins (ibid. 7). Shotter (1994) has now shown that these Neronian coins may be markers for pre-Flavian or early Flavian contacts with the Brigantes, and while he now accepts a (late) Flavian origin for Maryport (see below, p. 136) he did not include the Maryport coins in his 1994 survey. The Neronian coins were already in the Netherhall collection before 1915 and their provenances are not recorded, except for an *aureus* which was found somewhere 'upon the sea shore, within flood mark' (p. 132). This underlines the likelihood that the collection derives from other sources than just the fort. There may, therefore, be some significance to the contrast between the sample collected in the 1966 excavations and the wider sample. The 1966 fort group confirms the evidence of the pottery, that the excavated fort remains date from the reign of Hadrian (Jarrett 1976, 40-1). The wider general collection may point to an alternative location for the earlier fort(s).

Rome and Brigantia

Having seen the evidence, both direct and circumstantial, for a Flavian and Cerialan presence at Maryport, we may now look at how this might fit into the wider picture of the Roman occupation of Brigantia (Fig. 2.1). The process of conquest began with a rift in AD 69 between Cartimandua, the pro-Roman queen, and her consort, Venutius, who responded to his deposition by revolting and seizing the kingdom. Cartimandua was rescued by Roman soldiers led by the governor, Vettius Bolanus. Full conquest was left to the next governor, Petillius Cerialis (Tacitus, *Histories* III, 45; Hanson and Campbell 1986).

Cerialis, a Flavian partisan and probably son-in-law of Vespasian, arrived in Britain as governor in AD 71, having just suppressed the revolt of Civilis on the Rhine. He brought with him *Legio II Adiutrix*, replacing *Legio XIV*, which had been withdrawn in AD 66, and a number of auxiliary units (Holder 1982, 16). Tacitus acknowledges that Cerialis was active against the Brigantes and in pursuit of Venutius, although the details are uncertain. 'There were many battles, and sometimes they were not without bloodshed' (*Agricola* 17). Agricola, as legate of *Legio XX*, took part in this campaign.

While Tacitus is usually factually accurate (Wellesley 1969, 65), his use of barbed phrases, such as that quoted, innuendo

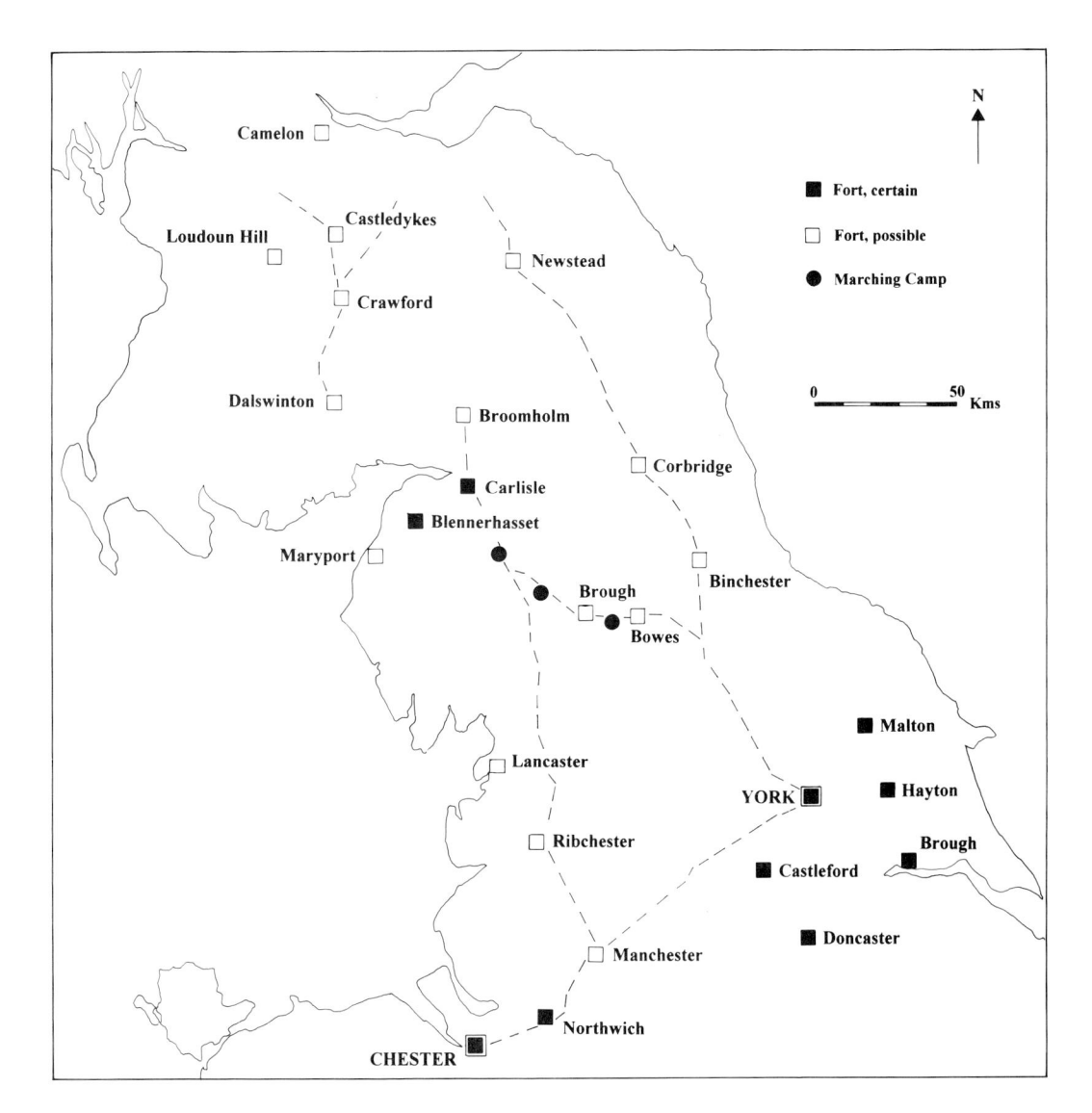

Fig. 2.1 Map of northern Britain indicating fortresses, forts and marching camps built either certainly (solid black symbol) or possibly (open symbol) during the governorship of Petillius Cerialis

(Ryberg 1942), and reporting of unfavourable rumour, intentionally diminishes the achievements and successes of more prominent governors, such as Cerialis and Frontinus, to the benefit of Agricola (A. Birley 1973, 186, 188). Cerialis was not the only one to suffer. A tradition more favourable to Bolanus than Tacitus, who stresses the failure to suppress Venutius, is contained in Statius' *Silvae* (5, 2, 142-9). Moreover, the elder Pliny, writing, according to Birley, between AD 70 and 72, in a work published in AD 77, speaks of Roman arms coming into contact with the Caledonians no more than thirty years from the start of Claudius' conquest (*NH*

IV, 102). Taken literally, this must mean that Roman armies had reached at least to the Forth-Clyde by AD 72 (E. Birley 1946).

There is, therefore, despite the influence of the Tacitean narratives, another group of ancient texts which suggest that governors prior to Agricola were responsible for much of what is attributed to Agricola in his early campaigns.

The process of conquest

In attempting to reconcile two conquests of Brigantia both by Cerialis and by Agricola in his second campaign, the first invasion is usually envisaged as not leading to permanent control, while Agricola is credited with lasting conquest (Frere 1978, 123; 1987, 90). We must now examine the possibility of reconstructing the conquest through Cerialis' activities, and consider how much is left to the credit of Agricola.

Venutius' last stand was once thought to have been at Stanwick, at the eastern end of the Stainmore route from York to Carlisle (Wheeler 1954). However, if Stanwick was Cartimandua's stronghold, as could be inferred by the quantity of Roman material at the site, the logic of the situation makes it more likely that Venutius held out elsewhere (Hanson and Campbell 1986, 86).

Many years ago Richmond identified the invasion route through Stainmore, by which he thought Cerialis had attacked the northern part of the Brigantian tribal area. The invading army was identified by its marching camps on this route, at Rey Cross, Crackenthorpe and Plumpton Head (Richmond and McIntyre 1934; Frere 1978, 120; 1987, 85), marked by the three solid circles on Fig. 2.1, and they point the direction of march northwards. Their date, as with all temporary camps, is difficult to establish, but the clue for Richmond was the fact that the Roman road from York to Carlisle, which he assumed to be Agricolan in origin, cuts through the camp at Rey Cross and is later than it.

Since Richmond and McIntyre wrote, there have been two significant developments which justify looking again at their arguments. Firstly, in Scotland much work has been done in identifying various series of temporary camps, grouped according to shared gate forms and to similarity of the area enclosed within the ramparts (e.g. St Joseph 1969; Hanson 1978). There is a strong case to be made that these series represent the passage of armies on the march. Secondly, the recent publication by the RCHME (Welfare and Swan 1995) of its survey data and transcriptions from aerial photographs of Roman temporary camps in England enables us to place the Stainmore camps in context.

The first point to make about Richmond's Stainmore camps is that they immediately stand out from the mass of English sites (ibid. 12-13, fig. 6, nos. 6, 15, and 23). They are characterised by irregular shapes, an area of 8.1-9.5 ha. (20-23.5 acres), and multiple gates on each side. The gates have the form of a traverse (*tutulus* or *titulum*).

Secondly, the series must be incomplete at its northern end, and we should anticipate a further camp at, or just south of, Carlisle. Whether there ought to be camps south of Rey Cross might depend whether the army started from Stanwick (see above) or York. If it departed from York, camps from this series might be expected at Catterick, where the recorded site is no more than a possibility (ibid. 136-7), Bootham Stray, and other unidentified sites between.

The distribution of temporary camps (of whatever function) in England makes it reasonably clear that the use of such camps was probably only coming into fashion in the late Neronian or Flavian period (ibid. 4, fig. 2). They are sparsely represented in the south-west, but the main clusters begin at Wroxeter and westwards, and from the Nottinghamshire and West Lincolnshire area northwards. They appear to be absent from south-east England in areas where campaigning took place in the 40s and 50s.

Consolidation

The new date for Carlisle's foundation provides firm, independent corroboration of the non-Agricolan historical traditions. However, Carlisle's foundation in AD 72/3 carries with it implications for the date of many of the forts of northern England. When the early date for Carlisle was only a suspicion, commentators were unwilling to build broad speculations on such insecure foundations. Frere, for example, merely suggested that an early fort at Carlisle may have been an advance base to make contact with the sea (1978, 119; 1987, 84).

Furthermore it is often assumed that the Roman conquest was a process of land-grabs behind an ever advancing front-line, whereas it actually proceeded as a series of takeovers of existing geo-political entities. The Romans worked either with or against the pre-existing tribal structures and their rulers, and it was this primary contact which determined the consequent treatment of the different tribal groups (Millet 1990). Despite the less developed political structures of the Brigantes, by comparison with the southern tribes, the implication of the intervention against Venutius and the planting of a fort at York and at sites in south Yorkshire (Breeze and Dobson 1985) is that the Brigantes were henceforward regarded as a subject tribe. It is not, therefore, surprising to find forts at the north-western limits of Brigantia being founded at the same time or very close to those south of York.

Since it is inconceivable that Carlisle was an isolated outpost, it is worth re-examining the position in the rest of Brigantia (Fig. 2.1). We must envisage, as a very minimum, that the whole of the Stainmore passage from York to Carlisle, was garrisoned at regular intervals with forts perhaps at Aldborough, Catterick, Carkin Moor, Brough-under-Stainmore and Brougham (Hartley 1980, 4). In the absence of excavated structures firmly tied to good dating evidence, it is necessary to use references to certain diagnostic finds, but, since the samian specialists have been vindicated over the foundation date of Carlisle, we need no longer be quite so circumspect in reaching tentative conclusions based on this evidence. Pre-Agricolan samian is recorded from Bowes (Hartley 1971, 58) and Brough-under-Stainmore (ibid. 66, n. 29). Brougham, however, looks as though its position is determined by the road junction and may not, therefore, be part of the primary system. Recent work at Old Penrith favours a foundation date there in the 80s AD (Austen 1991). As an alternative, if the earliest route through Stainmore came via Kirby Thore, it may have continued down the Eden valley rather than the Petteril, and there may be an unknown early fort in the Eden valley spanning the gap between Kirby Thore and Carlisle.

If the western route to Scotland was laid out, it is probable that Dere Street with its forts also was. Moreover, it is likely that there was direct access to the south via Low Borrow Bridge, Burrow-in-Lonsdale and Ribchester. Some evidence for the early Flavian date of this route exists, based on samian and coins from Manchester (Jones and Grealey 1974, 81-3,185; Shotter 1994, 30; for an affirmation of an Agricolan date, see Bryant et al. 1986, 141), and the coinage at Ribchester (Edwards and Webster 1985, 88; Shotter 1993a, 4), although the early date for Walton-le-Dale indicated by Hanson (1987, 65 and fig. 4) has not been sustained by full analysis of the finds. Recent excavations at Ribchester have produced some early coarse wares, including Lyon ware (Hird, pers. comm.). The coin-list from Lancaster may also the presence of a pre-Agricolan fort there (Shotter 1994).

Apart from the Lancashire forts, there is little modern excavated evidence from forts in England to confirm these suppositions. The earliest Corbridge fort, at Red House, was clearly dated to the Flavian period by the finds, and the excavators suggested occupation occurred within the range c. AD 75 - c. AD 90 (Hanson et al. 1979, 41-2). While the terminal date of c. AD 90 matches the start of occupation on the main Corbridge site, the start date at Red House is arguably too late. Some of the samian was Neronian/early Flavian (ibid. 36, nos. 1, 3, 4; 40, a & b), and there was a flagon with close parallels at Claudio-Neronian Richborough (ibid. 55; Dore 1981, 65-6). Similar flagons have also been noted at Hayton and Camelon (Dore 1981, 66), the first certainly an early Flavian fort. Lyon ware is present at Binchester (Dore 1981, 65).

Among other recently excavated sites, Chesterholm, like Old Penrith, seems to date from the 80s (R. Birley 1989, 277) and Watercrook to the 90s (Potter 1979, 358). Neither, however, is necessarily relevant to the argument since they were probably founded, as Potter suggests, during a later period of consolidation.

A cautious approach to dating the foundation of northern forts produces a 'hardly credible' distribution map, confined to south-east Yorkshire, of forts in existence by AD 75 (Breeze and Dobson 1985, 3 and fig. 1). This map is almost identical to that produced by Ogilvie and Richmond (1967, fig. 2) to show the state of the garrison before Agricola. The legionary fortress at York, usually dated to Cerialis (Wenham 1971, 47), is at the outer limit of Roman occupation. If it can be shown, as is argued here, that northern England must have had a network of garrison forts extending at least to the Tyne-Solway (Fig. 2.1), the extent of direct Roman control in the 70s becomes more credible. The legion at York is no longer exposed but takes its place behind a wide screen of auxiliary forts. Moreover, the revision in the pace of progress makes it all the more plausible that there was an early military phase at York prior to the foundation of the fortress (Wenham 1971, 48; but note the reservations of Hartley 1971, 56 and 1980, 2).

While there has in the past been some critical discussion of the dates for the earliest forts in the north of England, forts north of the border are all, except one, assumed to be no earlier than Agricola. The exception is Dalswinton, where four periods, all arguably Flavian, are visible on aerial photographs (St Joseph 1977, 131-2; Hanson 1987, 61 and fig. 7). Four Flavian periods, but no pottery later than c. AD 90, are known from Loudoun Hill (Hartley 1972, 14). Early Flavian rather than Flavian-Trajanic occupation might be the solution.

There are slight hints of possible earlier dates in other lowland forts. Lyon ware has been found at Newstead and Camelon (Dore 1981, 65). The latter site also has between twelve and fifteen vessels of *terra nigra* (Maxfield 1980, 77). The only piece of samian known from Crawford is a Form 29 dated c. AD 60-75 (Maxwell 1972, 189, no. 1; Hartley 1972, 10), and the site has, for the Flavian period, an old-fashioned form of barrack (Breeze and Dobson 1976, 128). Broomholm has an early Form 27 (Hartley 1972, 10 and 12). Castledykes has five vessels of early Flavian date (Robertson 1964, 175, 178-9, 186-89) and one Form 37 of early to mid-Flavian date (ibid. 190). Since all the Flavian samian dates to before AD 85, there is a greater possibility that the earlier material is not residual.

The evidence for most lowland sites is not strong, but, equally, little excavation has taken place on most sites except Newstead and Castledykes. Forts such as Easter Happrew, Bothwellhaugh and Raeburnfoot have produced no Flavian samian at all (Hartley 1972, 9-11). Much depends on the life expectancy of an individual pot. Caution dictates that too much should not be built on isolated sherds, but in the light of the hints listed here, and the context of the Carlisle date, the foundation date of any lowland fort needs to be carefully argued on archaeological grounds and without recourse to the *Agricola*.

To put the other side of the picture, it is only fair to point out several pieces of evidence which run counter to the argument here. The samian from Strageath, a fort north of the isthmus, contains a very small quantity of late Neronian-early Flavian sherds, similar to that cited above, though the proportion of the total is very small. Likewise the roads leaving Newstead and Crawford on Fig. 2.1 imply the need for another fort between Camelon and Newstead. Elginhaugh is the obvious candidate, and the site has produced *terra nigra* and some evidence for rebuilding within the single-period fort (Frere et al. 1987, 313 and fig. 8). However, the foundation date of the fort is currently thought to be after AD 77, assuming that a hoard in a wall trench of the *principia* was a foundation deposit (Hanson, pers. comm.).

Agricola and the *Agricola*

Where does this leave Agricola? It seems to me that the removal of Carlisle from the list of Agricolan foundations and the other new dates, both known and presumed, provide a wider challenge to the authority of the *Agricola* as a historical source. In particular it is worth re-examining Tacitus' descriptions of Agricola's conquests.

The implication of Tacitus' use of *expeditio* (years 3 and 5), and the almost invariable translation of *aestas* (years 1, 2, 4, and 6) as campaign season, conveys a series of summers filled with military manoeuvres. From this we derive our picture of seven active campaigns by Agricola, with an army in pursuit of conquest. If it is now accepted that Brigantia was under Roman control by AD 73, the achievements of the second season, incorporating new territory, receiving hostages and building a network of forts round the surrendered tribes (*multae civitates . . . praesidiis castellisque circumdatae*: *Agricola* 20), begin to look, at best, an exaggeration. Hanson has already queried how much had already been achieved by Frontinus in north Wales prior to Agricola's first 'campaign', and suggested that perhaps only Pen Llystyn and Caernarfon need be Agricolan foundations, rather than earlier (1987, 50-1). It becomes ever more important to look critically at the reality behind the descriptions of each year's progress.

The third season is characterised by further advance as far as the Tay, with new tribes encountered (*Agricola* 22). Military activity is not stressed, though 'territory was laid waste', and modern commentators have emphasised fort-building and the creation of roads (Ogilvie and Richmond 1967, 57; Frere 1978, 125; 1987, 91). The same applies to the fourth season with activity located in west central Scotland, securing territory overrun, and the creation of a frontier on the Forth-Clyde isthmus (*Agricola* 23).

Arguably, only in the fifth, sixth and seventh seasons is there a clear sense of aggressive military activity taking place. The nature of the fifth season's enterprise is somewhat problematical. The *Agricola*

(24) appears to refer to a crossing of the Clyde, although the name is not spelled out. Some commentators have tried to place all the action in south-west Scotland (Ogilvie and Richmond 1967, 58-60; Frere 1978, 127; 1987, 92), but the textual analysis is not entirely convincing (Reed 1971). Reed argues that a separate venture in the same year took the troops to Galloway, facing Ireland (ibid. 147). For the sixth year, an army group was assembled, and the hostile territory was penetrated in force. Only at this stage has archaeology shown the marching camps of a field army on the move (Hanson 1978; 1987, 121-36), and there is description of an actual battle. Even here, it is open to doubt how large a Roman force was involved (Hanson 1987, 135).

A close reading of the *Agricola* actually gives a picture of active campaigning confined to the sixth and seventh seasons, with a reconnaissance in force in the fifth year. The first four summers are described in not dissimilar terms. Tacitus' intention may well have been to convey the impression that a lot of campaigning was under way, but the substance of the narratives amounts to very little except that Agricola spent the summers touring the frontier parts of his province. Once we acknowledge, from the archaeological dates, that Tacitus has falsely managed to imply that the second season was one of conquest, we should be wary of accepting that the third and fourth seasons, described in comparable language, were also extending the limits of the province. (Were new forts built on the Tay in year 3?). No doubt much useful work was undertaken in these tours, including diplomacy, military consolidation and planning for the real campaign. However, since it is impossible to identify actual fighting, and the status of Agricola as a military leader of exceptional merit cannot be sustained (Hanson 1987, 174-9),

the *Agricola* must be used with exceptional care in interpreting remains on the ground. In particular, care must be taken not to use the excavated remains of forts as a commentary on the *Agricola*, but rather to test all dating by independent criteria.

Conclusion

This paper has shown that the newly attested foundation dates for Roman Carlisle and Blennerhasset point inexorably to the need for a contemporary site at Maryport. Some casual finds from Maryport lend support to a Flavian presence, but, perhaps apart from the coin evidence, they are not sufficiently well dated to support a Cerialan foundation date in the early 70s. The location of the early site at Maryport remains a mystery. Stone paving and walls south of the Ellen mouth recorded in 1886 and 1920 have been suggested as precursors to the visible fort (Bailey 1926). The known fort is almost certainly Hadrianic in date, and Bailey thought that these remains by the harbour were probably Agricolan. The use of stone at this period makes this highly unlikely, and recent observations of machine-dug test-pits in the same area indicates that Bailey's stonework was, in fact, the sandstone bedrock underlying river silts (Turnbull 1996, 235). Turnbull's critique of the arguments which have led to a belief in the existence of a major Roman naval base at Maryport are valid, but he overstates the case in arguing in general terms against the existence of a harbour, built or natural, as this paper has tried to show.

Bailey was correct in assuming that an earlier fort need not necessarily underlie the known fort. There is increasing evidence from the region (e.g. Old Penrith, Beckfoot) that second-century forts did not necessarily directly overlie their first-century predecessors. If this was so at Maryport, then we have to admit to complete ignorance of the position of the early fort. However, one possibility worth considering is that it does lie beneath the Hadrianic fort. Jarrett and his co-excavators in 1966 disagreed about the status of some deposits beneath the Hadrianic rampart. Their published section strongly suggests that the Hadrianic rampart lies on top of an early rampart (Jarrett 1976, fig. 5). Shotter has noted that an aerial photograph appears to show crop-marks of 'a large fort-like structure' underlying the known fort (1993b, 15). This evidence appears to be rather slender, and such a fort was not picked up by the RCHME (Lax and Blood, this volume, pp. 52-66).

Whatever the force of these suggestions, there is enough evidence to propose the existence of a fort at Maryport in Flavian times. Its location seems to suggest that its function was to form a link in a maritime supply line in support of units at Carlisle and on the main route axis through Brigantia and into Scotland. We should note also how the earliest Roman coinage in the north-west is also concentrated in coastal locations, as if it is also reflecting fleet activity (Shotter 1994, 26).

The implications of the early military occupation of this route from Maryport to Carlisle is that the Roman army was fully in control of the northern parts of Brigantia by about AD 72. I have tried to point out archaeological evidence to question the Agricolan foundation dates attributed to a number of other forts in northern England and southern Scotland. This evidence is anything but conclusive, but is sufficient to warrant a re-examination of the pace of conquest. I have suggested that the combination of archaeology, the non-Tacitean historical traditions, and a re-reading of the *Agricola* allow a history to be constructed that minimizes Agricola's role in the conquest of northern England, and possibly also southern Scotland.

Circumstantial evidence suggests that Maryport came into being in the early stages of consolidating the Roman hold on the north-west, when it had a role in supplying the Roman army. How long the first occupation lasted is a more difficult point. Blennerhasset appears to be a single-period and short-lived fort. Carlisle was not intensively occupied in the early years of Agricola's governorship, perhaps until a rebuilding which occurred around AD 83 (Caruana 1992). A wide spread of military sites in north-west Cumbria in the late-first and early-second centuries points to a fluid situation that is not properly understood (Jones 1982). This and the presence of a Flavian-Trajanic fort at Kirkbride (Bellhouse and Richardson 1982) means that Maryport may not have had an enduring role, and we need not necessarily expect continuity of occupation at Maryport throughout the Flavian and Trajanic periods. Re-occupation occurs only at the point when Maryport was brought into the Hadrianic system of coastal defences.

Acknowledgements

I am grateful to David Breeze, Philip Cracknell, Bill Hanson, Louise Hird, David Shotter, and Humphrey Welfare for information and discussion of various points. This should not be taken to imply that they necessarily agree with the ideas presented here.

References

ANDERSON, A. S. 1984 *Roman military tombstones* (Princes Risborough)

AUSTEN P. S. 1991 *Bewcastle and Old Penrith* [CW Research Series No. 6] (Kendal)

BAILEY, J. B. 1915 'Catalogue of Roman inscribed and sculptured stones, coins, earthenware, etc., discovered in and near the Roman fort at Maryport, and preserved at Netherhall', CW^2 15, 135-72

BAILEY, J. B. 1926 'Further notes on Roman

roads at Maryport and on the Netherhall collection', *CW² 26*, 415-22

BELLHOUSE, R. L. and RICHARDSON, G. G. S. 1982 'The Trajanic fort at Kirkbride: the terminus of the Stanegate frontier', *CW² 82*, 35-50

BIRLEY, A. R. 1973 'Petillius Cerialis and the conquest of Brigantia', *Britannia 4*, 179-90

BIRLEY, A. R. 1981 *The Fasti of Roman Britain* (Oxford)

BIRLEY, E. B. 1946 'Britain under the Flavians: Agricola and his predecessors', *Durham University Journal*, June 1946, 79-84 (= BIRLEY 1953, 10-19)

BIRLEY, E. B. 1952 'The Brigantian problem, and the first Roman contact with Scotland', *Transactions of Dumfries and Galloway Natural History and Archaeological Society* ser. 3, 29, 46-65 (= BIRLEY 1953, 31-47)

BIRLEY, E. B. 1953 *Roman Britain and the Roman army* (Kendal)

BIRLEY, R. E. 1989 'Vindolanda', *Current Archaeology 116*, 275-9

BRAILSFORD, J. W. 1962 *Hod Hill Volume I: antiquities from Hod Hill in the Durden Collection* (London)

BRANIGAN, K. (ed.) 1980 *Rome and the Brigantes: the impact of Rome on northern England* (Sheffield)

BREEZE, D. J. and DOBSON, B. 1976 'A view of Roman Scotland in 1975', *Glasgow Archaeological Journal 4*, 124-43

BREEZE, D. J. and DOBSON, B. 1985 'Roman military deployment in North England', *Britannia 16*, 1-20

BRYANT, S., MORRIS, M. and WALKER, J. S. F. 1986 *Roman Manchester: a frontier settlement* (Manchester)

BUSHE-FOX, J. P. 1913 'The use of samian pottery in dating the early Roman occupation of the north of Britain', *Archaeologia 64*, 295-314

BUTLER, R. M. (ed.) 1971 *Soldier and civilian in Roman Yorkshire* (Leicester)

CARUANA, I. D. 1992 'Carlisle: excavation of a section of the annexe ditch of the first Flavian fort, 1990', *Britannia 23*, 45-109

CARUANA, I. D. forthcoming *The Roman forts at Carlisle: excavations at Annetwell Street, 1973-84*

CASEY, J. 1976 'Coins', in Jarrett 1976, 46-8

COLLINGWOOD, R. G. and RICHMOND, I. A. 1969 *The archaeology of Roman Britain*, 2nd. ed. (London)

DORE, J. 1981 'Flavian coarse pottery in northern Britain', in *Early technology in north Britain* (Scottish Archaeological Forum 11), 62-9

DOREY, T. A. (ed.) 1969 *Tacitus* (London)

EDWARDS, B. J. N. and WEBSTER, P. V. 1985 *Ribchester Excavations. Part I: excavations within the Roman fort, 1970-1980* (Cardiff)

EVANS J. and SCULL, C. 1990 'Fieldwork on the Roman fort site at Blennerhasset, Cumbria', *CW² 90*, 127-37

FERGUSON, R. S. 1880 'Excavations at the Roman camp near Maryport', *Proceedings of the Society of Antiquaries of London² 8*, 392-5

FRERE, S. S. 1978 *Britannia: a history of Roman Britain*, 2nd. ed. (London)

FRERE, S. S. 1987 *Britannia: a history of Roman Britain*, 3rd. ed. (London)

FRERE, S. S., HASSALL, M. W. C. and TOMLIN, R. S. O. 1985 'Roman Britain in 1984', *Britannia 16*, 251-332

FRERE, S. S., HASSALL, M. W. C. and TOMLIN, R. S. O. 1987 'Roman Britain in 1986', *Britannia 18*, 301-77

GROVES, C. 1990 *Tree-ring analysis and dating of timbers from Annetwell Street, Carlisle, Cumbria, 1981-84* [A. M. Lab. Report 49/90] (London)

HANSON, W. S. 1978 'Roman campaigns north of the Forth-Clyde Isthmus: the evidence of the temporary camps', *PSAS 109*, 140-50

HANSON, W. S. 1987 *Agricola and the conquest of the north* (London)

HANSON, W. S., DANIELS, C. M., DORE, J. N. and GILLAM, J. P. 1979 'The Agricolan supply base at Red House, Corbridge', *AA⁵ 7*, 1-88

HANSON, W. S. and CAMPBELL, D. B. 1986 'The Brigantes: from clientage to conquest', *Britannia 17*, 73-89

HARTLEY, B. R. 1971 'Roman York and the northern military command to the third century A.D.', in Butler 1971, 55-69

HARTLEY, B. R. 1972 'The Roman occupation of Scotland: the evidence of samian ware', *Britannia 3*, 1-55

HARTLEY, B. R. 1980 'The Brigantes and the Roman Army', in Branigan 1980, 2-7

HATTATT, R. 1982 *Ancient and Romano-British brooches* (Sherborne)

HAWKES, C. F. C. and HULL, M. R. 1947 *Camulodunum* [Society of Antiquaries Research Report No. 14] (London)

HIGHAM, N. J. 1986 *The northern counties to AD 1000* (Harlow)

HOBLEY, B. 1969 'A Neronian-Vespasianic military site at "The Lunt", Baginton, Warwickshire', *Transactions of the Birmingham Archaeological Society* 83, 65-129

HOLDER, P. A. 1982 *The Roman army in Britain* (London)

JARRETT, M. G. 1958 'The pre-Hadrianic occupation of Roman Maryport', CW^2 58, 63-7

JARRETT, M. G. 1976. *Maryport, Cumbria: a Roman fort and its garrison* [CW Extra Series No. 22] (Kendal)

JONES, G. D. B. 1982 'The Solway frontier: an interim report 1976-81', *Britannia* 13, 283-97

JONES, G. D. B. and GREALEY, S. 1974 *Roman Manchester* (Manchester)

MACKRETH, D. F. 1969 'Report on the brooches', in Hobley 1969, 107-11

MANN, J. C. 1985 'Two "topoi" in the *Agricola*', *Britannia* 16, 21-4

MAXFIELD, V. A. 1980 'The Flavian fort at Camelon', *Scottish Archaeological Forum* 12, 69-78

MAXWELL, G. S. 1972 'Excavations at the Roman fort at Crawford, Lanarkshire', *PSAS* 104, 147-200

MILLETT, M. 1990 *The Romanization of Britain* (Cambridge)

OGILVIE, R. M. and RICHMOND, I. A. (eds.) 1967 *Cornelii Taciti 'De Vita Agricolae'* (Oxford)

POTTER, T. W. 1979 *Romans in North-west England* [CW Research Series No. 1] (Kendal)

REED, N. 1971 'The fifth year of Agricola's campaigns', *Britannia* 2, 143-8

RICHMOND, I. A. and McINTYRE, J. 1934 'The Roman Camps at Rey Cross and Crackenthorpe', CW^2 34, 50-61

ROBERTSON, A. S. 1964 *The Roman Fort at Castledykes* (Edinburgh)

RYBERG, I. S. 1942 'Tacitus' art of innuendo', *Transactions of the American Philological Association* 73, 383-404

ST JOSEPH, J. K. S. 1969 'Air reconnaissance in Roman Britain, 1965-68', *JRS* 59, 104-28

ST JOSEPH, J. K. S. 1977 'Air reconnaissance in Roman Britain, 1973-6', *JRS* 67, 125-61

SHOTTER, D. C. A. 1980 'The Roman occupation of North-west England: the coin evidence', CW^2 80, 1-15

SHOTTER, D. C. A. 1993a 'Coin-loss and the Roman occupation of North-west England', *British Numismatic Journal* 63, 1-19

SHOTTER, D. C. A. 1993b *Romans and Britons in North-west England* (Lancaster)

SHOTTER, D. C. A. 1994 'Rome and the Brigantes: early hostilities', CW^2 94, 21-34

SNAPE, M. E. 1993 *Roman brooches from North Britain: a classification and a catalogue of brooches from sites on the Stanegate* [BAR British Series No. 235] (Oxford)

STEAD, I. M. and RIGBY, V. 1989 *Verulamium: the King Harry Lane Site* [English Heritage Archaeological Report No. 12] (London)

TOMLIN, R. S. O. 1992 'The Twentieth Legion at Wroxeter and Carlisle in the first century: the epigraphic evidence', *Britannia* 23, 141-58

TURNBULL, P. 1996 'The supposed Roman harbour at Maryport', CW^2 96, 233-5

WEBSTER, J. 1986 'Roman bronzes from Maryport in the Netherhall collection', CW^2 86, 49-70

WELFARE, H. and SWAN, V. 1995 *Roman camps in England: the field archaeology* [RCHME] (London)

WELLESLEY, K. 1969 'Tacitus as a military historian', in Dorey 1969, 63-97

WENHAM, L. P. 1971 'The beginnings of Roman York', in Butler 1971, 45-53

WHEELER, R. E. M. 1954 *The Stanwick fortifications, North Riding of Yorkshire* [Society of Antiquaries Research Report No. 17] (London)

3 The earthworks of the Maryport fort: an analytical field survey by the Royal Commission on the Historical Monuments of England

Amy Lax and Keith Blood

Introduction

The Roman frontier defences of the Cumbrian coast were the subject of a detailed survey by the Newcastle office of the RCHME during 1992-93.[1] It was inevitable, given their importance and their good state of preservation, that the earthworks of the fort at Maryport should be singled out for particular attention. Like so many Roman forts in Britain, Maryport had never been planned in detail. The results of the analytical survey carried out by the writers are presented here.

The fort lies on the cliff top near the summit of a broad hill, at about 55 m above OD. The River Ellen flows through the southern outskirts of Maryport from the north-east, joining the sea to the south-west of the fort but never coming closer to the site than 500 m. From the fort itself there is good visibility in almost all directions. Most notable are the extensive coastal views to Allonby Bay in the north, south to Workington, and across the Solway Firth to Galloway. On a clear day the Isle of Man is visible. To the north-east the outlook is slightly restricted by the top of the rise, 300 m away. The site itself is not entirely level: between the highest point of the fort platform, in the north-east angle, and the lowest point at the west gate,[2] the ground level drops by 6 m. The ground on which the fort lies is very poorly-drained clay and sand subsoil. The earthworks of the fort are now the only visible remains, although some elements of the wider Roman landscape have been recorded in the past. The surviving earthworks lie within a pasture field enclosed by a substantial stone wall next to the former Battery, which is now the Senhouse Roman Museum. Beneath the fields that extend for 375 m to the north of the fort, known as the Borough Fields,[3] and in the fields directly to the west of Camp Farm, lie the remains of the *vicus*, a cemetery, and the road running from the north gate to Old Carlisle (Fig. 3.2). Unusually, it has been claimed that the sites of two parade grounds can be identified (but see now below, p. 69); an original second-century one lay 300 m north-east of the fort and is known from the fine set of dedicatory altars recovered there in 1870,[4] now on display in the museum. Nothing is now visible of this alleged parade ground, or of its replacement which lay 140 m south-west of the fort.[5] Good-quality building stone for the fort was readily available from the cliff face; it is said that when a new quarry was opened up in 1880 the rock-faces exposed showed signs of earlier working.[6] The full archaeological history of the site, including a detailed discussion of the garrison, is dealt with by Jarrett[7] and elsewhere in the present volume, and is not discussed here.

The first antiquary to visit the site, Camden, in 1599, wrote that 'Corne growes where the towne stood; neverthelesse many expresse footings thereof are evidently to be seen'. It is not clear from this account whether Camden was referring to the fort, the *vicus*, or both. Certainly John Senhouse, the landowner, had already begun to explore the site, and other early accounts suggest that the *vicus* was heavily robbed at a comparatively early date before attention returned to the fort.[8] The Senhouse family continued to rob the fort of its stone, or to excavate the site for nearly 200 years, and there can be no doubt that the configuration of the majority of the earthworks visible today is a direct result of their activities. For example, Colonel Humphrey Senhouse excavated the north gate and the commanding officer's house during the 1780s and was reported to keep 'a man daily at work in searching, and clearing the walls within the fort....'.[9] It is likely that the foundation of the town of Maryport in 1749 by Humphrey Senhouse accelerated the robbing process. Collingwood[10] reported being told that up to the middle of the nineteenth century it was not uncommon for the inhabitants of Maryport to sound for building stone inside the fort, an anecdote which is consistent with the piecemeal early nineteenth-century robbing identified during excavation in 1966.[11] This excavation, carried out by Michael Jarrett and Anthony Birley, occurred in the north-east angle and is the only modern excavation of the site to have taken place.[12] There have been implicit suggestions – not surprising in themselves – that this long history of robbing was well under way in the medieval period. The chancel arch of the Norman church of St John the Evangelist at Crosscanonby, 3.5 km to the north-east, may be of Roman origin, reset.[13] If the arch is from Maryport and was incorporated into the fabric of the church, then it might also imply that the fort survived in relatively good condition at least until the Norman period. Against this, perhaps, there is a tradition, still current in Maryport, and apparently coming from the Senhouse family, concerning the discovery of a complete fallen arch at the fort and its removal to the church during the eighteenth century. There are no known documentary sources to confirm this.

THE DEFENCES (Fig. 3.1)
The fort wall and rampart

The fort is almost square in shape with an internal area of approximately 1.87 ha (4.6 acres); between the crests of the ramparts it measures 135 m from north to south by 139 m transversely. Excavation has shown that the defences consisted of a stone wall, 2 m wide, with a rubble core and a substantial clay rampart-backing, fronted by ditches,[14] but except for fragments of the north gate (NG on Fig. 3.1), no stonework is now visible within any part of the fort. In 1725 Stukeley visited the site and mentioned the 'stone wall on the high vallum';[15] by 1880, however, the fort was almost in its present state, although two courses of masonry were visible adjacent to the north gate.[16] The excavation plans published by Jarrett[17] suggest that the course of the fort wall is usually represented on the surface by the narrow terrace that interrupts the principal external scarp of the defences along the greater part of its length; this terrace marks the line of the robber-trench dug into the side of the defences to extract the masonry of the wall. Despite this wholesale robbing, the eastern defences stand to a maximum height of 1.6 m above the bottom of the ditch; on this side the terrace marking the position of the wall is up to 1.3 m wide. The northern end is 1.2 m

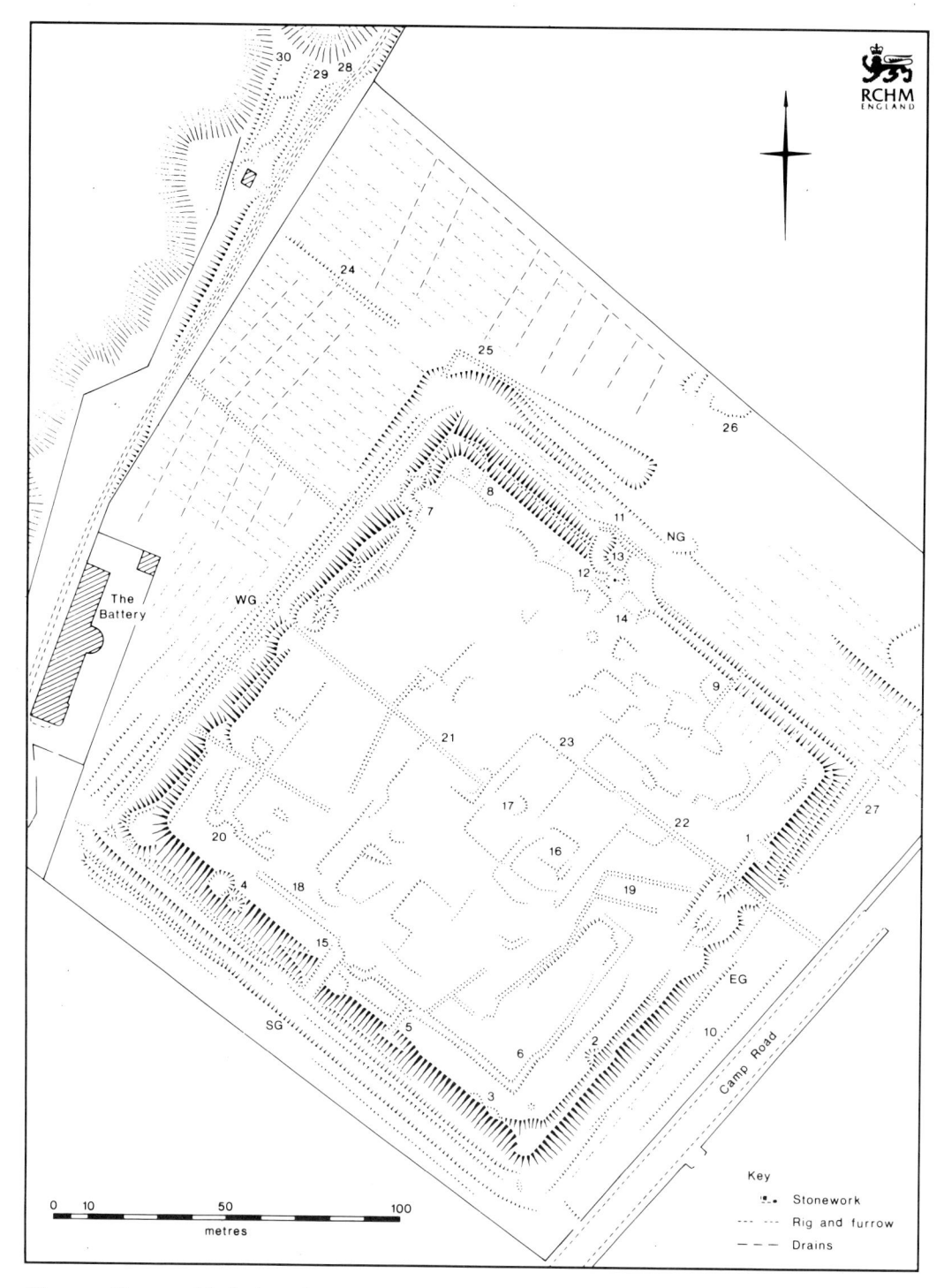

Fig. 3.1 Topographical plan of the earthworks of the Roman fort, as surveyed by the RCHME

above the bottom of the ditch, and here the terrace is less well defined and at a marked angle to the rest of the rampart; this may well be as a result of the ploughing that has evidently taken place across the top of the defences after the robbing of the stone wall. Mid-way between the site of the east gate (EG) and the north-east angle, a shallow amorphous scoop measuring 5 m by 5.5 m (1) has been cut down through this area of ploughing into the top of the rampart and into its internal scarp. A wide crescentic cut (2), 5.5 m by 4.0 m across, likewise interrupts the line of the rampart between the gate and the south-east angle. These seem to be robber trenches; their location suggests, in each case, a search for the better quality stonework that might be found in the remains of an interval tower. The south-east angle is marked by a platform measuring 5.4 m by 9 m, where the angle tower has been quarried away. This robbing interrupts the outer scarp but is continuous with the terrace marking the robbed-out wall. The base of the slope around the angle extends beyond its normal line; this phenomenon can be seen at other points along the perimeter and appears to be due to spoil being thrown down the outer scarp of the defences during the course of stone robbing. The existence of a corner bastion, added as part of the development of Roman coastal defences in the fourth century, has also been suggested and remains a possibility.[18] A late coastal fort with at least one external bastion is known at Lancaster,[19] but there the new fort was built close to the end of the Roman period to a wholly different plan from those of its predecessors.

The southern side of the fort at Maryport shows little sign of the robber-trench following the line of the fort-wall, perhaps due to the differential deposition of material resulting from ploughing of the interior. Here the earthworks reach a maximum height of 2.7 m externally. Two shallow semi-oval cuts (3) into the top of the rampart are probably later robbing, post-dating the ploughing, as are the pair of larger crescentic scoops (4) towards the western end of the outer scarp; these measure 7.7 m by 8.4 m, and 5 m by 4.5 m, respectively. A trench, 2 m wide (5), cuts across the rampart and runs into the very marked internal robber-trench (6); the former may have been utilized as a drain at a later date. At the south-west angle, the foot of the principal outward-facing scarp has again been pushed outwards, producing a platform 2.3 m high, and 10.5 m by 5.5 m across. This is evidently the debris left behind when the angle tower was robbed away. Subsequently the outline of the upper portion of the angle has been smoothed and restored, probably as a result of ploughing within the interior.

The earthworks of the western defences are the most complex. The maximum height of the outer scarp above the bottom of the ditch is 3.1 m. Between the south-west angle and the west gate (WG) the line of the principal robber-trench for the fort-wall becomes little more than a change of slope. A crescentic platform 9.5 m across, projecting from the crest of the rampart, clearly marks the robbing of another interval tower. A field drain cuts through it. The northern interval tower on this side is not so easily recognisable due to further mutilation of the north section of the defences; however, it is most likely to lie where the foot of the major scarp reaches its maximum westward extent, mid-way between the gate and the north-west angle. At (7) a series of small scarps form a zig-zag trench across the rampart and the outer scarp at a point where they are both very abraded. This is now utilised by a drain, but its angular route suggests that it follows the line of one or more old robber-trenches; certainly, the robber-trench of the fort-wall

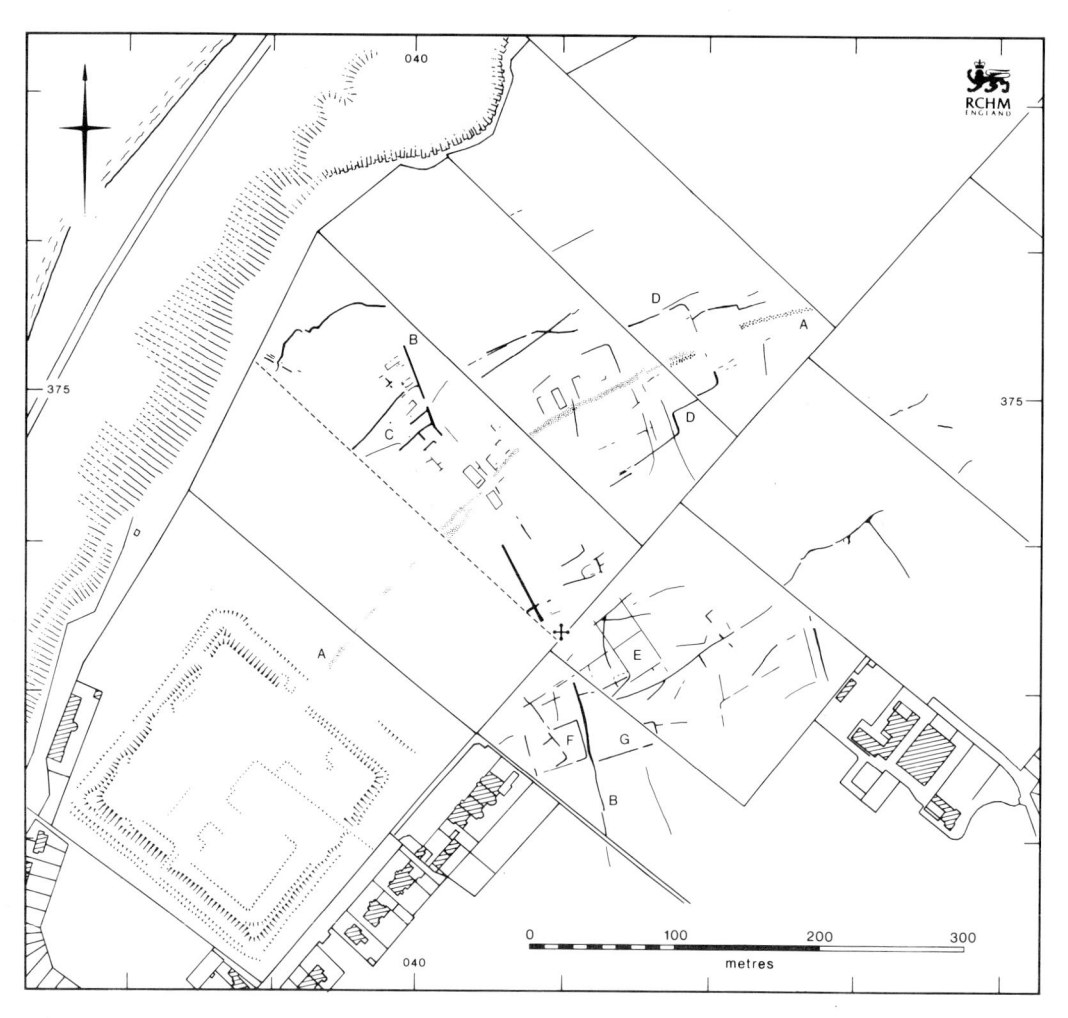

Fig. 3.2 Topographical plan of crop-marks and other features noted from aerial photographs of the fields lying north of the Roman fort, as surveyed by the RCHME. The cross near the centre marks the approximate position of the rectangular temple excavated in 1880 and re-excavated in 1885.

seems to be one element of its course. It is conceivable that a latrine which drained through the wall and rampart was situated here; this would be one of the few structures built of better-quality blocks which would cross the line of the wall, and which could thus have attracted stone-robbers in this way. As on the south side, the northwest angle also displays a small platform, 5 m by 2.5 m, mid-way down the outer scarp which is 3.3 m high at this point. This platform is not as well marked as those at the south-east and south-west angles; in this case, later disturbance on the top of the rampart may have produced spoil that has partially obscured the platform.

Along the western section of the north perimeter the robber-trench of the fort wall is 1.3 m wide and is easily visible. The only exception to this is below the point where a narrow trench (8), 2.4 m wide, cuts the top of the rampart. This may once have been a drain, but the inner scarp between the angle and the gate is formed by a series of shallow crescentic scoops which suggest that this area has been nibbled away either by robbing or by excavation; the precise reason for this is unclear. The section of defences to the east of the central gate on this side, and to the west of a drain (9), is in a subtly altered form and on a slightly different alignment to that along the east and west ends. Here we have evidence that the whole central range of the fort, extending north-south, has not in the past been heavily ploughed, whereas the *praetentura* and *retentura* have been extensively cultivated. In this section the robber-trench is also wider (up to 2 m) and seems to have suffered less subsequent disturbance than elsewhere. The difference in appearance might suggest that this robbing is of a different period from that of the rest of the rampart, but the traces immediately to the east of ridge-and-furrow may indicate that the section between the north gate and the drain (9) has only been lightly ploughed. The drain (9), which coincides with the end of the middle section of the defences, seems to have been a recut of an earlier feature separating the differing sections of rampart on either side. It is unlikely to have originated as a robber-trench since it presumably crosses through the intervallum road and the rampart. In its original form it may have been a field boundary cut along the western edge of the arable ground: between the drain and the northeast angle the profile of the rampart is smoothed by the northern end of some narrow ridge-and-furrow, whereas (as noted above), the strip immediately to the west, relatively unploughed, coincides with the central range of buildings of the Roman fort. As at Haltonchesters[20] this area would have contained the best-quality stone, and was thus more attractive to the stone-robber than to the ploughman. A comparable change is visible in the crest-line of the rampart on the southern side, presumably indicating that none of the central range has been subsequently cultivated for any length of time.

The ditches

Outside the wall of the fort, the most recent excavations[21] revealed three certain ditches and, peripheral to these, a fourth less certain ditch. The Roman ditches have evidently undergone extensive reshaping and there may be little on the surface that survives from that phase. The overall pattern of the earthworks is of two shallow ditches separated by a low, flat-topped bank. In the early eighteenth century, Gordon[22] remarked on the depth of the ditches, and later Bruce[23] also commented that the ditches were remembered as being 'much deeper within living memory, than at present'. Certainly, all the ditches show signs of having been ploughed along their linear axes and/or having been recut to form drains at a later date. However, it seems likely that the ditches visible on the surface correspond in terms of their position to the two innermost ditches excavated by Jarrett and Birley, despite being much damaged in form.[24] On the east side of the fort the single ditch is 5 m wide but is poorly defined by a degraded and interrupted counterscarp. Once again it seems likely that ploughing is responsible for the poor quality of these remains. It is possible that the long scarp (10) beyond this ditch is the outer scarp of another ditch equating to Jarrett's third ditch.

Along the southern perimeter are two fairly flat-bottomed ditches separated by a low bank 6 m wide. The inner ditch narrows from a breadth of 3.5 m at the east end to a sharper V-shape at the west end, where the debris from the wall and rampart seem to have impinged upon it, and it has then been recut as a drain. The outer ditch narrows in the same manner from a maximum basal width of 3.2 m to 1 m. The north-facing scarp of this ditch is 0.6 m high. The southern field boundary lay along the top of this scarp before the boundary wall was rebuilt a few metres farther to the south, sometime between 1863 and 1900.[25] On the northern side of this wall lay a footpath which followed the course of the outer ditch prior to the change in the boundary; scouring along the line of the path may account for the accentuation of the scarp on the south side of the ditch. Both ditches are interrupted at points close to each other; the break in the southern scarp of the medial bank may represent the last vestiges of the causeway of the south gate (SG).

Along the west face, the line of the Roman ditches has been repeatedly cut by drains, now visible only as shallow grooves 0.15 m deep, approximately at right angles to the rampart. These evidently carried water into the two ditches, which show signs of extensive reshaping. The inner and outer ditches are separated by a small bank and a berm which are up to 3.5 m wide overall. Where the inner ditch is overlain by spoil from the robbing of the wall and the towers of the fort, it is difficult to ascertain its true width from surface remains alone. The width of the outer ditch ranges from 2 m to 5.5 m, although its outer scarp is discontinuous. At its northern end the field drains have collapsed in several places. At first sight, due to the natural rise of the land, the ditches that formed part of the northern defences of the fort appear to have survived best; in fact it seems that little of them remains visible on the surface. Along the eastern half of the rampart the ditches are obscured by narrow ridge-and-furrow. Immediately to the west, the lower scarp of the rampart curves round to create the western edge of a basin which may have been a later pond. This suggestion is strengthened by the fact that a small culvert drains into its western end. Another drain (11) leads from this depression, skirting the spoil-heap adjacent to the north gate, running into the remnant of the inner ditch which has also been incorporated into the drainage system. Part of drain 11 may have been formed by recutting a section of the furrow that continues west beyond its end. Two furrows separate this ditch from the outer ditch which is 4 m wide. It appears that this is the original Roman line but the profile of this ditch has also been altered by ploughing along its axis.

The gates

The positions of the gates and the inferred sites of the interval towers indicate that the fort faced west. In many of the early accounts of the fort, it is described as having four gates, although Stukeley's account,[26] memorable for its detail and apparent accuracy, only mentions three. The north gate was excavated by Colonel Senhouse in 1787 when 'in digging in front of the gateway, they found the arch entire which had covered the gate but, Col. Senhouse being unfortunately from home at that time, the arch was destroyed, and the stones carried away for the repair of walls'.[27] A sketch and a plan of one guard-chamber and the sill stone of one carriageway were published by Rooke in his description of the excavations.[28] His drawings and description suggest that the rutted stone sill and three of the four other blocks which survive beside the west gate are the remains, still *in situ*, of the westerly guard-chamber and carriageway. Any further remains of the guard-chamber must be marked by the square mound (12) which is 3.5 m across. The shape and dimensions of this mound strongly suggest that it is the undisturbed internal fill of the guard-chamber left behind by the excavators, who were only interested in investigating and then robbing the walls of the building. To the north of this lies a sub-rectangular flat-topped mound (13), measuring about 8 m by 9 m and 1.5 m high, which appears to be the major spoil-heap from the clearance of the gateway. A small rectangular platform (14), measuring 4.5 m by 5.5 m, appears to be the result of robbing of the east guard-chamber; if that were so, the gateway would have had a single portal, either by original design, which would be unusual, or by modification, a far more common phenomenon. Comparison of the earthworks of the north gate with other Hadrianic gate-plans suggests that the earthworks at 14 are misleading and that there was a double portal gate. The position of the south gate, at the other end of the *via principalis* is only recognisable by the trenches dug by stone-robbers, who no doubt were attracted by the high quality masonry that the entrance structures would have yielded. A wide steep-sided trench (15) 4.7 m wide and 16 m long, with a depth of up to 0.4 m, cuts right across the rampart. Its centre is directly opposite the presumed centre of the north gate. The rectangular platform, measuring 4.5 m by 5.0 m, to the east of the gate may represent the robbing of a guard-chamber. Although interrupted by the recutting of the ditches, the slight rise of the ground surface noted here may represent the remnants of the causeway. The guard-chambers of the west gate (which should, in theory, have been the principal entrance to the fort) also appear to be marked by curving scarps that protrude from the base of the rampart. The scarps and hollows around the northerly guard-chamber suggest major robbing here, and possibly that of other structures too. A later field drain cuts through the gateway. The rise of the causeway across the ditches is plainly visible here. The position of the east gate is marked by little more than a break in the crest of the rampart. A rectangular depression to the south may be the site of a guard chamber or another building, now robbed away. The causeway is visible as a small, unsurveyable rise.

THE INTERIOR

Despite the long history of excavation by the Senhouses, relatively little is known of the internal buildings of the fort. The excavations of 1966 have shown that a pair of barracks, superseded by stables or storerooms, lay in the north-east angle, with their long axes parallel to the eastern rampart.[29] Details from the Senhouse excavations that appear on the first edition 25-inch Ordnance Survey maps[30] show that the headquarters building occupied the usual central position, and that to the north of this, as would be expected, was the commanding officer's house. The earthworks indicate the presence of these buildings but most of the scarps in the interior appear to be due to post-Roman activity, namely stone-robbing, excavation, ploughing and drainage. As noted above, most of the robbing has been concentrated on the central range of buildings where better quality stone would have been used for construction.

Within the area where the headquarters building should lie is a series of long straight low scarps, nearly all of which lie parallel or perpendicular to one another. They define an area measuring approximately 35 m by 37 m. Some of these scarps must have been caused by robbing of the walls of the headquarters building, but to equate them all with the specific parts of a structure with any accuracy is difficult. The strongroom of the headquarters building, within the rear range of rooms, was opened in *c.* 1686 and again in 1766. Its stone floor was removed when it was first excavated, but its walls still survived to a metre in height, and the steps were intact when it was reopened.[31] Its remains probably lie below the two right-angled scarps (16) that together form a square measuring 10.3 m. The headquarters building is also known to have had a stone-lined well, 0.9 m in diameter, in its front courtyard. The well was first mentioned by Bruce in 1851; by 1867 it had been excavated and was already collapsing inward and silting up.[32] No definite traces of it were found during the present survey, but a semi-circular depression (17) probably marks its spot.

The commanding officer's house, situated to the north of the headquarters building, was excavated by Colonel Senhouse in 1788. The report describes a well-built structure, as would be expected, including a private bath.[33] A number of small scarps and depressions cover this area; some are linear, but none can be readily correlated with a particular part of a building.

The roads within the fort are described in one early account as being built of flagstones,[34] but Pennant[35] also mentions 'stones from the shore', presumably indicating cobbled road surfaces too. Two of the roads are just visible: the *via principalis* and the *via praetoria*. The course of the *via principalis* is marked by a drainage ditch that extends from the west gate to the site of the headquarters building. The drain seems to have been cut into a slight depression that is likely to have been caused by the robbing of flagstones. The *via praetoria* is marked on its east side by the broken line of scarps between the north and south gates.

The most obvious feature of the interior of the fort is the series of very deeply cut robber-trenches which runs discontinuously round the southern side from the east gate to the west gate, roughly parallel to and inside the line of the rampart. Along with the robber-trench (15) that crosses the area of the south gate, trenches (6) and (18) appear on the first edition 25-inch Ordnance Survey map of 1863-5. It is probable that these trenches are roughly contemporary, and their good preservation suggests they are relatively late in the sequence of robbing and excavation. Oddly, no upcast from the trenches is visible.

Robber-trench (6), in the southern half of the *retentura*, extends approximately from the east gate to the south gate, forming a right-angle. Both parts of the trench are straight, except at a point where the easterly ditch kinks inward at a distance of 12.5 m from its south-east corner. It is likely that it marks the robbed remains of the east and south walls of a barrack block with detached officers' quarters, such as those excavated in the north-east angle.[36] Farther to the west, the trench turns outwards just before ending beside the south gate. This westerly section of (6), cutting through the central range, must have been dug in order to rob a separate structure, which in this area is most likely to have been a double granary or a workshop. A field drain, a continuation of the two parallel drains at (19), meets the trench here; a small cut, linking the end of the trench with (15), carries the water away.

Trenches (18) and (20) are slightly narrower, being 2.5 m wide, and at 0.3 m deep are shallower. Trench (20) may represent robbing of a barrack block, as in the south-east angle, although its convoluted course suggests that more than one building has been robbed. In the *praetentura* little else is visible. A field drain (21) runs along the line of the *via principalis* with two tributary drains running into it. A further drain cuts across the south-west quadrant and through the interval tower of the west rampart.

The twentieth century has left few distinctive earthworks. During the 1966 excavations in the north-east angle of the fort,

Jarrett and Birley cut a narrow section (22), 2 m wide and 71.5 m in length, across the eastern defences; their trench is still visible on the surface, surviving to a maximum depth of 0.2 m. A separate trench (23) continues west along the same axis for a further 13 m where it then becomes a north-facing scarp. This alignment is coincidental, and the apparent extension to the excavation trench would appear to derive from Colonel Senhouse's excavation of the commanding officer's house. Surprisingly, the scarps recognisable to the north of the long section (22) do not correspond to those that would be expected from the plans.[37] The excavators identified two phases of post-Roman stone-robbing: a systematic removal of building walls, and one later, randomly dug, pit. Other late features to the north of the excavated area, between the east rampart and trench (9), are the remains of ridge-and-furrow running onto the top of the rampart; the furrows are neither truly parallel nor evenly spaced. Examination of air photographs[38] taken prior to the 1966 excavations shows that the ridging then extended just beyond the southern limit of the excavated section. It is surprising that the robbing of stonework within the interior of the fort has left behind minor scarps rather than open trenches; this is probably because of the ploughing that has evidently taken place over the sites of the buildings long after they had been robbed of most of the best of their dressed stone. Subsequent robbing, and the antiquarian investigations following the period of cultivation, have left behind those trenches and pits that are visible, for instance 4-9, 15-18, and 20. If these later excavation trenches and drainage ditches are ignored, the earthworks in the interior of the fort are concentrated in the central range, underlining the limited amount of cultivation in this sector, compared with the *praetentura* and *retentura*.

In summary, a general sequence of events can be understood from the documentary sources and the earthworks, particularly in the north-east quadrant. We know from Camden that there was cultivation in or around the fort from at least 1599. If Stukeley's description of an upstanding wall is to be believed, then it must have been robbed after the 1720s, after the earliest documentary evidence for digging in the fort (c. 1686). After this the line of the wall was ploughed over as the interior of the fort was cultivated. It seems that the whole area was ploughed but the earthworks of the central range suggest that cultivation of this sector was abandoned after a relatively short period. It is possible that ploughing had already commenced before the robbing of the fort walls and that their removal was carried out in order to facilitate cultivation. The substantial robber-trenches in the southern half of the fort do not give the impression of being ploughed and must therefore post-date this phase. These are overlain by two of the drainage ditches.

Other earthworks within the fort field

Most of the available ground lying outside the fort but within the same modern field is covered by narrow ridge-and-furrow overlain by field drains. The ridges are straight, between 3.5 m and 4.5 m apart, and only 0.2 m in maximum height. The ridging on the west side, running in a north-south direction, is overlain by the Battery and must be earlier than 1885. A small bank (24), 3.2 m wide, may be an earlier field boundary connected with this cultivation. Another field-drain (25) empties into the ditches from a natural hollow. The hollows (26) to the north of the north gate are probably the result of the robbing, before cultivation, of Roman roadside buildings. Extending beyond the north-east angle of the fort is a low bank (27) overlain by the ridge-and-furrow. It is not clear whether this is of Roman origin, relating to the ditches, or whether it is a later field boundary.

The cliff top

To the west and north-west of the fort much of the archaeology within the strip of land between the cliff face and the Borough Fields has been obscured by landscaping. Nevertheless, three fairly substantial banks, lying almost parallel to the cliff edge, survive by the wind shelter just beyond the Battery. The inner bank (28) has been extensively remodelled in recent times although there is some indication that its northern end is cut by the quarry for the new Maryport dock of 1880.[39] The middle bank (29) is 0.4 m high and was also truncated by the quarry. Near its centre is a rectangular platform measuring about 5 m by 11 m. Along the cliff edge the outer bank (30), standing 0.2 m high, may skirt around the perimeter of the wind shelter, and thus may be relatively recent, although this relationship is unclear due to the interference of the present fence along the cliff boundary. What these earthworks represent is uncertain, although they may be related to the large building discovered on the cliff top by Robinson, which he described as being in approximately this location.[40]

The civilian settlement (Fig. 3.2)

A large civilian settlement (the *vicus*) is known to have existed in the fields to the north and east of the fort, although no surface remains are visible due to extensive ploughing dating from the sixteenth century or earlier. Air photographs show archaeological remains beneath the Borough Fields, and in the fields adjoining them to the north-west of Camp Farm; a transcription of these photographs is shown in Fig. 3.2, and the results are discussed below. Whether the *vicus* extended around the other sides of the fort is difficult to ascertain because buildings now obscure the area. However, an observation by Stukeley that 'on the north side of this castrum lay the city'[41] suggests that the *vicus* was mainly on this side of the fort, along the road to the fort at Old Carlisle. Like the fort, this area was extensively robbed by the Senhouse family. Gordon[42] complained that 'too many of the Stones have been dug up for making Walls and Enclosures', and Stukeley[43] wrote that 'the family of the Senhouses and the Eaglesfields . . . have been continually digging here'.

In 1880 Joseph Robinson[44] excavated in the first, second and third of the Borough Fields. He uncovered several 'strip-houses' along the roadside in the first and second fields; one of them he excavated fully. A cemetery also lay to the north of the fort. Robinson excavated burials on both sides of the main Roman road in the fourth Borough Field to the north. In the second of the Borough Fields he found burials in the vicinity of the strip-houses, strongly suggesting that a military cemetery predated the *vicus*. Collingwood[45] drew attention to Robinson's report of the sagging foundations of the Roman buildings in the first Borough Field and concluded that this might have been caused by underlying burial pits. The burials included urned cremations, some of which were in stone-lined cists. Robinson also traced the course of the road from the north gate, and uncovered several sections, one measuring 6.4 m wide. A number of inscribed altars were also recovered during the excavations, and a piece of phallic sculpture known as the Serpent Stone (see pp. 121-3 below) was removed from the fourth field.

Perhaps the most important of Robinson's discoveries were the two large stone buildings, probably temples, in the south-east corner of the second Borough Field (NY 0410 3734). Both buildings had been heavily robbed and plough-damaged; they survived as clay and cobble foundations for part of their length. Recently published photographs of this excavation demonstrate that afterwards the buildings were left open, remaining in good condition for at least five years.[46, 47] Unfortunately, no traces can be seen today, either on the ground or on air photographs.

Bailey[48] reported the existence of a bank enclosing part of the *vicus*, which he interpreted as a later annexe to the fort. This bank originated at a point mid-way along the western boundary (NY 0408 3731) of the first field, continued round along the northern boundary between the second and third Borough Fields, turned south along the cliff-top, and was then lost under the Battery; possible outworks were noted along its western extent. A section of the bank was excavated (at an unspecified point) by Collingwood,[49] who found that it lay above third-century Roman remains. During the course of the present survey none of the earthworks on the west side of the fort could be identified as the outworks described by Bailey. The field boundaries on the seaward side of the Borough Fields are situated on a lynchet, which may be the 'bank' that Bailey identified as the western side of his annexe. There seems to be no compelling reason to ascribe this feature to the Roman period; furthermore, no separate feature can be distinguished from the field boundary between the second and third Borough Fields as Bailey claimed. Only a short section of bank, 0.6 m high, running east-west from the western end of the field boundary between the second and third fields to the cliff face, may be confidently identified as part of his 'annexe'; there is no reason to doubt that this is anything but a relatively recent field boundary. The supposed course of the enclosure does not sit easily within the pattern of remains revealed by air photographs. It therefore seems unlikely that any of the earthworks that Bailey saw were Roman.

The cropmarks

The transcription of the cropmarks (Fig. 3.2) was prepared by the Air Photography Unit of the RCHME with the aid of the AERIAL 4.20 computer program. Two areas are relatively blank on the transcription. The first of Borough Fields (NY 0398 3738) showed few cropmarks, except for discontinuous traces of the Roman road; conditions in this area so far have not been conducive to the recording of cropmarks, or else the archaeology may have been destroyed through agricultural practices. In the second area (NY 0425 3745) numerous cropmarks were showing on poor-quality oblique photographs, but few could be reliably distinguished as archaeological features from the background of geological cropmarks.

The Roman road (A) issuing from the north gate of the fort is visible as an intermittent parch-mark up to 6 m wide, which is flanked by a broad, shallow ditch beside part of its northern section. It has been generally supposed that the road from the fort forked at approximately NY 0417 3752,[50] with one road (NAR Linear RR750) continuing north-eastwards along the coastal defences to Silloth, and a second road (NAR Linear RR754) branching off in an east-north-easterly direction towards Old Carlisle. In fact, although the bend in A coincides with the accepted start of RR754, RR750 is not visible beyond this point. The absence of this postulated section of a coastal route (RR750) is further demonstrated by the presence of other features in the *vicus* which clearly do not respect any such road. In addition, the fact that both the buildings and the enclosures in fields 3 and 4 are arranged parallel to RR754 shows that linear development of the *vicus* occurred, but that only one route for that development existed. The exact course of RR750 between the fort and Bankend, 1.5 km to the north-east, remains unknown. Similarly the recorded line of the Maryport-Papcastle road (RR751) has been slightly inaccurate. On Ordnance Survey maps it is still depicted as joining the fort a little to the north of the east gate, a nonsensical alignment, but one aerial photograph,[51] not transcribed, shows slight earthwork remains curving south-westwards to meet at the east gateway.

Flanking the main road are a number of 'strip-houses', rectangular buildings with their short axis facing the street. One group of these buildings is partially surrounded by a ditched enclosure (NY 0413 3753). Three are complete, measuring approximately 6 m x 12 m, 6 m x 11 m and 7 m x 15 m, the latter showing an internal partition. A broad linear feature (B), seen as a positive crop mark extending discontinuously SW-NE, probably represents the remains of a secondary road or trackway; this too is partly lined by rectangular buildings although they are smaller than the others, measuring only 3 m in width. They also may be accompanied by ditched enclosures (C).

Towards the north-eastern end of the main road (A) are a number of ditched enclosures with rounded angles (D), flanking the road, that decrease in width in a series of steps. Their orientation in relation to the road suggests that they are later than the establishment of the road, but were contemporary in use; they may be property boundaries of the general kind seen elsewhere in roadside settlements,[52] or they may have defined the extent of the cemetery belonging to the pre-*vicus* phase. It is also possible that this exposed position answered a more pressing need by providing a light defensive enclosure for the *vicus*. No close parallel has been found for this arrangement.

Around the southern half of trackway B is a concentration of cropmarks that also extend north-east, gradually becoming more diffuse. Elements of this group appear to be set off this road as it bends to the north-west; however most of the features are very fragmentary and it is unlikely that all are contemporary. The two adjacent square enclosures (E) and two other less complete examples (F, G) may represent small fields. No bath-house has been identified and nothing resembling one is visible on the air photographs. Nowhere in the immediate vicinity of the fort would a plentiful supply of water have been readily available. The building 'of very fine building blocks'[53] at NY 0382 3742, partly destroyed by cliff erosion and quarrying in March 1880, may have been a bath-house or alternatively a *mansio*.

Acknowledgements

Access to the site was kindly granted by Mr H. Messenger, Camp Farm. Thanks are due to Lt Cdr Brian Ashmore for helpful comments about the site. The late Professor Michael Jarrett assisted by confirming points about the excavation of 1966. The cropmarks of the *vicus* were transcribed and a separate report prepared by Yvonne Boutwood of the Air Photography Unit, RCHME. The survey was undertaken by K. Blood and A. Lax and the text was written by A. Lax with the assistance of H. Welfare. The illustrations were prepared for publication by P. Sinton and are Crown Copyright: RCHME. This paper is published by courtesy of the Commissioners.

Notes

1 The survey methods employed were the same as those described in Blood and Bowden 1990, 61, note 1.
2 The axis of the fort is actually NW-SE but in

concordance with earlier writers the seaward face of the fort has been described as west and the other gates, angles and sides accordingly.
3 The fields are numbered 1-4 from SW to NE consecutively, after Robinson 1881. The field boundary separating fields 1 and 2 has now been removed but in the text the original numbering has been retained to avoid confusion.
4 Bruce 1874
5 Birley 1961, 222
6 Robinson 1881
7 Jarrett 1976; Jarrett and Stephens 1987, 61; Birley 1961, 216-22
8 Gordon 1727, 98; Stukeley 1776, 50
9 Rooke 1792, 142
10 Collingwood 1936, 86
11 Jarrett 1976, 36
12 Jarrett 1976
13 Pevsner 1967, 113-114
14 Jarrett 1976, 31-2
15 Stukeley 1776, 50
16 Bailey 1881, 181
17 Jarrett 1976
18 Higham 1993, 46-7
19 Jones and Shotter 1988, 225
20 Blood and Bowden 1990
21 Jarrett 1976, 31-2
22 Gordon 1727, 98
22 Bruce 1853, 339
24 Jarrett 1976, Fig. 5
25 Ordnance Survey 1st and 2nd edition 6-inch maps
26 Stukeley 1776, 50
27 Rooke 1792, 141
28 Rooke 1792, 141, plate opposite page 140
29 Jarrett 1976, 33-41
30 1853
31 Anon. 1773
32 Bruce 1851, 361; 1867, 289
33 Rooke 1792
34 Lysons 1816, cxii
35 Pennant 1790, 63
36 Jarrett 1976, 34
37 Jarrett 1976, figures 5 and 7
38 CUCAP DL22
39 Robinson 1881, 137
40 Robinson 1881, 240
41 Stukeley 1776, 50
42 Gordon 1727, 98
43 Stukeley 1776, 50
44 Robinson 1881
45 Collingwood 1936, 90
46 Bellhouse 1992
47 National Monuments Record : BB92/17981, 91, 92, 97
48 Bailey 1923, 151-3
49 Collingwood and Taylor 1924
50 Margary 1967, 397-9
51 NLAP NY.437/11
52 Finch Smith 1987, 22-3
53 Robinson 1881, 237

References

ANON. 1773 'An account of some Roman monuments found in Cumberland, 1766', *Archaeologia* 2, 58-9

BAILEY, J. B. 1880 'The Maryport camp: its history, its explorations, and its present aspect', *Transactions of the Cumberland Association for the Advancement of Literature and Science* 5, 181-90

BAILEY, J. B. 1923 'Maryport and the Tenth Iter', *CW*² 23, 142-53

BELLHOUSE, R. L. 1992 *Joseph Robinson of Maryport* (Otley)

BIRLEY, E. 1961 *Research on Hadrian's Wall* (Kendal)

BLOOD, K. and BOWDEN, M. C. B. 1990 'The Roman fort at Haltonchesters', *AA*⁵ 18, 55-62

BRUCE, J. C. 1851 *The Roman Wall* (London)

BRUCE, J. C. 1853 *The Roman Wall*, 2nd. ed. (London)

BRUCE, J. C. 1867 *The Roman Wall*, 3rd. ed. (London)

BRUCE, J. C. 1874 'On the altars recently found in the Roman camp at Maryport', *CW*¹ 1, 175-88

CAMDEN, W. 1600 *Britannia*, translated into English 1637 (London)

COLLINGWOOD, R. G. and TAYLOR, M. V. 1924 'Roman Britain in 1924', *JRS* 14, 206-51

COLLINGWOOD, R. G. 1936 'The Roman fort and settlement at Maryport', *CW*² 36, 85-99

FINCH SMITH, R. 1987 *Roadside Settlements in Lowland Roman Britain* [BAR British Series No. 157] (Oxford)

GORDON, A. 1727 *Itinerarium Septentrionale* (London)

HIGHAM, N. J. 1993 *The Kingdom of Northumbria* (Stroud)

JARRETT, M. G. 1976 *Maryport, Cumbria: a Roman fort and its garrison* [CW Extra Series No. 22] (Kendal)

JARRETT, M. G. and STEPHENS, G. R. 1987 'The Roman garrisons of Maryport', CW^2 87, 61-66

JONES, G. D. B. and SHOTTER, D. C. A. 1988 *Roman Lancaster* [Brigantia Monograph No. 1] (Manchester)

LYSONS, D. and S. 1816 *Magna Britannia* IV: Cumberland (London)

MARGARY, I. 1967 *Roman Roads in Britain* (London)

PENNANT, T. 1790 *A Tour in Scotland and the Hebrides 1772*, pt.1 (London)

PEVSNER, N. 1967 *Buildings of England: Cumberland and Westmorland* (Harmondsworth)

ROBINSON, J. 1881 'Notes on the excavations near the Roman camp, Maryport', CW^1 5, 237-55

ROOKE, H. 1792 'An account of some Roman antiquities in Cumberland hitherto unnoticed', *Archaeologia* 10, 137-42

STUKELEY, W. 1776 *Itinerarium Curiosum*, vol. II (London)

4 The regiments stationed at Maryport and their commanders

David J. Breeze

Introduction

Maryport is unique among the forts in Roman Britain for preserving an almost complete run of what are believed to be annual dedications, erected during the occupation of the fort by one of the regiments stationed there, the *cohors I Hispanorum*. These particular dedications are often called 'Jupiter altars', for they were dedicated to Iuppiter Optimus Maximus, Jupiter Best and Greatest, the chief god in the Roman pantheon, by the commanding officer on behalf of the regiment. These altars, together with those of other units, cast a fascinating light on the commanding officers, the nature of the dedications, and the altars and their decorations. They are supplemented by later annual dedications and other inscriptions, which provide further information about the regiments based at Maryport and their commanding officers.[1]

Seventeen altars were found at Maryport on 18th April 1870 in pits about 350 yards to the north-east of the fort during the explorations of Humphrey Pocklington Senhouse (Fig. 1.6).[2] Many of these altars were dedicated to Jupiter: others in the pits were dedicated to Mars and to Victory. None of the inscriptions found in this area appears to date later than the second century.

The altars located in 1870 form the majority of the twenty-two altars (together with a probable twenty-third, now fragmentary) dedicated to Jupiter which have been found at Maryport.[3] They were erected by at least three regiments, the *cohortes I Hispanorum*, *I Delmatarum* and *I Baetasiorum*, and together list ten commanding officers, either tribunes or prefects, of these units.

The inscriptions on the altars are generally brief: the dedication to Jupiter, the name of the commanding officer, sometimes the name of the unit, and a final word or phrase, for example: *I. O. M. coh. I Hisp. cui prae. M. Maenius Agrip. tribu. posuit*: 'To Jupiter, Best and Greatest, the First Cohort of Spaniards, which is commanded by M. Maenius Agrippa, tribune, set this up'.

The inscriptions do not all follow the same formula, but adopt slightly different styles. On the four altars each dedicated by the commanding officers Maenius Agrippa and Caballius Priscus (Figs. 4.1 and 4.6), only one each bears the names of the unit and the commanding officer (in that order): the other three carry only the name of the commanding officer. This order – unit and officer – is followed on the single inscriptions of Helstrius Novellus, Antistius Lupus Verianus, Attius Tutor, Caecilius Vegetus and Cornelius Gaius, as well as on four other inscriptions to other gods. This suggests that in this series the commanding officer, on his first occasion, dedicated on behalf of himself and the unit, while later he himself only dedicated, presumably with the unit's involvement understood. On the altars of one commanding officer, Cammius Maximus, the order is not only reversed but both officer and unit are named on all three of his dedications: this order is also followed by the single inscription of Censorius Cornelianus. Interestingly, both officers have additional information to impart – a new appointment in each case – but the other stones of Maximus follow the same pattern. One inscription only records the unit but not the commanding officer.

There are other distinctions. The altars of Cammius Maximus (e.g. Fig. 4.9) all indicate that *cohors I Hispanorum* was *equitata*, that is, it contained cavalry as well as infantry. All the altars of Maenius Agrippa, Caballius Priscus, Cammius Maximus, Helstrius Novellus, Caecilius Vegetus, Attius Tutor and Postumius Acilianus are relatively simple, offering little more than the dedication and the name of the commander and regiment. One of the stones of Cammius Maximus, together with the single inscriptions of Censorius Cornelianus and Antistius Verianus, provide further information, including further appointments in the first two cases, and the city of origin of the officer in the latter two instances. Furthermore, all three stand out as the most highly decorated stones at Maryport.

The form of the dedication is also worth consideration. Nearly all the altars are dedicated simply to *I. O. M.* Novellus dedicated to *Iovi Op. M.*, while two of Maenius Agrippa and one dedicated by the unit alone are to *Iovi Op. M.* or *I. O. M.* and *Num. Aug.* The altar erected by Censorius Cornelianus is to *Iovi Aug* (Fig. 4.8). Three of the stones of Maenius Agrippa (e.g. Fig. 4.6) end with 'pos(uit)', 'set this up', those of Cammius Maximus and Censorius Cornelianus with VSLLM, 'gladly, willingly and deservedly fulfilled his vow' (Figs. 4.8 and 4.9). Helstrius Novellus used 'fecit', 'made this', while Caballius Priscus and Antistius Verianus had no final word or phrase.

The lettering and decorations on the altars are important not just in their own right, but because they have implications for the date and grouping of the stones. The style of ornament and lettering on the altars dedicated by Ulpius Titianus and T. Attius Tutor, prefects of *cohors I Baetasiorum*, has led to the suggestion that all five were carved by the same mason, while the altars of *cohors I Hispanorum* bear distinctive decorations: these altars will be discussed further below.[4]

Occasion and location of the dedications

The formulaic nature of the inscriptions has led to the suggestion that these Jupiter altars form part of a regular series of dedications to the god. There were a number of occasions when such dedications might be made. These were the 'holy days' recorded in the fragmentary third-century Feriale Duranum. This list of official festivals, dating to about AD 223-227, was found at Dura Europos on the river Euphrates. Most of the occasions when sacrifices should be made were the anniversaries of the accession, the birthdays of the deified emperors, and the birthdays of their wives. By the early third century there were at least twenty-six such anniversaries to celebrate, and perhaps, bearing in mind the fragmentary nature of the document, a total of forty.[5]

Two dates were particularly important, 3rd January and the anniversary of the reigning emperor's succession. On 3rd January, two days after every unit in the Roman army had renewed its oath of loyalty to the emperor, vows were paid and undertaken for the welfare of the emperor and for the eternity of the Empire. This ceremony is recorded by the younger Pliny. In 112, when governor of Bithynia and Pontus, he wrote to the Emperor Trajan, 'We have made our annual vows, Sir, to ensure your safety and thereby that of the State, and discharged our vows for the past year, with prayers to the gods to grant that they may be always then discharged and confirmed'. Trajan responded, 'I was glad to hear from your letter, my dear Pliny, that you and the provincials have discharged your vows to the immortal gods on behalf of my health and safety, and have renewed them for the coming year'. A year later Pliny and Trajan had a similar exchange of letters.[6]

The wording of the correspondence on the anniversary of the emperor's accession is on the same lines. Pliny wrote in 112, 'we have celebrated with appropriate rejoicing, Sir, the day of your accession whereby you preserved the Empire; and have offered prayers to the gods to keep you in health and prosperity on behalf of the human race, whose security and happiness depends on your safety. We have also administered the oath of allegiance to the troops in the usual form, and found the provincials eager to take it, too, as a proof of their loyalty', and this too was acknowledged by Trajan.[7]

Pliny wrote in very different tones to report the celebration of the birthday of Trajan in 112: 'it is my prayer, Sir, that this birthday and many others to come will bring you the greatest happiness, and that in health and strength you may add to the immortal fame and glory of your reputation by ever new achievements'.[8] There is no hint of a special ceremony on this anniversary.

The Jupiter altars from Maryport, apparently the only annual series of altars known from any Roman fort, dedicated to the chief god of the Roman pantheon, are presumably those dedicated on either 3rd January or on the anniversary of the emperor's succession. As Pliny's descriptions of the form of services on these two days are so similar, it is not possible to determine which occasion the Maryport altars commemorate: possibly they relate to both. Whichever day, the appropriate sacrifice to Jupiter was probably an ox.[9]

It is usually presumed that the Jupiter altars were erected beside the fort's parade ground where the troops were drawn up for the appropriate ceremonies, and from this it has been inferred that there was a parade ground north of the fort at Maryport in the area where the altars were found. As a parade ground is known to have been located south of the fort,[10] this has led to the further elaboration that the fort's parade ground was moved at some stage during the occupation of the site. There is, in fact, no necessity to assume the existence of an early parade ground north of the fort.[11]

There is no specific evidence from Pliny that the troops were involved in the religious activities, only in the renewal of the oath of allegiance. There may have been two separate ceremonies on the anniversary of the emperor's accession. The recent discoveries at Osterburken in Germany (Fig. 6.1 on p. 93) and at Sirmium in Serbia of two groups of altars, each dedicated by soldiers, arranged in rows, some still standing on their bases, may offer parallels to Maryport, where Peter Hill has suggested that the altars also stood in rows.[12] A shrine similar to those at Osterburken and Sirmium may have existed north of the fort at Maryport where the altars were dedicated, and this receives some support from the discovery in the nineteenth century of civilian buildings in this general area, including two possible temples (see further above, pp. 30-2).[13] The thin slab bearing an inscription to Iuppiter Optimus Maximus for the welfare of Antoninus Pius, found in one of the pits in 1870, may have commemorated the renewal of this shrine rather than a repair to the *tribunal* beside the parade ground.[14] It is possible that the altars were buried when they had used up all the available space, this being a straightforward way of allowing new stones to be erected.[15]

In summary, it is argued that the only parade ground at Maryport lay south of the fort, that a shrine to Jupiter lay to the north, and that it was here that the annual dedications were made.

The inscriptions found at Maryport demonstrate that several units were based there during its occupation. These units, and their commanding officers, are listed and discussed below.

1. Cohors I Hispanorum milliaria equitata
The regiment
The regiment was raised in Spain and is first attested in Britain in the late first century. An inscription at Ardoch is of the style usual in the first century, and therefore presumably relates to the occupation of that fort during the 80s.[16] *Cohors I Hispanorum* is recorded on diplomas, the certificates of privileges issued to auxiliary soldiers, dating to AD 98, 103, 105, 122, 124 and 146: no diploma records the unit as being *equitata* or *milliaria*.[17]

Two units of this name may have served in Britain. This was first proposed over 40 years ago by Eric Birley on the basis of his study of the diplomas. His analysis led him to conclude that the diplomas of AD 98 and 105 were issued to soldiers in the group of auxiliary regiments in the area of command of *legio XX Valeria Victrix* based at Chester, while that of AD 103 listed the units in the command of *legio II Augusta* based at Caerleon. *Cohors I Hispanorum* appears in all three diplomas. Birley suggested that, rather than there being an overlap between the two areas of command, there were two units of the same name in the province.[18]

A newly discovered diploma issued to an auxiliary soldier in AD 178 lists two *cohortes Hispanorum*.[19] One is *cohors I Aelia Hispanorum*, but unfortunately it is not possible to determine the number of the other *cohors Hispanorum*, as the diploma is damaged at that point. The former is presumably the *cohors I Aelia Hispanorum milliaria equitata* which is recorded at Netherby, just north of Hadrian's Wall, in the early third century.[20] The *cohors I Hispanorum* recorded at Axelodunum in the *Notitia Dignitatum* may not be the same regiment, as *Aelia* is omitted from its title, contrary to the normal practice in this section of the *Notitia*.[21] For reasons to be discussed below, it seems probable that the Maryport unit was not *cohors I Aelia Hispanorum*. Both *cohortes Hispanorum* were 1000 strong (*milliaria*), although we only know this for the Maryport unit because, for part of its residence at the fort, it was commanded by a tribune, the normal title for a commander of a unit of such size: 500-strong units were usually commanded by prefects.[22] As we have seen, the altars of Cammius Maximus reveal that *cohors I Hispanorum* was a mixed infantry and cavalry unit (*equitata*).

The records of *cohors I Hispanorum* at Maryport are particularly interesting because they record two different titles for the commanding officer, prefect and tribune. As we have seen, a prefect normally commanded a 500-strong regiment and a tribune a 1,000-strong unit. This suggests that the unit changed its size while based at Maryport, but was it increased or reduced in size? Analysis of the commanding officers and their inscriptions suggests that the regiment was reduced in size while at Maryport.

TABLE 1. The *cohortes I Hispanorum*: a possible allocation

Date	coh. I Aelia Hisp. mill. eq.	coh. I Hisp. mill. eq.
Hadrianic		Maryport
Antonine		listed on diploma of 146
	listed on diploma of 178	
early 3rd century	Netherby	
c. 400 (*Not. Dign.*)		Axelodunum

The size of the fort is also relevant to this problem. The visible fort covers 6.5 acres (2.64 ha) over the ramparts. This is too large for a 500-strong infantry cohort and suggests that the fort, normally considered to have been built under Hadrian, was erected for a larger unit: a 1000-strong mixed infantry and cavalry unit would not have been an inappropriate regiment. One building inscription indicates that a fort was built at Maryport under Hadrian, while another shows that the builders were *cohors I Hispanorum*.[23]

The altars associated with *cohors I Hispanorum* are particularly distinctive as they bear a range of ornamental motifs. One group includes wheels, triangles, tendrils, demi-lunes and zig-zags, and another dot-and-circle and concentric circles motifs.[24] The style is so distinctive that it enables us to associate an uninscribed altar to *cohors I Hispanorum*, and to assign to the Hadrianic period a building inscription of *cohors I Hispanorum* on which appear dots and concentric circles. Decorations appear on other stones, for example, rosettes on some Antonine inscriptions, while the connection between Jupiter and the wheel appears elsewhere;[25] but these altars of *cohors I Hispanorum* form a clear group.

The style of decoration on the altars of this unit helps us group the inscriptions. The dot-and-circle and concentric circle motifs appear on the altars of Maenius Agrippa (Figs. 4.2 and 4.7), Caballius Priscus and an unknown commander, while the dot-and-circle alone is used on the stone of Helstrius Novellus (Fig. 4.3). The wheel appears on the altar of Antistius Lupus Verianus (Fig. 4.4) and one each of the altars of Caballius Priscus and Cammius Maximus. This last altar also bears tendrils, triangles, demi-lunes and zig-zags (Fig. 6.4, p. 100). Demi-lunes and zig-zags appear on the altars of Censorius Cornelianus and Antistius Lupus Verianus, the last also in combination with circles (Fig. 4.4), while demilunes and circles also appear together on another altar of Cammius Maximus (Fig. 4.5).

The decorations have been re-examined by P. R. Hill (pp. 92-104), who comments that the wheel motif is of particular interest as it appears in three different forms. One stone of Caballius Priscus has the remains of a wheel which appears to have been a simple representation of spokes and rim. Two altars of Maenius Agrippa have wheel-like ornament which consists of six triangles in a circle. One dedication by Cammius Maximus carries what most resembles a Gothic wheel window, with spaces between the spokes having sub-circular foil shapes to the outer edges: the dedication slab of legions II and XX carries what was possibly a similar foil design.[26]

Fig. 4.1 Altar dedicated to Jupiter Optimus Maximus by cohors I Hispanorum *while C. Caballius Priscus was its tribune (RIB 817)*

The officers
1. M. Maenius Agrippa
Agrippa was born at Camerinum in Italy. His career inscription erected there proudly commences with the statement that he was a friend of Hadrian. His subsequent career certainly suggests high-level support and favour. The inscription also records that he took part in the *expeditio Britannica* during the reign of Hadrian. It is now accepted that this expedition was that in 122 when Hadrian visited Britain, and not an unrecorded later occasion.[27]

While serving in the British expedition, or immediately afterwards, Agrippa became tribune of *cohors I Hispanorum*. He is recorded on four Jupiter altars at Maryport (two are illustrated in Figs. 4.6 and 4.7), and we can thus date his dedications at Maryport to AD 123-126 or 124-127. Two of his altars (including *RIB 824*: Fig. 4.7) were dedicated to Jupiter and to the Divine Power of the emperor. Only one other altar at Maryport bears the same dedication. This was found in one of the pits in 1870 and bears the dot-and-circle motif. It is possible that this stone, erected by the regiment only, may also date to the time of Maenius Agrippa.[28]

An inscription at Camerinum details the rest of Agrippa's career. His previous, and first, appointment as an auxiliary commanding officer had been as prefect of *cohors II Flavia Brittonum* in the province of Moesia Inferior on the Lower Danube. Following service at Maryport, on the second rung of the promotion ladder of equestrian officers, he returned to Moesia Inferior to command a cavalry regiment, the *ala Gallorum et Pannoniorum catafractariorum*. His last two appointments were back in the west, as prefect of the British fleet and procurator of Britain. His son rose even higher, becoming a senator.

The dating of Agrippa's career to the 120s and his title of tribune allow us to place him first in the order of commanding officers, and determine that when the regiment took up residence at Maryport it was at full strength.

2. C. Caballius Priscus
This tribune is named on four Jupiter altars (e.g. *RIB 817*, Fig. 4.1).[29] He may have been a native of Verona, as another soldier with the same name had a link with that city.[30]

Fig. 4.2 Detail of the decoration on the top of the altar dedicated by cohors I Hispanorum *under the command of Marcus Maenius Agrippa (RIB 826)*

Fig. 4.3 Detail of the decoration on the top of the altar dedicated by cohors I Hispanorum *under the command of Helstrius Novellus (RIB 822)*

The occurrence of the same decorations on the altars of Agrippa and Priscus suggests that the one followed the other as commanding officer. This is supported by the title of Priscus, tribune.

3. M. Censorius M. f. Voltinia Cornelianus
Cornelianus was a native of Nîmes (Nemausus) in the province of Narbonensis. He is only recorded on one Jupiter inscription, among the most difficult to read of the entire collection (Fig. 4.8):[31]

Iovi Aug(usto)
M(arcus) Censorius
M(arci) fil(ius) Voltinia (tribu)
[C]ornelianus c(enturio) leg(ionis)
[X Fr]etensis prae-
[ ]tus coh(ortis) I u
[ ]is(panorum) ex provincia
Narbone[n(si)] domo
Nemauso [v(otum)] s(olvit) l(ibens)
  m(erito)

The dedication does not start with the usual, abbreviated *I.O.M.* formula, and may therefore not be one of that series but erected on a different occasion.

The name of the regiment is not entirely certain. All that can be seen on the stone is .]is[.. Between *coh I* and the unit's name is a symbol which appears to be u with a subscript bar. It has been suggested that this resembles a Greek μ and interpreted as the *milliaria* (thousand) sign.[32] This sign, however, normally follows the regimental name, and is rendered as oo, not as a single o. A single o might be best interpreted as indicating that the unit was only half *milliaria*. Such a symbol is unknown, but as this particular symbol has no parallel, such an explanation may not be too fanciful. A unique symbol would only, it might be expected, be used in unusual circumstances, such as the reduction in size of a thousand strong unit to one half that strength.

The rank of the commanding officer is not clear. It has been restored both as *praepositus* and *praefectus*. The former was an acting commander and later the permanent commander of an auxiliary regiment, and the restoration of the title has depended upon different interpretations of the career of Cornelianus. *Praepositus* has been restored on the basis that he held a legionary centurionate and was serving as acting commander of *cohors I Hispanorum*. *Legio X Fretensis*, however, was stationed in Judaea at the opposite end of the Roman Empire. Accordingly, a refinement has been offered, namely that he was acting commander while serving in a British legion, and had just received notice of his new posting when he erected the dedication. *Praefectus* has been restored on the basis that it was possible to transfer from one post to the other.[33]

In summary, the unit recorded on this stone is presumably *cohors I Hispanorum*; it may have been recently reduced in size from a nominal strength of 1000 to 500; and it is more likely to have been commanded by a prefect, the appropriate title for the commander of a 500-strong cohort.

Promotions from the legionary centurionate to the command of an auxiliary unit are not known after the mid-first century, but movement in the other direction continued. Such a move was to a post of lower social status, but a legionary centurion was paid the same as the prefect of a 500-strong cohort, and the transfer offered certain advantages, particularly permanency. An auxiliary commanding officer was only appointed for one tour of duty, and he had no guarantee of a further post: a centurion had no fixed term of office, and might continue in post for decades.[34]

A suitable occasion has been sought for the transfer of Cornelianus from Britain to Judaea. In 132 the governor of Britain, Iulius Severus, was transferred to the Eastern frontier to command the Roman armies against the Jewish rebels. This would be a convenient time for Cornelianus to receive a posting taking him across the whole length of the Empire, and to the province where Severus took up his command: such appointments were in the gift of governor.[35] It would have been coincidental if Cornelianus learnt of his appointment at the time that he was to make an official dedication. It is more likely that he fulfilled his vow to Jupiter when he received word of his move. The slightly different dedication, to *Iovi Aug.*, and the highly ornate nature of the stone, might be taken as support for this suggestion. A location with the other Jupiter altars may have seemed the most appropriate place to erect another dedication to the same god.[36]

Cornelianus' title appears to have been prefect. It would appear, therefore, that the unit was reduced in strength. One way this might have occurred was through the detaching of part of the regiment for service elsewhere, leaving the equivalent of a 500-strong unit at Maryport. Although no such detachment is known, this does seem the simplest way to account for the sudden appearance of the title prefect. It has been suggested that Severus took the detachment with him to the East, when he may also have taken *cohors III Bracaraugustanorum* from Britain.[37] Cornelianus could not have accompanied the detachment, as he clearly remained in command of the rump at Maryport, but he may have been sent for later by Severus.[38]

It is on the basis of the possible connection with Iulius Severus that the altar of Cornelianus is placed first in the series of prefects of *cohors I Hispanorum*. The altars of Cornelianus and Maximus are decorated with demi-lunes and zig-zags, suggesting a proximity of date. These two decorations also appear on the altars of Verianus, but the appearance of wheels on the stones of Priscus and Maximus would suggest that Maximus rather than Verianus followed Cornelianus. There are also similarities in the manner in which the die is recessed into the stone on inscriptions of Cornelianus, Maximus and Verianus, which may point to these officers serving close together at Maryport.

In summary, Cornelianus and the remaining commanding officers to be considered were all prefects. The transfer of Iulius Severus from Britain to take command of the Roman armies against the Jewish rebels would have been a suitable occasion for a move from an auxiliary unit in Britain to *legio X Fretensis* based in Judaea. This proposition does not explain the detaching of a vexillation from *cohors I Hispanorum* for service elsewhere, unless we accept another connection with Severus, and propose that he took the detachment with him, thus reducing the status of the commanding officer at Maryport to that of prefect. If this was the event which led to the creation of the detachment, we might suppose, however, that it returned on completion of the Jewish War; yet it did not, since there are three other prefects attested at Maryport, and the cohort is not attested as *milliaria* again. The detachment, which does not appear to be attested anywhere, may have been permanently separated from its parent unit, as was the case with other vexillations.

Fig. 4.4 Detail of the decoration on the top of an altar dedicated by cohors I Hispanorum *under the command of L. Antistius Lupus Verianus (RIB 816)*

Fig. 4.5 Detail of the decoration on the top of an altar dedicated by cohors I Hispanorum *under the command of L. Cammius Maximus (RIB 828)*

Fig. 4.6 Altar dedicated to Jupiter Optimus Maximus by cohors I Hispanorum *while Marcus Maenius Agrippa was its tribune* (RIB 823)

Fig. 4.7 Altar dedicated to Jupiter Optimus Maximus and the Divine Power of the Emperor by cohors I Hispanorum *while Marcus Maenius Agrippa was its tribune* (RIB 824)

4. L. Cammius Maximus

Three dedications to Jupiter record this prefect: in one (Fig. 4.9: *RIB* 827) he states that he was tribune of *cohors XVIII Voluntariorum*.[39] This information was squeezed in at the end of the dedication, giving the impression that it was an addition to the main text. Presumably Maximus had just been notified of the appointment, but had not yet taken it up. This regiment is known to have been stationed in Upper Pannonia on the middle Danube between AD 138 and 154. A date in summer for the transfer, that is, about the time of the anniversary of Hadrian's accession on 11th August, would have been more sensible than January, though, as with Censorius Cornelianus, this may have been a separate dedication.[40]

It has been suggested that Cammius Maximus is the same man as the person of that name who was a *decurio* (town councillor) of Solva in Noricum, in modern Austria.[41]

5. *L. Antistius L. f. Quirina Lupus Verianus*
Only one Jupiter inscription (Fig. 4.10a) mentions this prefect.[42] This records that he came from Sicca in Africa, modern Le Kef in western Tunisia. This is the third most highly decorated stone at Maryport (Fig. 4.4), inviting comparison with those of Cammius Maximus and Censorius Cornelianus.

6. *Helstrius Novellus*
This prefect is recorded on two altars, one to Jupiter (Fig. 4.10b) and the other to Vulcan, the last providing his full name.[43] The dot-and-circle is the only decoration used on the Jupiter altar (Fig. 4.3), and as this appears on several stones it is of no help in relating this prefect to any other. The simple style of the decorations may suggest that this prefect should come earlier in the sequence, but that would create other problems (see the discussion under Censorius Cornelianus above).

Summary
Cohors I Hispanorum was based at Maryport during the Hadrianic period. It probably arrived early in the building programme for the frontier, perhaps even in 123 if Maenius Agrippa was in Britain with Hadrian in 122. While at Maryport the regiment lost a detachment for service elsewhere. While the detachment was away, one commanding officer, M. Censorius Cornelianus, was appointed centurion in *legio X Fretensis*, which was stationed in Judaea. The likely period for such a transfer was AD 132/135, following the appointment of the governor of Britain, Iulius Severus, to take command of the Roman forces against the Jewish rebels. Severus could have taken Cornelianus with him if the detachment of *cohors I Hispanorum* had already left Maryport, but it is possible that Severus took the detachment himself, subsequently sending for the prefect. It appears that the detachment never returned to Maryport, and possibly not to Britain, thereafter.

An inscription to be discussed below suggests that *cohors I Delmatarum* may have arrived at Maryport by AD 139. *Cohors I Hispanorum* presumably left at that time, perhaps to take part in the re-conquest of southern Scotland in 139-142. However, if the detachment did not return, it is more likely to have been the other *cohors I Hispanorum* which was awarded the title *Aelia* for meritorious conduct during those campaigns, since it is that unit which is later attested as *milliaria*.

If this analysis of the commanding officers is correct, we may be able to date them notionally as follows:

123-126	M. Maenius Agrippa, tribune
127-130	C. Caballius Priscus, tribune
131	?
132	M. Censorius Cornelianus, prefect (detachment formed and sent on service elsewhere, perhaps to Judaea)
133-135	L. Cammius Maximus, prefect
136	L. Antistius Lupus Verianus, prefect
?	Helstrius Novellus, prefect
?	unknown[44]

Assuming that the altars all related to one of the two main annual ceremonies, it seems that we possess almost a full sequence of commanders for the period of residence of *cohors I Hispanorum*, depend-

Fig. 4.8 Altar dedicated to Jupiter Optimus Maximus, badly damaged but still legible, by M. Censorius Cornelianus, commanding officer of cohors I Hispanorum *(RIB 814)*

Fig. 4.9 Altar dedicated to Jupiter Optimus Maximus by Lucius Cammius Maximus, prefect of cohors I Hispanorum, *revealing his promotion to become tribune of the* cohors XVIII Voluntariorum *(RIB 827)*

ing on when the regiment arrived and departed. There are some areas of uncertainty, including the date when *cohors I Hispanorum* arrived at Maryport, and whether the two altars of Censorius Cornelianus and Cammius Maximus, on which they indicated other appointments,

Fig. 4.10 Altars dedicated to Jupiter Optimus Maximus by cohors I Hispanorum: (a) left, while Lucius Antistius Lupus Verianus was prefect (RIB 816); (b) right, when the prefect was Helstrius Novellus (RIB 822); cf. Fig. 4.3

were normal Jupiter altars. If the unit did not arrive until 124, and if the two altars were normal Jupiter dedications, then the series is complete.

Two commanders dedicated four altars each, one three and three one each, with one unknown. The average time each commander stayed at Maryport was therefore nearly two and a half years. Bearing in mind, however, that we may be missing two altars, the average would be a little over two and a half years. This is close to the three-year period usually presumed to be the norm.

2. Cohors I Delmatarum
The regiment
This regiment was raised in modern Croatia. It is recorded in Britain on diplomas of AD 122, 124 and 135.[45] It was stationed at Maryport during the reign of Antoninus Pius, and was later at Chesters on Hadrian's Wall, probably before about 180. A fragmentary inscription at High Rochester north of Hadrian's Wall may also refer to this unit.[46]

The officers
1. Paulus P. f. Palatina Postumius Acilianus
This commanding officer is attested on three altars, one to Jupiter, one to 'the gods and goddesses', and a fragmentary third, from which the dedication is missing, found half a mile to the north of the fort, at Cross Canonby. His name also appears on two slabs, one dedicated to Antoninus Pius, and the other to Jupiter but also mentioning Antoninus Pius.[47] The last (Fig. 4.11) was found in a pit near the main group of altars. It does not give Antoninus Pius the title *pater patriae*, which he accepted in 139. If this is not an accidental omission it does indicate that *cohors I Hispanorum* had left by that year, when prepara-

Fig. 4.11 Altar dedicated to Jupiter on behalf of the emperor's safety by Paulus Postumius Acilianus, prefect of cohors I Delmatarum (RIB 832)

tions commenced for the re-occupation of southern Scotland, and its place was taken by *cohors I Delmatarum*.[48] It has been suggested above that the two slabs may record work on the Jupiter shrine.

The prefect was probably a descendant of a freedman of Postumius Acilianus of Cordova, a procurator under Trajan.[49]

2. L. Caecilius Vegetus
Only one Jupiter stone attests the presence of this prefect.[50]

Summary
Cohors I Delmatarum was probably at Maryport from AD 139 to either 158 or the mid- to late 160s, with a preference for the latter date, which is the suggested date for the arrival of *cohors I Baetasiorum*. For that period of twenty years or so, we only have four Jupiter dedications erected by two commanding officers.

3. Cohors I Baetasiorum civium Romanorum ob virtutem et fidem
The regiment
This cohort was originally raised in Lower Germany, but had been in Britain since at least 103; it is also recorded on diplomas of 122, 124 and 135.[51] It was stationed at Bar Hill on the Antonine Wall during the reign of Antoninus Pius, when it first used the title *c(ivium) R(omanorum) ob vi[rtutem et fi]dem*. The award of Roman citizenship to the soldiers of the unit was probably the result of meritorious conduct during the Antonine re-conquest of southern Scotland in AD 139-142.[52] An inscription also attests its presence at Old Kilpatrick on the same frontier. This inscription has been variously dated to the second Antonine period (*c.* 158-163) and to the early third century. The unit is recorded at Reculver on the Saxon Shore in the third century, and was still listed there in the *Notitia Dignitatum*.[53]

The officers
1. *Ulpius Titianus* (Fig. 6.3a-b on p. 98)
Titianus is twice attested as prefect on dedications to Military Mars and to the Emperor's Victory, which were found, like those of Attius Tutor, with the Jupiter altars in 1870.[54]

Fig. 4.12 Altar dedicated to the Victory of the Emperor by cohors I Baetasiorum *while its prefect was Titus Attius Tutor (RIB 842)*

2. *T. Attius Tutor* (Fig. 4.12 and Fig. 6.2b on p. 96)
Tutor is recorded on three altars, as a prefect.[55] One of these is the annual Jupiter dedication, the other two are to Military Mars and to the Emperor's Victory. Tutor was a native of Solva in Noricum, where his career inscription was erected.[56] After service as a *decurio* (town councillor) of Solva, Tutor's first post was with *cohors I Baetasiorum*. He then became tribune of *legio II Adiutrix*, based at Aquincum (Budapest), prefect of *ala I Tungrorum Frontoniana*, probably in Dacia, and prefect of *ala I Batavorum milliaria*, again in Dacia and one of the top-flight auxiliary appointments.[57]

Summary
Cohors I Baetasiorum was probably at Maryport from the abandonment of the Antonine Wall in the mid- to late 160s until at least the early 180s, when there appears to have been a major re-organisation in the location of the frontier regiments.[58] The dedications to Mars and Victory may have been an acknowledgement of the unit's distinguished service during the re-conquest of southern Scotland.[59]

The Third Century
After the copious evidence for the second-century units based at Maryport, the evidence for the third century is very poor. Two commanding officers may date to this time.

C. Cornelius Peregrinus
This tribune is recorded on a dedication (Fig. 4.13) to the *genius loci*, Fortune the Home-Bringer, Eternal Rome and Good Fate.[60] He came from Saldae in Mauretania Caesariensis, where he was a *decurio* (town councillor). This stone is dated to the third century because on it appears a *signum*, or personal name, Volantius, a feature which

is generally thought not to occur before that time. It has, however, been suggested that the altar does date to the second century, with the *signum* possibly an addition to the stone,[61] although this seems unlikely.

Peregrinus was a tribune and therefore should have commanded a 1000-strong cohort. In the third century, the known 1000-strong cohorts all appear to be located on, or beyond, Hadrian's Wall, leaving none available for Maryport.[62] There is another possibility. By the end of the fourth century, the distinction between milliary and quingenary units had disappeared (and all had been reduced in strength). All cohorts now were commanded by tribunes, as is witnessed by the *Notitia Dignitatum*. The third century was a time of transition, and it is possible that Peregrinus, though a tribune, may have commanded a 500-strong regiment during that period.[63]

P. Cornelius P. f. Gaius

Cornelius is only recorded on one altar, as prefect.[64] The stone is now lost, but a drawing shows that it bore the letters EQ where the unit's title would be expected. This suggests that Gaius' regiment was *equitata*, and the only such unit known at Maryport is *cohors I Hispanorum*. The form

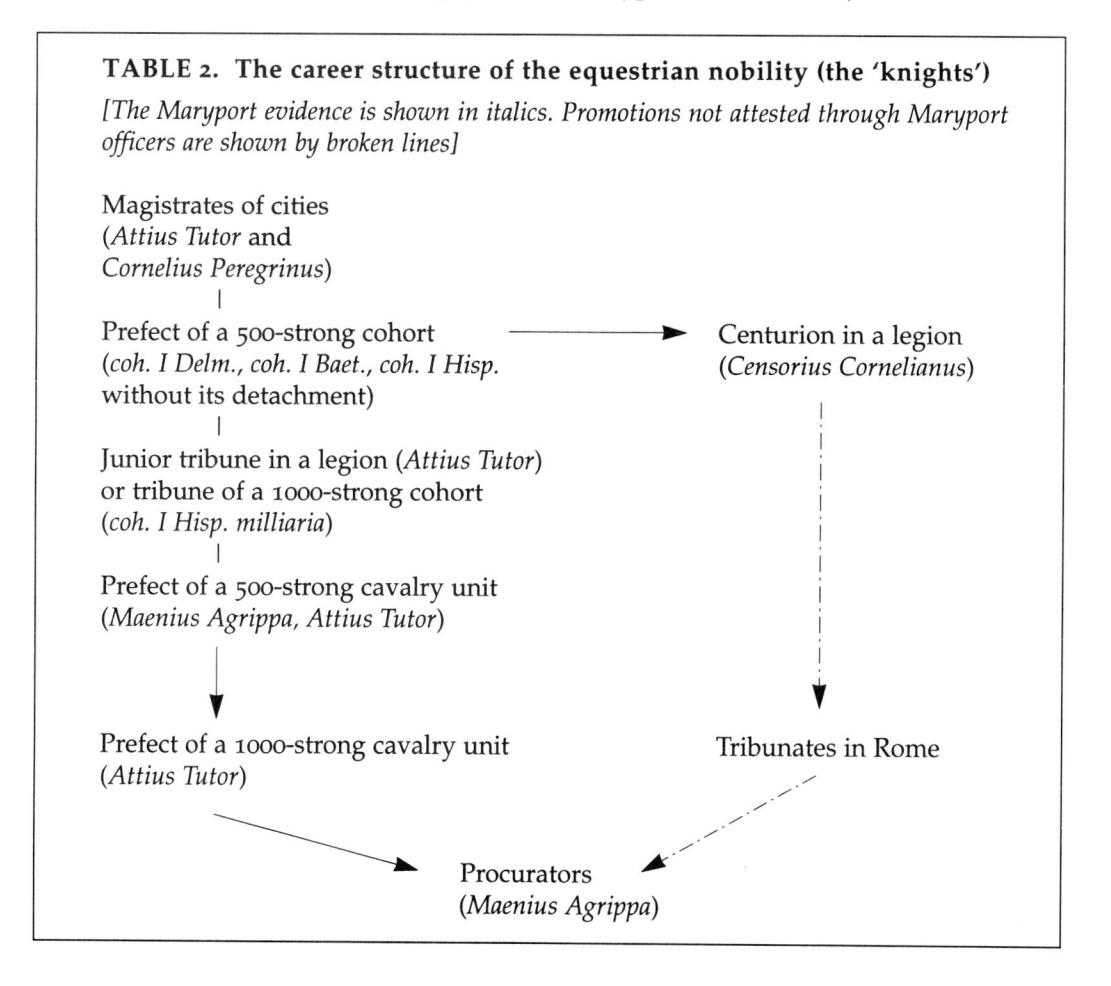

TABLE 2. The career structure of the equestrian nobility (the 'knights')

[The Maryport evidence is shown in italics. Promotions not attested through Maryport officers are shown by broken lines]

Magistrates of cities
(*Attius Tutor* and
Cornelius Peregrinus)
|
Prefect of a 500-strong cohort ⟶ Centurion in a legion
(*coh. I Delm., coh. I Baet., coh. I Hisp.* (*Censorius Cornelianus*)
without its detachment)
|
Junior tribune in a legion (*Attius Tutor*)
or tribune of a 1000-strong cohort
(*coh. I Hisp. milliaria*)
|
Prefect of a 500-strong cavalry unit
(*Maenius Agrippa, Attius Tutor*)
|
↓
Prefect of a 1000-strong cavalry unit   Tribunates in Rome
(*Attius Tutor*)
        ↘   ↙
            Procurators
          (*Maenius Agrippa*)

Fig. 4.13 Altar dedicated to the Genius loci, *to Fortune the Home-Bringer, to Eternal Rome, and to Good Fate by C. Cornelius Peregrinus, tribune (RIB 812), which left the Senhouse Collection when it was given by John Senhouse to Sir John Lowther in 1683; it is now on display in the British Museum. The largest of all the Maryport altars, it stands a massive 1.52 m (5 ft) high (for the dimensions of the other illustrated altars, see pp. 162-3).*

of the officer's name would support such a date, but the abbreviation of the formula *cui praeest* to *c.p.* usually only occurs in the third century.

The inscription of Cornelius Gaius implies, therefore, that there was a *cohors quingenaria equitata*, a 500-strong mixed infantry and cavalry regiment, stationed at Maryport in the third century. This would not be at variance with the evidence provided by the inscription of Cornelius Peregrinus, if the title tribune was not being used in its exact second-century sense.[65]

Other units

Three inscriptions at Maryport record legionaries building at the site.[66] One of these stones apparently recorded *legio XX Valeria Victrix* building under the Emperor Gordian (238-44). This legion is recorded by itself on an undated stone, and with *legio II Augusta* on a second undated stone. There are a number of building stones recording these two legions in northern Britain, and it is possible that some at least date to the third century, when they were both stationed in the southern British province, but sent detachments north to aid their colleagues in the northern province. However, a commemorative slab recording the same two legions is known at Bar Hill on the Antonine Wall, and therefore presumably belongs to the mid-second century, while P. R. Hill has drawn my attention to the appearance of the same unusual wheel motif on a dedication by Cammius Maximus, probably dating to the 130s, and on the stone of legions II and XX, also supporting a mid-second-century date for the inscription.[67]

Other soldiers

Few other soldiers are recorded at Maryport.[68] The tombstone of a centurion recorded that he lived 40 years, while an *optio*, Julius Civilis, dedicated an altar to the northern British god Belatucadrus. A doodle of a face and body had scratched beside it SIG, presumably *signifer*, another post in the century. A dedication in Greek to Asclepius (the Roman equivalent of Aesculapius) may have been by a doctor, many of whom were Greek.

Conclusions

The Maryport inscriptions are important in a variety of ways. Firstly, those of *cohors I Hispanorum* form a unique collection, illustrating the nature of the annual ceremony when vows were made for the welfare of the emperor and the state, on 3rd January and on the anniversary of the emperor's accession. Only at Maryport in the entire Roman Empire does there survive a series of altars presumably relating to one or other of these occasions, and representing nearly every year of a regiment's residence. This also helps us to appreciate the subtle differences between the annual dedications.

It might be asked why more such annual dedications have not survived at other Roman forts. Certainly some are known, for example, those at Birdoswald on Hadrian's Wall, but not as many as might be expected if every unit in the army erected an altar every year. It is possible that, rather than erect an altar, some units may have chosen to mark the annual dedication in another way, perhaps limiting themselves to the sacrifice of an ox, the animal specified for this day on the Feriale Duranum.[69] Such action was presumably taken on the other 'holy days': the Feriale probably listed, as we have seen (p. 68), some forty festivals, each with the appropriate sacrifice for the day, including most of the accession-days and birthdays of the emperors and their wives from Augustus onwards; even the birthday of the deified Julius Caesar appears.

Secondly, the altars illustrate the position of the commanding officers within the framework of imperial administration and military organisation. There were four rungs on the ladder of promotion for auxiliary commanding officers, members of the equestrian nobility. The three regiments attested at Maryport lay on either the first or second rung. The bottom rung was command of a 500-strong regiment. The prefects of *cohors I Baetasiorum* and of *cohors I Delmatorum* both lay at this level, as did the command of *cohors I Hispanorum* once it had lost a detachment.

Cohors I Hispanorum at full strength lay on the second rung. Thence promotion was possible to a 500-strong cavalry regiment, and, beyond that, to a 1000-strong cavalry regiment. Maenius Agrippa's post as tribune was on the second rung, and he moved from there to command a cavalry unit before passing on to the next group of posts. By the time Cammius Maximus arrived at Maryport to take over command of *cohors I Hispanorum*, it had lost a detachment for service elsewhere, and thus his post as prefect was on the first rung of the ladder. While at Maryport he learnt of his next appointment: to the command of a cohort of 'Volunteers' (Fig. 4.9). Commanding officers of these cohorts were entitled 'tribune' because they were citizen units, in spite of the fact that they were only 500-strong.

Attius Tutor, prefect of *cohors I Baetasiorum*, passed through all four levels of the hierarchy. His second appointment was not as tribune of a 1000-strong cohort but the alternative, junior tribune in a legion, in his case *legio II Adiutrix*. Tutor was privileged to pass through all four grades, as the number of posts available reduced at each level, and therefore promotion was never guaranteed: this, no doubt, was one way of weeding out the unsuccessful commanding officers. There were about 270 quingenary (500-strong) cohorts throughout the Empire. Thus, there were about ninety vacancies available each year at the lowest level: the evidence from Maryport for the length of service of each appointment being about three years is important here. At the next level there were about sixty vacancies each year, and then perhaps thirty as prefect of a 500-strong cavalry unit. There were only ten 1000-strong cavalry units in the whole Empire, with three or four posts falling vacant each year: these posts were indeed only for the very best auxiliary commanding officers.[70] Attius Tutor was, however, surpassed by Maenius Agrippa, who reached one of the highest posts in the Empire, retiring as procurator of Britain.

An alternative path to such top posts was through the centurionate. Entry to the centurionate was usually from the ranks (Julius Civilis, the *optio* at Maryport, may have had his hopes for promotion to centurion), but a direct commission was also possible. This appears to have been the path chosen by Censorius Cornelianus when he moved from command of *cohors I Hispanorum* to a centurionate in *legio X Fretensis*.[71] He will have received no extra pay as a result of the move, but he exchanged the uncertainty of the career structure of the auxiliary commanding officer for the permanency of the legionary centurionate. It has been calculated that the number of vacancies for legionary centurions each year was about ninety, the same as for commanding officers of 500-strong cohorts, so entry to the centurionate was no easier. Both appointments, too, had to be obtained from the governor; hence the attraction of a link between Censorius Cornelianus and the governor Iulius Severus.[72]

Commanding officers and legionary centurions entering on direct commission were also often about the same age when taking up their appointments, that is about thirty, although the centurion rising from the ranks was normally a little older.[73] Commanding officers had sometimes held magistracies in their own home towns before taking up a military career: Attius Tutor and Cornelius Peregrinus are examples of this at Maryport.

The careers of the commanding officers at Maryport indicate the integrated and cosmopolitan nature of the equestrian aristocracy in the Roman Empire in other ways. The officers at Maryport came from Italy, Provence, Noricum (modern Austria), north Africa and possibly Spain. They moved between posts in Britain and in provinces of the middle and lower Danube, including both Upper and Lower Pannonia, Lower Moesia and Dacia, as well as Judaea, travelling almost literally from one end of the Empire to another to take up their next appointment.

The altars are an important source of information for the length of service of commanding officers of auxiliary units. The best evidence relates to *cohors I Hispanorum*. Four inscriptions have survived of two commanders of this unit, three of a third, while three prefects have left us only one altar each, although others may have existed; in addition there is an altar dedicated by the unit alone, and one clearly assignable to the unit on the basis of its decoration, but which has lost its inscription. The number of altars dedicated by individual commanders suggest that the average duration of a post at Maryport was about three years.

The history of *cohors I Hispanorum* also illustrates another aspect of Roman army organisation, the creation of temporary detachments. In part this was the result of the increasing immobility of the army as it settled down on the frontiers such as Hadrian's Wall. By the middle of the second century it was so rare to move a legion that new field armies were created through the formation of legionary detachments, some of which eventually became separate units. The despatch of a detachment from *cohors I Hispanorum* was at an early stage of this relatively new trend.

Finally, we see the rewards available to soldiers through their own actions in war. Both *cohors I Baetasiorum* and the other *cohors I Hispanorum* appear to have been given special honours through their conduct during the re-occupation of southern Scotland in 139-142 under Antoninus Pius. Maryport, its units and its commanders are indeed true reflections of the Roman army.

This is by no means the last word on the Maryport altars. There is still much to be learnt about them, their decoration and the form of the dedications, as well as about the commanding officers and their careers.

Acknowledgements

I am grateful, as ever, to Dr Brian Dobson for reading and commenting on earlier drafts of this paper and discussing particular problems with me; to Peter Hill for so readily responding to my request that he re-examine the stones and for producing a contribution to this volume at short notice; to Professor J. C. Mann who has also prepared a contribution on the altars (Ch. 5 below); to Miss Shirley Waldock for providing me with access to her unpublished thesis and for much stimulating discussion about the Maryport material, and to Ian Caruana and Dr M. M. Roxan for discussing various points with me.

Notes

1. For discussion of the altars and the regiments attested at Maryport see Wenham 1939; Jarrett 1965; 1966; 1976a; 1976b, 147-9; Davies 1977; Jarrett and Stephens 1987; Jarrett 1994, 46-8, 52-4. This paper owes much to the detailed studies of the Maryport inscriptions by the late Professor M. G. Jarrett over many years.
2. *RIB* 815-817, 819, 822, 824-828, 830-832, 838, 842, 843 and 846; Bruce 1875, facing p. 429 ; Wenham 1939, 20.
3. The dedications to Jupiter include altars found at others times: *RIB* 814, 818, 820, 821, 823, 829, 833, 834 and 835: the Jupiter altars are *RIB* 814-835. Other altars relevant to this study are: 810, 812, 837, 838, 842, 847, 850. The decoration on *RIB* 836 allows it to be assigned to *cohors I Hispanorum*. It was found (see Fig. 1.6) about 20 yards from a Jupiter inscription of *cohors I Hispanorum* and therefore may have been dedicated to the same god.
4. Jarrett 1976a, 10-12. See Hill in this volume, pp. 95-8.
5. P.Dura 54 = Fink 1971, no. 117.
6. 1st January: Tacitus, *Histories* 1, 55; Suetonius, *Galba* 16. 3rd January: Pliny, *Ep.* 10, 35 and 36; 100 and 101 (Penguin translation). See also *Digest* 50, 16, 239, 1, quoting Gaius.
7. Pliny, *Ep.* 10, 102 and 103.
8. Pliny, *Ep.* 10, 88 and 89.
9. Feriale Duranum: P.Dura 54 = Fink 1971, no. 117.
10. Birley, E. 1961, 218, 222, fig. 34.
11. Miss Shirley Waldock kindly brought to my attention the lack of evidence for a parade ground north of the fort (see Waldock 1995, 72).
12. Schallmayer 1983; 1990, 131-60; Popovic 1989; Hill in this volume, pp. 93-5. See also Thornborough 1959 for a possible shrine at South Shields.
13. Robinson in Bellhouse 1992, 36-53.
14. I. A. Richmond, quoted by Jarrett 1965, 126. See Waldock 1995 for doubts concerning this suggestion, and on the assumption that the civilian settlement expanded over the site of an earlier parade-ground.
15. See Hill elsewhere in this volume and for a discussion of the date and purpose of the burial of the altars.
16. *RIB* 2213.
17. *CIL* XVI, 43, *RIB* 2401.1; 2; *CIL* XVI, 69; *RIB* 2401, 6; 10; Jarrett 1994, 46-8.
18. Birley, E. 1952-53. As there appear to have been two *cohortes I Hispanorum* in Britain, it is not clear which unit appears on which

diploma listed in note 17. That of 146, which records *cohors I Hispanorum* without the title *Aelia* presumably awarded about 142/3, probably refers to the other cohort: Davies 1977, 15, n. 50. An inscription published in 1972 (*AE* 1972, 226) recorded a tribune in command of *cohors [ ] Hispanorum tironum*, i.e. a newly-recruited regiment. The officer went on to command the *ala Gallorum Petriana civium Romanorum milliaria*. This appointment must date between 98, when the cavalry regiment was still quingenary (500-strong), and the reign of Hadrian when a new tier was created in the hierarchy of command. This *cohors Hispanorum* may be one of the two recorded in Britain, but as several units of that name are known, there is no certainty of this. For the latest discussion of these units, see Jarrett 1994, 46-8.
19 Roxan 1994, no. 184.
20 *RIB* 968 and 976-80 (dating to 213-222); Breeze and Dobson 1987, 251, 273.
21 Jarrett 1994, 48. The location of *Axelodunum* is not known: cf. Breeze and Dobson 1987, 273, and notes 2 and 42 of Chapter 1, pp. 33 and 36 above.
22 Jarrett 1976a, 20-21; Jarrett 1994, 47.
23 *RIB* 851 and 855; Jarrett 1976b, 148-9. On fort sizes generally, see Austen and Breeze 1979, 124 (= Breeze and Dobson 1993, 488).
24 Jarrett 1976a, 10.
25 *RIB* 836; Jarrett 1976a, 12; *RIB* 855. Other Antonine stones: *RIB* 832 and 833. On the connection between Jupiter and the wheel, see, for example, Green 1986: I owe this reference to Miss S. A. Waldock.
26 *RIB* 817, 823, 826, 827, 852. I am grateful to Mr Hill for this information.
27 *CIL* XI, 5632 = *ILS* 2735. Jarrett 1976b, 147-9; Birley, A. R. 1979, 292-3.
28 *RIB* 823-6; Wenham 1939, 24; Jarrett 1965, 124-6; Davies 1977; Jarrett and Stephens 1987, 61. The third altar is *RIB* 815; for further discussion of this point see the paper by J. C. Mann below (pp. 90-1).
29 *RIB* 817-20; Jarrett 1965, 123-4.
30 Birley, E. 1952-53, 90-91.
31 *RIB* 814; Jarrett 1965, 120-22. Davies 1977, 9; 1981, 198-201.

32 Davies 1981, 198-201.
33 Davies 1977 suggested that the shadow of 'ec' was visible on the stone, but the whole surface has flaked off at this point, and the surviving marks are only coincidental. I am grateful to Ian Caruana for discussing this with me. Davies' reading is accepted by Jarrett 1994, 47.
34 On the background to such promotions see Dobson 1972 (= Breeze and Dobson 1993, 186-200) and Birley, E. 1983, 78 (= 1988, 226). Birley's suggestion was linked to the reading of *prae[ ]tus* as *praepositus*.
35 See note 72 below.
36 Jarrett 1976a, 22; 1976b, 149; 1994, 47. Davies 1977, 9 saw this dedication by Cornelianus as not being within the normal series.
37 Roxan 1994, 297, n. 10.
38 I owe the suggestion that Severus may have sent for Cornelianus after his arrival in Judaea to Dr Brian Dobson. The fact that the detachment does not appear to have returned to Maryport (no other commander is entitled tribune) renders Davies' suggestion (1977, 9), that Cornelianus may have accompanied the cohort on its return to Maryport from the East, improbable.
39 *RIB* 827-29; Jarrett 1965, 120-2.
40 On the transfer to *cohors XVIII Voluntariorum* see Birley, E. 1952, 187-8 (= 1988, 296-7).
41 Birley 1952, 187 (= 1988, 296); *CIL* V, 961; Jarrett 1965, 123; cf. also Dobson 1978, 247-8.
42 *RIB* 816; Jarrett 1965, 120.
43 *RIB* 822, 846; Jarrett 1965, 120.
44 *RIB* 836.
45 *CIL* XVI, 69; *RIB* 2401, 6; 8.
46 Chesters: *JRS* 47 (1957) 229, no. 4. Cf. Breeze and Dobson 1987, 244 and 254. High Rochester: *RIB* 1289.
47 *RIB* 810, 832, 833, 847, 850; Jarrett 1965, 126.
48 Jarrett 1965, 126-7.
49 Jarrett 1965, 127.
50 *RIB* 831; Jarrett 1965, 126.
51 *RIB* 2401.1; 6; *CIL* XVI, 69; *RIB* 2401. 8.
52 Davies 1977, 170 suggested that the unusually full expression of the title on *RIB* 2170 might indicate that the unit had recently

been awarded it, and that the most likely time is during the Antonine advance; hence also the regiment was probably at Bar Hill in the first Antonine period. This might support its appearance at Old Kilpatrick in the second Antonine period: Breeze and Dobson 1969-70, 120, n. 48 (= 1993, 402, n. 48).

53 *RIB* 2170; cf. *RIB* 2169; *Britannia* 1 (1970), 310, no. 20. Breeze and Dobson 1969-70, 120, n. 48 (= 1993, 402, n. 48) argue for an Antonine II date; Birley, E. 1983 (= 1988, 221-231) for a Severan date. *RIB* 2468; *Notitia Dignitatum*, Occ. 28, 18.
54 *RIB* 838, 843; Jarrett 1965, 128.
55 *RIB* 830, 837, 842; Jarrett 1965, 128.
56 *CIL* III, 5331 = *ILS* 2734.
57 Jarrett 1965, 128. Birley, E. 1966, 57 (= 1988, 352).
58 Breeze and Dobson 1987, 130-3.
59 Davies 1977, 8-9; Jarrett 1994, 47.
60 *RIB* 812; cf. *RIB* 840; Jarrett 1965, 128-9.
61 Davies 1977, 9.
62 Jarrett and Stephens 1987, 63; Breeze and Dobson 1987, 129-40; 247.
63 Davies 1977, 16, n. 61; Jarrett and Stephens 1987, 63.
64 *RIB* 821; Jarrett 1965, 129-30; Davies 1981, 201-2.
65 Jarrett and Stephens 1987, 63. Davies 1977, 10-11 (cf. Davies 1981, 183-214) brought together several fragmentary pieces of evidence to suggest that the other *cohors I Hispanorum* was at Maryport in the third century. Davies himself acknowledged the weakness of his case and his arguments are rebutted by Jarrett and Stephens 1987, 63-5. If Maryport was *Alauna*, *cohors III Nerviorum* was here in the late fourth century (*Notitia Dignitatum*, Occ. 40, 53) and possibly earlier, and this may be supported by an inscription reading IIX. . . ER (*Britannia* 22 [1991] 295-6, no. 2).
66 *RIB* 852-854: *legio XX Valeria Victrix* is identified on this last inscription through the appearance of its emblem, the boar.
67 Breeze 1989, 28; *RIB* 2171. See above, p. 71.
68 *RIB* 858, 809, 871, 808.
69 I owe this suggestion to Professor J. C. Mann.
70 Birley, E. 1966 (= 1988, 349-363).
71 Dobson 1972 (= Breeze and Dobson 1993, 186-200) for a comparison of the pay and prospects of legionary centurions and equestrian officers.
72 Birley, E. 1952-53, 141. Tacitus, *Annals* II, 55 records that Piso replaced centurions and tribunes in Syria with his own appointments.
73 Dobson 1972, 194 (= Breeze and Dobson, 1993, 187); Breeze 1974, 276 (= Breeze and Dobson 1993, 11-58).

References

AUSTEN, P. S. and BREEZE, D. J. 1979 'A new inscription from Chesters on Hadrian's Wall', *AA*[5] 7, 115-26 (= BREEZE and DOBSON 1993, 479-90)

BELLHOUSE, R. L. 1992 *Joseph Robinson of Maryport: archaeologist extraordinary* (privately printed)

BIRLEY, A. R. 1979 *The People of Roman Britain* (London)

BIRLEY, A. R. 1981 *The Fasti of Roman Britain* (Oxford)

BIRLEY, E. 1952 'Noricum, Britain and the Roman Army', *Beiträge zur alteren europaischen Kulturgeschichte* 1, Festschrift R. Egger (Klagenfurt), 175-88 (= BIRLEY, E. 1988, 284-297)

BIRLEY, E. 1952-3 'Roman garrisons in Wales', *Archaeologia Cambrensis* 102, 9-19

BIRLEY, E. 1953 *Roman Britain and the Roman Army* (Kendal)

BIRLEY, E. 1961 *Research on Hadrian's Wall* (Kendal)

BIRLEY, E. 1966 'Alae and cohortes milliariae', *Corolla Memoriae Erich Swoboda Dedicata* (Römische Forschungen in Niederösterreich V), 54-67 (= BIRLEY, E. 1988, 349-64)

BIRLEY, E. 1983 'A Roman altar from Old Kilpatrick and interim commanders of auxiliary units', *Latomus* 42, 73-83 (= BIRLEY, E. 1988, 221-31)

BIRLEY, E. 1988 *The Roman Army, Papers 1929-1986* [MAVORS IV] (Stuttgart)

BREEZE, D. J. 1974 'The organisation of the career structure of the immunes and principales of the Roman army', *Bonner Jahr-*

bücher 174, 245-92 (= BREEZE and DOBSON 1993, 11-58)

BREEZE, D. J. 1989 *The Second Augustan Legion in North Britain* (Cardiff)

BREEZE, D. J. and DOBSON, B. 1969-70 'The development of the Mural Frontier in Britain from Hadrian to Honorius', *Proceedings of Society of Antiquaries of Scotland* 102, 109-21 (= BREEZE and DOBSON 1993, 391-403)

BREEZE, D. J. and DOBSON, B. 1987 *Hadrian's Wall* (London)

BREEZE, D. J. and DOBSON, B. 1993 *Roman Officers and Frontiers* [MAVORS X] (Stuttgart)

BRUCE, J. C. 1874 'Altars recently found in the Roman camp at Maryport', CW^1, 175-88

BRUCE, J. C. 1875 *Lapidarium Septentrionale* (London and Newcastle upon Tyne)

COLLINGWOOD, R. G. 1936 'The Roman fort and settlement at Maryport', CW^2 36, 85-99

DAVIES, R. W. 1976-77 'Roman Scotland and Roman auxiliary units', *PSAS* 108, 168-73

DAVIES, R. W. 1977 'Cohors I Hispanorum and the garrisons of Maryport', CW^2 77, 7-16

DAVIES, R. W. 1981 'Some Roman commands from Roman Britain', *Epigraphische Studien* 12, 183-214

DOBSON, B. 1972 'Legionary centurion or equestrian officer? A comparison of pay and prospects', *Ancient Society* 3, 193-207 (= BREEZE and DOBSON 1993, 186-200)

DOBSON, B. and JARRETT, M. G. (eds.) 1966 *Britain and Rome: essays presented to Eric Birley* (Kendal)

DOBSON, B. 1978 *Die Primipilares* (Köln)

FINK, R. O. 1971 *Roman Military Records on Papyrus* (Cape Western Reserve University)

GREEN, M. J. 1986 'Jupiter, Taranis and the Solar Wheel', in Henig and King 1986, 64-75

HENIG, M. and KING, A. (eds.) 1986 *Pagan gods and shrines of the Roman Empire* [Oxford University Committee for Archaeology, Monograph 8] (Oxford)

JARRETT, M. G. 1965 'Roman officers at Maryport', CW^2 65, 115-32

JARRETT, M. G. 1966 'The garrison of Maryport and the Roman army in Britain', in Dobson and Jarrett 1966, 27-40

JARRETT, M. G. 1976a *Maryport, Cumbria: a Roman fort and its garrison* (Kendal)

JARRETT, M. G. 1976b 'An unnecessary war', *Britannia* 6, 145-51

JARRETT, M. G. 1994 'Non-legionary troops in Roman Britain: Part One, The Units', *Britannia* 25, 35-77

JARRETT, M. G. and STEPHENS, G. R. 1987 'The Roman garrisons of Maryport', CW^2 87, 61-6

POPOVIC, V. 1989 'Une station de bénéficiaires à Sirmium', *Comptes Rendues de l'Académie des Inscriptions et Belles-Lettres* 1989, 116-22

ROXAN, M. M. 1994 *Roman Military Diplomas 1985-1993* (London)

SCHALLMAYER, E. 1983 'Ausgrabung eines Benefiziarier-Weihebezirkes und römischer Holzbauten in Osterburken, Neckar-Odenwald-Kreis', *Archäologische Ausgrabungen in Baden-Württemberg 1982* (Stuttgart), 138-46

SCHALLMAYER, E. 1990 *Der römische Weihebezirk von Osterburken I, Corpus der griechischen und lateinischen Benefiziarier-Inschriften des Römischen Reiches* (Stuttgart)

THORNBOROUGH, J. W. 1959 'Report on the excavations at Beacon Street, South Shields, 1959', *South Shields Archaeological and Historical Society Papers* 1.7, 8-25

WALDOCK, S. A. 1995 *A study of the auxiliary forts along Hadrian's Wall, and some associated forts, to ascertain possible locations of cavalry and infantry parade grounds* (University of Durham, unpublished BA thesis)

WENHAM, L. P. 1939 'Notes on the garrisoning of Maryport', CW^2 39, 19-30

5 A note on the Maryport altars

J. C. Mann

An important religious point emerges from Professor Breeze's discussion of the Maryport 'Jupiter' altars. Although the whole process of paying vows for the past year, and making vows for the coming year, seems to have had a firm official basis, in fact it represents private actions by the men of the unit and their commanders. Although perhaps they were enjoined to do so by higher authority, it had nothing to do with the official 'State Religion', so-called.

This unauthorised title, 'State Religion', is an attempt to indicate the vital relationship between Rome and her guardian gods, particularly but not exclusively the Capitoline triad, Jupiter, Juno and Minerva. This relationship existed at a simple, primitive level. Basically, the body of Roman citizens, acting primarily through their elected priests, the *pontifices*, sought to propitiate, by means of sometimes complex ritual actions, the deities who presided over the fortunes of the Roman state, before they took it upon themselves to vent their anger on the citizen body. The gods were envisaged as at least irritable, if not permanently angry, and liable to strike without mercy unless they were mollified by the appropriate sacrifices and rituals. In this so-called 'State Religion', action was taken, by the priests on behalf of the citizens, *before* the gods could do anything amiss. If the gods, in spite of this, did in fact display displeasure, there were precise rituals by which the situation could be retrieved.

The resultant tranquil relations established between Rome and her gods was called the *pax deorum*, the peace of the gods. That it truly existed was quite clear to the Roman from the fact that since her earliest days Rome had prospered, not least in military affairs. This would not have happened if the gods did not approve. From the fact that the gods approved, Romans concluded that the propitiatory sacrifices and rituals were the correct ones to please the gods, and therefore they had to be maintained. Their importance is illustrated by the fact that in the third century Christians were persecuted because, as atheists, their presence was polluting the sacrifices and incurring the wrath of the gods, in turn causing military defeats.

In his personal relations with the gods, the individual Roman took a more sophisticated view. He now made bargains with the gods. He vowed that if a particular god or goddess would protect or favour him in particular circumstances – preserve his life in battle, ensure his safety on a voyage, or ensure his child's recovery from illness or his family's survival when faced with plague – he would do something to please that deity, whether it was simply to make a sacrifice of an animal, or set up an altar, or even build a shrine: he would 'pay his vow'. The frequency with which this contract was made with a deity is indicated by the number of times that the letters *v. s. l. m* appear on dedications: 'he paid his vow willingly and deservedly'. This could almost be blackmail. A merchant, setting sail from York for Bordeaux in AD 237, vowed that if he arrived safely he would set up an altar to the guardian deity Boudiga (*AE* 1922, 116; Ottaway 1993, pl. 31). He took the altar (of Yorkshire millstone grit) with him. If the deity did not get his ship safely to Bordeaux, she would lose her altar.

The annual vows by army units and/or their commanding officers were not propitiatory, nor part of the 'State Religion'. They were personal actions, corporately or individually. They were nevertheless made in response to instructions laid down in documents like the Feriale Duranum. Their purpose was not to convert members of the army to the religion of Rome, a fatuous idea which does not need refutation, but to instil in them loyalty to the emperors and obedience to their army and unit commanders. It may well be that the altars or sacrifices had to be paid for by the men themselves and/or the commanders. Thus it may be that when a new commander appears, commander and unit made and paid a joint vow, but thereafter usually only the commander could afford an altar. Perhaps the men had to be content with the sacrifice of an animal – except perhaps in the case of *RIB* 815, on which only the unit name and not its commander appears.

Reference

OTTAWAY, P. 1993 *English Heritage Book of Roman York* (London)

6 The Maryport altars: some first thoughts

P. R. Hill

Introduction

In February 1995, following a suggestion from Dr D. J. Breeze, all the Maryport altars were inspected, and about a dozen examined in some detail, measured, and recorded.[1] The other altars were taken into consideration but not recorded in detail. It is hoped that a full survey of all the Maryport altars will be prepared for publication in the near future. In the following pages particular reference is made to the group of altars discovered in April 1870, in a series of pits some 300 m to the north-east of the fort, in an attempt to elucidate the reason for, and the date of, their burial. Sixteen inscribed altars were found,[2] in nine pits, along with other stone artefacts. The method of assessment used was in line with the recommendations made by the author in 1981,[3] but with the essential addition of the author's masonry skills and experience.

General description

In view of the presumed importance to the unit of the *I.O.M.* altars, one might expect them to have been worked to a consistent, high standard. In reality, the workmanship varies over a wide range, perhaps reflecting the immediate availability of skilled craftsmen at given periods, and perhaps for other reasons. The very poor standard of *RIB* 819 (Caballius Priscus) is in sharp contrast to, say, *RIB* 825 (Maenius Agrippa), which in its original state was of much better quality. As only one of the Priscus altars (Fig. 4.1 on p. 72: *RIB* 817, probably the first[4]) rises above the mediocre, it is tempting, if a little fanciful, to suggest that, although the *I.O.M.* altars marked official ceremonies, the commanding officer paid for them out of his own pocket.[5] Perhaps the first of the series was paid for out of unit funds as part of the commanding officer 'reading himself in'. Surprisingly, not one of the altars was worked to the highest standards, although in almost every case the front was significantly more accurately worked than the sides, which were probably not intended to be easily visible. In general every element of the front was worked to a straight edge with deviations of only one or two millimetres at most. The returns are sometimes square, but more often several millimetres over or under, and rising to twenty millimetres in a few cases; the sides are worked significantly hollow. It is not uncommon for the top to be out of alignment with the base, giving the altar a leaning appearance, and for the mouldings to run at an angle across the face.

The sides are generally rather better preserved than the faces, and there is some indication that on many of the altars one side may have been better protected than the other. This could have been due to the prevailing wind striking one side or the other according to how they were sited, but it may indicate that they stood close together, perhaps in pairs, or against some sort of shelter. Further examination will be needed to confirm this differential weathering, but it does raise the question of how they were displayed. One might presume that a newly dedicated altar was held in some sort of reverence, at least for the current year. In that case it would hardly have been stood simply at the edge of the parade ground for animals to rub against, or worse. One might reasonably expect some sort of demarcation of the area in which the new altar and its many predecessors[6] were set up. This need not have been elaborate, but might have been a simple affair of wattle hurdles on three sides, open to the parade ground. The greater degree of weathering on the tops of the altars suggests that the sanctuary was not roofed in any way.

It must be pointed out that the reference to the altars standing beside a parade ground continues the supposition which was first put forward in 1939[7] and not seriously questioned until recently (see p. 69 above). Two slabs set up under Antoninus Pius by Postumius Acilianus have been supposed to represent the building or rebuilding of a *tribunal*,[8] but there is no evidence that the stones formed part of such a structure; they could equally well have been associated with a temple. One[9] is dedicated to Jupiter Capitolinus and the welfare of the emperor (Fig. 4.11, p. 80), the other[10] only to the welfare of the emperor. Their format and style are dissimilar, and there is no reason to suppose that they were dedicated at the same time. Acilianus also set up the Jupiter column, and it may be that he was given to making dedications without specific purpose. There is in fact no evidence for a parade ground to the north of the fort other than the presence of the altars and these two slabs: there may well have been, of course, such a parade ground, but in the absence of supporting evidence the argument is in danger of assuming the curved posture so familiar in studies of Roman Britain.

A degree of support for the presence of an enclosure comes from the excavations at Osterburken (Fig. 6.1).[11] Here, a number of the altars were within some sort of timber barrier which may have served to delin-

Fig. 6.1 Osterburken (Baden-Württemberg, Germany), reconstruction sketch showing the altars dedicated by beneficiarii *as they may have appeared in a sanctuary outside the fort*

eate a part of the 'consecrated ground'. To one side was a temple to Dea Candida,[12] a situation not wholly unlike that at Maryport where a supposed temple lies 120 m to the south of the 1870 pits. There is no suggestion that the Osterburken altars stood alongside a parade ground; the altars were set up by *beneficiarii* stationed at or near the fort, and were generous in the range of deities included. One stone, for example, was dedicated not only to Jupiter, Best and Greatest, but also to Juno, Mars Exalbiovix, All Gods and Goddesses, and to the *Genius Loci*.

At Stockstadt successive *beneficiarii* set up altars similarly dedicated to multiple deities, and apparently erected them on the river bank adjacent to their 'station' which was near the jetty.[13] Some of the altars were dedicated to *I.O.M.* (sometimes with other gods), and may have been annual dedications made in somewhat similar fashion to those at Maryport; but the parallel is not a clear one. Neither at Osterburken nor at Stockstadt were the altars buried, but seem to have been gradually overwhelmed by changes in the courses and levels of the respective rivers near which they stood. In both cases the quality of workmanship appears (from photographs) to be generally superior to that of the Maryport altars; the reason for this is not immediately obvious, but may reflect the generally lower standards of workmanship obtaining in Roman Britain as compared to the mainland of Europe. The Osterburken and Stockstadt altars were provided with moulded stone bases, something which has not been found at Maryport. This may again reflect provincial differences, although three bases were found adjacent to a presumed parade ground at South Shields.

The South Shields altar bases were discovered in 1959,[14] 66 yards north-east of the north-east corner of the fort. A series of narrow trenches revealed three altar bases, an altar lying a few feet away, and the head and torso of a statuette attributed to Mars and Jupiter, or to Brigantia/Victory.[15] No fence or other division was found, possibly owing to the limited area of the excavation. The discovery of 'a substantial structure of large cobbles . . . [forming] a rough mound or platform of stones approximately 6 feet square and 3 feet high' was interpreted as forming the base of a *tribunal*;[16] hence the theory that the altars lay beside a parade ground. However, it is now believed, on topographical grounds, that the altars and the statuette relate to a temple rather than a parade ground.[17] If this is so, the situation at South Shields is not dissimilar to that at Osterburken, and perhaps to that at Maryport.

An apparently closer parallel is to be found at Mainhardt, on the Lorch-Miltenburg stretch of the *limes* of Antoninus Pius in Upper Germany. Here, nine altars and three Mother Goddess reliefs were found in 1944 and in subsequent excavations.[18] Five of the altars were dedicated to *I.O.M.* on behalf of *cohors I Asturum equitata* by successive prefects; two of the altars were dedicated by a single prefect. There is little doubt that these were annual, or perhaps bi-annual, dedications at New Year and/or the beginning of a new regnal year. The interpretation was of a cult centre to Jupiter.[19] As at Osterburken and Stockstadt, the Mainhardt altars appear, from photographs, to be of relatively high quality workmanship as compared to those at Maryport. Professor Baatz noted subsequently that they were found 'between the Kastell and the *limes* where the parade ground is assumed to be'.[20] He also notes that 'from time to time space had to be made for new altars and so the oldest altars at the time were carefully buried. In this way . . . the altars were preserved'.

However, there is no evidence that these altars had been been deliberately buried. The excavator, O. Paret, considered that '... because they were lying partly on their backs and partly on their faces, they were silted up with the clay in which they lay'.[21] Goessler suggests that in fact they were found '... in approximately the original places of falling ... In no way would such heavy stones have been transported by human hand from further away'. They were discovered 0.5 m below the turf, and there is no indication of any kind of pit. No bases were discovered, and no fence or barrier was recorded. The suggested proximity to the parade ground remains speculative, as does the suggestion of burial, and both of these hypotheses have perhaps been influenced by the received theory on Maryport.

Much better evidence for the manner of display and the disposal or otherwise of altars comes from the Roman town of Sirmium, some 40 miles west of Belgrade in what is now Serbia. Here, yet another station of *beneficiarii*, again on a river (the Save), has yielded an exceptional discovery.[22] A group of eighty-five altars, both whole and fragmentary, and almost all *in situ*, came to light in 1986 in the course of a rescue excavation. They stand close to a building of unknown purpose; it is suggested, from the 'coarseness of the architecture',[23] that it may have been part of a barracks. The altars stood in an open court, surrounded on at least two sides by screens. A single row runs across the back of the court, while the remainder are set in one complete U-shape and one half-U. They are all packed tightly together, with little, if any, space between adjacent altars or between the two U-shapes. They are not only mostly *in situ* but are still more or less upright. Being stood so close together would give them considerable protection from the weather except on their tops; this is very reminiscent of the condition of the altars at Maryport. The earliest altar carries a consular date of 157, after which there is a long interval until the next consular date of 185; from then they run through to 231 apart from a gap between 209 and 220.

The parallel is again not an exact one, as the Sirmium altars are dedicated by *beneficiarii* and not by prefects or tribunes, but it gives a clear indication of the way in which altars were set out, and shows that old altars were permitted to remain indefinitely and not buried as part of a ritual disposal. This is despite the apparent destruction of the buildings during the Marcomannic war, and the subsequent rebuilding.

The altars of Attius Tutor and Ulpius Titianus

This group was given particular attention at the request of Dr Breeze, especially in relation to a suggestion that they may all have been the work of one man.

Attius Tutor (RIB 830, 837, 842)
The simplest design is shown in *RIB* 842 (Fig. 4.12 on p. 81), with both the base and capital having two stepped square mouldings, a torus, and a broad fillet. *RIB* 837 (Fig. 6.2b) is similar, with the addition of a second fillet at the base separated by a quirk (the groove between the moulding elements). *RIB* 830 (Fig. 6.2a) is a development of *RIB* 837 in that the lowest moulding on the capital and the upper moulding on the base is in each case a second torus; the square mouldings, however, have been reduced to fillets, and the only step is from mouldings to die. The use of a torus mould is not common at Maryport, and to that extent these three altars form an identifiable group and may represent the work of the same mason. The only remaining decoration is on the left-hand roll of *RIB* 830 where, despite damage and erosion, there are what seem to be concentric circles.

Fig. 6.2 Altars dedicated by cohors I Baetasiorum *while its prefect was Titus Attius Tutor: (a) left, to Jupiter Optimus Maximus (RIB 830); (b) right, to Military Mars (RIB 837)*

Even allowing for the effects of weathering, it is clear that the faces of the altars were rubbed smooth before letter cutting began.

The standard of workmanship on the three altars is similar. All have angles which vary between square and up to 10 mm out of square; the steps on the mouldings are not quite square, and the quirks make uneven lines. The base mouldings on *RIB 830* do not run parallel with the top, but fall away to the right. In none of the altars are the quirks carefully worked, but seem to have been cut in largely with a punch.

It is interesting that there is no sign of axial chiselling on the rolls (as would be normal, and which survives on most other Maryport altars); however it is possible that weathering has removed all traces of tooling on the rolls other than that resulting from the use of a punch. *RIB 837* in particular is quite badly weathered, but the erosion on the face is probably due to its use in a house wall in the seventeenth century.

Turning to the lettering, it is quite possible that the same hand was at work on all three altars. If so, it is not unreasonable to see a progression as the man improved on the standard and style of his work. It is important to note that the lettering was not necessarily cut by the same man who worked the altars, although this may well have been the case.

RIB 842 (Fig. 4.12) is reasonably consistent in its letter forms, and certainly the work of a man with training in letter-cutting. The lines are well laid-out and placed centrally between the margins of the die. Most of the letters R and P have rather small bowls, especially on the ligatures. The cross bar on A is rather high. The three leaf stops are scribed in outline, while the triangular stops are cut in.

RIB 837 shows some improvement, with more consistency, although this is obscured to some extent by the severe weathering of the face. The layout was probably good, although the ends of lines 3–5 are now lost. R and P are of a better size than on the previous altar, but both Ms in the first line are very wide. The cross bar on A is in a similar high position to those on *RIB* 842. The treatment of the leaf and triangular stops is as on the previous altar.

On *RIB* 830 the letters are generally well cut, and consistent in form, although R and P still tend towards a small bowl at times, especially in the ligatures. Rather oddly, line 5 is not well laid out, with excessive space at the right-hand end being filled with a leaf stop which, like all stops on this altar, is a fully-cut leaf form. The first two letters on this line drop below the rest of the line. In line 6, the tails of the E and F slope upwards to their outer ends. The first L in the last line has a bad tail, perhaps partly due to the closeness of the line to the mouldings, but largely the result of carelessness on the part of a man who was certainly capable of cutting a good letter. He has aligned the upper lines with the capital and the lower lines with the base, which shows some regard for the finished appearance.

All three Tutor altars were lettered by a man who, while not in the highest rank of craftsmen, shows skills above the average and a care for his work. All three may well have been the work of one man.

Ulpius Titianus (RIB 838, 843: Fig. 6.3a-b)
Both altars show somewhat unusual mouldings, with *RIB* 838 having a wave moulding at top and bottom, and with a stepped square moulding against the die, and *RIB* 843 having at top and bottom, reading from the die outwards, a stepped square mould, a very shallow scotia, a torus, and a fillet. Not dissimilar styles of moulding can be seen in *RIB* 813 and 845 (both by Hermione, daughter of Quintus), and to a lesser extent *RIB* 819 (Priscus); but the two Titianus altars are sufficiently distinctive to suggest the same hand being responsible for both. No decoration survives on either altar.

The standard of workmanship is about the same as that of *RIB* 830, although within the overall standard the Titianus altars show a little less detailed care than the Tutor altars. The quirks are certainly no better worked. *RIB* 843 has something of a lean to the right due to misalignment of base and capital. Again, all elements of the face are more accurately worked than the sides, and were rubbed smooth before lettering.

The lettering on *RIB* 838 is not very consistent, and the letter forms are not cleanly cut; some straight lines are distinctly wavy. Letter C is shallow and open, and R and P have small tight bowls and straight spiky legs, except for the final R on line 1 which has a good bowl. The leaf stops are all triangular, fully cut in. The letter-cutter had certainly received some training, but was not especially competent or careful.

RIB 843 has marking-out lines at the top of the third line and the bottom of the fourth line; there may be signs of an upper one at the left-hand end of the first line, but if so it is touched only by the initial letter. Letter S is inconsistent and oddly shaped, especially in lines 4 and 7. Letter C is particularly poor on line 6. Letter A has an unusually low cross bar, unlike *RIB* 838 where the cross bar is rather high. The tails of E and F slope up in a manner reminiscent of *RIB* 830. The leaf stops, as on *RIB* 838, are triangles. The layout of the lines is fair, although the last two lines start too close to the left-hand edge of the stone. The lettering may have been cut by the same man as cut *RIB* 838; there are similarities but there are also differences. We may be looking at a careful but not wholly competent man who had no settled style.

The letters on all five altars were cut by a man with a care for the appearance of his work, as well as a degree of skill. This is sufficiently unusual to raise the question of

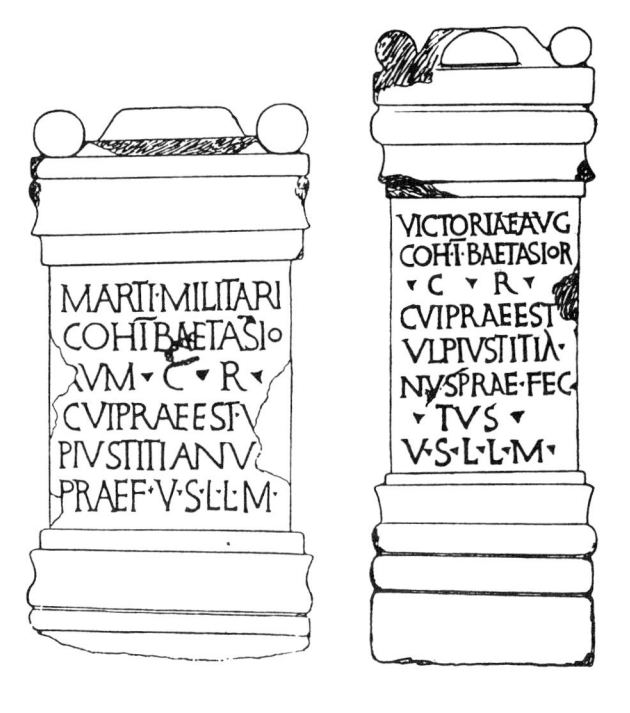

Fig. 6.3 Altars dedicated by cohors I Baetasiorum *while its prefect was Ulpius Titianus: (a) left, to Military Mars (RIB 838); (b) right, to the Emperor's Victory (RIB 843)*

whether the same man was responsible for the lettering for both Tutor and Titianus. If that were the case, then it is beyond doubt that Titianus held his command before Tutor, and we are seeing the development of the skills of this letter-cutter. The different characteristics exhibited by the two groups, however, raise such doubts that the question must remain open for the present. All five altars show considerable signs of weathering.

The date and purpose of the burial of the altars

Current thought on these questions tends to follow the hypothesis put forward by L. P. Wenham in 1939,[24] that they were 'honourably buried' immediately following upon the dedication of a new altar at the New Year or at the start of a new regnal year of the emperor. Wenham bases his reasoning on the grounds that the old altars '... would not be permitted to stand indefinitely on the parade ground ...' and that

'... they are so little weathered and ... in such remarkably fine condition ...'[25]

The length of time for which it is considered that altars might have been retained, or otherwise allowed to remain, must be a matter of the weight given to the evidence from Stockstadt, Mainhardt, Osterburken and Sirmium, but the date of burial judged in relation to the degree of weathering suffered by the altars is a question which, subject to one reservation, can at least be illuminated if not conclusively answered. One thing is certain; no altar in the collection is in pristine condition, and they all show noticeable signs of weathering.

Weathering

Weathering of sandstones is chiefly a matter of the breakdown of the cementing material, or matrix, which holds together the grains of sand.[26] The Maryport altars are in the local stone, which is of the type commonly known as New Red Sandstone, and more specifically as one of the St. Bees sandstones. This stone, from the Triassic series, has a quartz matrix and, unlike some other New Red Sandstones,[27] is a good, reasonably durable building stone with a fine grain; although it is by no means among the hardest sandstones, it does not show signs of weathering in a matter of a year or two. The remains of the north gate of the fort provide a good comparison, especially the threshold. This must have stood in the open for perhaps as much as two or three hundred years, quite apart from its modern exposure, and yet toolmarks on the upstand are still visible. The stone is worn and weathered but has not become unrecognisable, as it would have been were the weathering on the altars to represent only one year in the open air. The foundation block, now standing at present ground level, shows clear toolmarks on the sides; it seems, like the threshold, to have been exposed (there is no precise evidence) since the discovery and robbing of the gate in 1787. It must be borne in mind that stones from different beds in the same quarry are quite likely to respond differently to the weathering process, but such evidence as we have suggests that the stone quarried by the Romans was of a durable nature.

Toolmarks on buildings in Curzon Street, Maryport, built in 1870 from similar New Red Sandstone, still have bold and clear toolmarks even though the face is delaminating in places as a result of face bedding. The Midland Bank in Senhouse Street, built around the turn of the century or a little earlier,[28] shows that where the stone is most exposed to wind and rain, as on the corners, erosion will take place and crispness will be lost, although toolmarks do remain. The sides of the same building still show very crisp toolmarks even on the chiselled margins and picked panels of the projecting rusticated courses. Only the apparently protected sides of the altars show toolmarks with anything approaching the same degree of freshness, and in many cases even they are rather more weathered. It is perfectly true that the sides of the altars do show many toolmarks, but when trying to 'read' the marks it becomes clear that they are a little blurred and indistinct. The finely-picked backgrounds to the demi-lunes on two altars of Cammius Maximus, RIB 827 (detail in Fig. 6.4) and RIB 828 (Fig. 4.5 on p. 75), are probably the clearest and freshest looking marks on the altars, and look less weathered than the rather coarser picked work on the Midland Bank, but still they show signs of weathering. Although the stone of RIB 827 is given in RIB as being of light-coloured sandstone, it appears little different from the rest of the altars; it may have come from a different bed. The precise time it spent in the open air is impossible to determine, but a reasonable minimum might be between twenty and thirty years; it could well be much longer. Despite the extensive damage, the standard of the masonry work on this stone is among the best in the collection, but the letter cutting is rather poor.

The reservation mentioned above is the effect on their condition of the precise treatment and location of each of the altars since they passed into the hands of the Senhouse family. Looking first at the altars discovered before 1870, some details of their location and use are recorded: RIB 823 was in use as a sundial, and thus exposed to the weather. Others were built into garden walls, while RIB 834 was recorded as being in the orchard at Netherhall. RIB 837 was seen by Horsley built into the wall of a house on the fort site before being taken into the Senhouse collection. This doubtless accounts for at least some of the weathering to the face of this altar, but the rolls are also weathered; did this occur before or after its transfer to Netherhall?

Fig. 6.4 Detail of the decoration on the top of the altar dedicated by cohors I Hispanorum *while Lucius Cammius Maximus was its prefect (RIB 827); cf. Fig. 4.9*

The length of time each piece was in its recorded location in the collection is unknown, and thus the effect of that location must remain unknown. Lt Cdr Brian Ashmore, in the course of his rescue of the collection, records '... recovering 125 items ... lost amidst overgrown shrubberies and woodland'.[29]

We can be rather more certain about the treatment of those altars discovered in 1870, and of their condition at the time of excavation. It will be useful as a first step to see if any light can be thrown on the manner of their burial.

The 1870 altars
The method of burial
In a paper delivered in July 1870, Collingwood Bruce described the discovery and gave some indications as to the condition of the altars.[30] The first altar came to light as the result of moving a stone which had fouled the plough; it appears that the altar itself was not struck by the ploughshare.[31] Humphrey Senhouse then organised a search and the rest of the group was found in a number of pits. It thus seems unlikely that any of these altars suffered plough damage, although, as deep ploughing had been in progress, this is not impossible. Any damage is most likely to have occurred at or before the moment of burial.

Bruce describes something of the way in which they were buried: 'the altars have been placed in their beds with care'. But a little further on he also refers to 'marks of haste ... lying diagonally ... as if hurriedly thrown in . . . portions of the capitals have been broken off the altars, apparently by the force with which they have been projected into their places . . .'[32] This does not carry the signs of 'honourable burial', but rather the disposal of unwanted items. None of the inscriptions were found face-up, but any significance attaching to this, and to the covering of each altar of a multiple burial with earth and stones, is uncertain.

It is just possible that burial face-down is due more to the manner of burial, and perhaps to the way in which they had been displayed, than to any religious significance. If they were standing close to where they were buried, they would have been carried to the pits by hand. The first stage in moving them would have been to tip them to the horizontal so that several men (probably four) could lift and carry them. If they had been standing with their backs to a screen, they would have been tipped forward, and if they were then carried and dropped into the pits in one lift, as would be easiest, they would land face downwards, or if they turned a little in the act of tipping, on their sides. There is clearly a measure of speculation in this suggestion.

Since Bruce's day it has become clear that later altars were lying beneath earlier ones. It has been suggested[33] that earlier altars, accidentally discovered during the digging of fresh pits, were exhumed and re-buried on top of the later ones. According to this hypothesis, the burial of *RIB* 843, dedicated by *cohors I Baetasiorum*, must have involved the chance discovery, and the exhumation, of not one but two altars of *cohors I Hispanorum*. The notion of hauling stones weighing four or five hundredweight (200-250 kg) from pits up to six feet deep in order to project them in again with some force does not seem logical.

None of the above accords with the idea of careful burial as part of a regular pattern of annual interment. Nor, as some pits contained altars dedicated by more than one commander, was burial related to the appointment of a new commanding officer. For example, *RIB* 826, an *I.O.M.* altar of a tribune of *cohors I Hispanorum*, was in the same pit as *RIB* 838, an altar to Military Mars dedicated by a prefect of *cohors I Baetasiorum*.

The seventeen altars found in 1870 were in nine pits and 'several other pits . . . contained only portions of . . . some of the altars found before 1870 . . .'[34] The plan published by Collingwood Bruce, although inaccurate in its details, shows that a total of fifty-seven pits were excavated. 'Besides the pits which contained altars there were others in which fragments of inscribed stones were found, and others which were quite empty.'[35] If, as will be suggested below, all the burials took place at the same time, it would be likely that several gangs were at work; this would go some way towards explaining the number of pits.

The condition of the 1870 altars

Bruce gives little information about the condition of the altars, merely referring to the inscriptions as 'distinctly legible', 'the clearness and sharpness of their sculpture', and to one (*RIB* 826) as having been used as 'a common whetstone'.[36] The legibility of most of the altars is unquestioned, although they are by no means uniformly clear. His reference to their 'clearness and sharpness' is relative to his view that they were buried by the Romans long before their abandonment of Britain.

Bailey's catalogue of the Senhouse collection, published in 1915, has brief descriptions[37] of the 1870 altars, which were stored at that time in the portico[38] at Netherhall and thus had some protection from the weather. He gives the condition of three of them as 'splendid', 'nearly perfect' and 'excellent'.[39] He is referring here to the overall condition and completeness, and in as much as they are nearly 2,000 years old, and remarkable survivals, the descriptions are perfectly fair. His photographs however, although not as sharp as one would wish, clearly show that these and the other altars all shows signs of weathering over many years. Their condition is in fact, so far as one can judge, little different from that of today. It is not permissible to describe them as 'extremely fresh and unweathered'[40] or 'so little weathered'.[41]

All the 1870 altars show weathering on their faces, on the mouldings, on the tops, and, to a varying extent, on their sides. They are comparatively unweathered when set against altars which remained on the surface throughout the Roman period and beyond; but they are by no means pristine and fresh from the hands of the mason, as they would have been if exposed for only one year. They were buried early in their lives, but only after an interval which may be judged as somewhere between no less than twenty and no more than one hundred years. Some later altars seem a little less weathered than earlier ones (e.g. *RIB* 827 [Figs. 4.9 and 6.4] as against 824[42]), but it is not at present possible to say whether the differences are such as would be expected if the stones were all buried at the same time; the point is complicated by the effects of weathering on stones taken from different beds in the quarry.

The use of *RIB* 826 as a whetstone is of itself a rebuttal of the notion that each altar was carefully buried at the end of the year. It is inconceivable that the current altar, set up by the commanding officer as part of a solemn official ceremony, would be used in this casual manner before the year was out. It is far more likely that it was one of a number of old altars standing beside the parade ground or in some sacred place, a redundant relic of past ceremonies, convenient to use for secular purposes. At Birdoswald it seems likely that several altars dedicated in the third century were still standing beside the parade ground when the fort was abandoned over a century later.[43] The altars at Sirmium stood in their enclosure for up to seventy years while the station was in use, despite rebuilding of the adjacent structures following their destruction in the Marcomannic war,[44] and were left standing thereafter.

The date of the burial of the altars

If the idea of annual burial is to be discarded as inconsistent with the evidence, then some other occasion and motive must be found. R. G. Collingwood suggested[45] that the most likely occasion for the burial of the altars was the invasion of the Maeatae following the withdrawal of troops by Clodius Albinus in 196. Whether or not one accepts this invasion as having occurred, the timing is probably about right for the degree of weathering. Another possible reason for the burials is the move from a supposed parade ground north of the fort to a new one just to the south. Professor E. Birley[46] suggested that this move took place after the second century; Professor Jarrett,[47] on the other hand, believed that it may have occurred late in the second century. Such a move would have been an occasion for clearing up the site and disposing of altars which, although perhaps no longer regarded as having any religious significance, were still relics of official ceremonies and as such not to be left lying around for use as building materials or desecration by civilians. It might be one thing for soldiers to deface them by using them as whetstones, but quite another for civilians to do likewise. Disposal in a number of pits would be a satisfactory solution, and one would expect the altars to be buried in a 'nearest first' order which, especially with several gangs at work, would explain the random grouping of altars within the pits and the burial of later altars, which would be nearest the front, beneath earlier ones. A redundant parade ground would certainly provide a convincing reason for the burial of the altars. But if the idea of a northern parade ground is not tenable, as now seems likely (p. 69), then the burial might be the result of a general reorganisation of the area, in the course of its further development as the fort's *vicus*.[48]

It is clear from the title of this chapter that this contribution is in the nature of a preliminary view. The jury is still out, but, given the evidence presented above, there does seem to be *prima facie* a good case for a revision of current views on the following lines: the altars were retained alongside the sacred area (or parade ground) indefinitely; burial was not an annual event; no great care was taken in burying the altars; burial was not practised on any regular basis such as the end of a commander's period of service; and the most likely occasion for the burial was when the sacred area (or parade ground) was abandoned in the third century.

Notes

1. Thanks are due to Mr Finbar O'Súilleabháin of the Senhouse Roman Museum for his assistance and forbearance, to Mrs J. Watkinson for searching out references at short notice and for assisting with translations from the German, and to VSS who made possible the site visit. Dr D. J. Breeze both encouraged the survey and made a number of useful comments on the draft text. Professor J. C. Mann, Dr M. Roxan and Miss S. Waldock discussed the burials, German parallels, and parade grounds, respectively, and provided the references to Stockstadt, Mainhardt and South Shields. Dr B. Dobson encouraged greater clarity, and removed some ambiguities, as well as providing the reference to Sirmium.
2. *RIB* 815, 816, 817, 819, 822, 824, 825, 826, 827, 828, 830, 831, 838, 842, 843, 846, with one uninscribed altar. Three altars were buried singly, eight were buried in pairs, and six in triple burials.
3. Hill 1981, 4-6
4. Breeze (in this volume, pp. 67-8) suggests that altars which mention unit as well as commanding officer are probably the first to be dedicated by a new commander.
5. At Birdoswald, in the late third century, Pomponius Desideratus used a second-hand altar formerly dedicated *Deo Cocidio* for a Jupiter altar set up on behalf of *cohors I Dacorum*, and was content with perfectly appalling lettering and layout (*RIB* 1885).
6. See pp. 100-1 below, on the purpose of the burial of the altars.
7. Wenham 1939, 21, 22
8. E.g. Jarrett 1965, 117
9. *RIB* 832, discovered buried in a pit near to where the altars were found in 1870: Fig. 1.6
10. *RIB* 850, discovered before 1600.
11. Schallmayer 1983, 141 and fig. 114
12. Planck and Beck 1987, 54
13. Fabricius, Hettner, and von Sarwey 1914
14. Thornborrow 1959
15. Thornborrow 1959, 23
16. Thornborrow 1959, 9, 11-12
17. Paul Bidwell, personal comment.
18. Goessler 1943; *Berichte der Römisch-Germanische Kommission* 1959, 173-4; Filtzinger, Planck and Cämmerer 1986
19. Filtzinger, Planck and Cämmerer 1986, 438
20. Baatz 1993, 240
21. *Germania* 1943, 157
22. Popovic 1989, 117-22
23. Popovic 1989, 120
24. Wenham 1939, 22
25. Wenham 1939, 22
26. Hill and David 1995, chapter 3
27. For example, the New Red Sandstone taken (probably) from the Permian series in the Eden valley for the building of Carlisle cathedral is not as durable as St. Bees (Clifton-Taylor 1972, 126).
28. Information on the date of buildings in the

town was kindly supplied by Mr H. Jackson, 27 Curzon Street, Maryport.
29 Ashmore 1991, 3
30 Bruce 1874, 178. See note 2 for a list of the 1870 altars.
31 Bailey 1915, 137, disagrees with Bruce, claiming that the first 1870 altar to be found (Bailey no. 28 = RIB 828) was the stone struck by the plough. Bailey was writing 45 years after the event, Bruce only a few months.
32 Bruce 1874, 179
33 Jarrett 1965, 117
34 Bailey 1915, 137
35 Bruce 1875, 429 and facing plan
36 Bruce 1874, 175, 177, 180
37 Bailey 1915, 143-7 and plates I-V
38 Bailey 1915, 139
39 Nos. 28, 29, 30 respectively = RIB 828, 824, 831
40 Collingwood 1936, 95
41 Wenham 1939, 22
42 Breeze (in this volume, p. 77) argues that Cammius Maximus held his command some ten years later than Maenius Agrippa.
43 Jarrett 1965, 117
44 Popovic 1989, 121
45 Collingwood 1936, 97
46 Birley 1961, 222
47 Jarrett 1965, 131
48 Collingwood 1936, 88. It is important to remember that the burial, as with any other archaeological phenomenon, does not have to be linked to a specific historical event; a newcommanding officer may have ordered clearance of the site in order to prevent further desecration by sword sharpening, or for what might seem to modern minds to be some quite illogical reason. Professor Mann in discussion drew attention to the predilection of the Romans for burying personal articles, a category into which the altars may have been held to fall.

References

ASHMORE, B. 1991 *Senhouse Roman Museum* (Maryport)

BAILEY, J. B. 1915 'A catalogue of the Roman inscribed and sculptured stones, coins, earthenware, etc., discovered in and near the Roman fort at Maryport and preserved at Netherhall', CW^2 15, 135-72

BAATZ, D. 1993 *Der Römische Limes*, 3rd. ed. (Berlin)

BIRLEY, E. B. 1961 *Research on Hadrian's Wall* (Kendal)

BRUCE, J. C. 1874 'On the altars recently found in the Roman camp at Maryport', CW^1 1, 175-88

BRUCE, J. C. 1875 *Lapidarium Septentrionale* (London and Newcastle upon Tyne)

CLIFTON-TAYLOR, A. 1972 *The pattern of English building* (London)

COLLINGWOOD, R. G. 1936 'The Roman fort and settlement at Maryport', CW^2 36, 85-99

FABRICIUS, E., HETTNER, F. and VON SARWEY, O. 1914, 'Kastell Stockstadt', *Der Obergermanisch-Raetische Limes des Roemerreiches, Abteilung B, Kastell Nr. 33* (Heidelberg)

FILTZINGER, P., PLANCK, D. and CÄMMERER, B. (eds.) 1986 *Die Römer in Baden-Württemberg*, 3rd. ed. (Stuttgart)

GOESSLER, P. 1943 'Stein aus dem Kastell Mainhardt (Württemberg)', *Germania* 27, 157-68

HILL, P. R. 1981 'Stonework and the archaeologist', AA^5 9, 1-22

HILL, P. R. and DAVID, J. C. E. 1995 *Practical Stone Masonry* (London)

JARRETT, M. G. 1965 'Roman officers at Maryport', CW^2 65, 115-32

PLANCK, D. and BECK, W. 1987 *Der Limes in Südwestdeutschland*, 2nd. ed. (Stuttgart)

POPOVIC, V. 1989 'Une station de bénéficiaires à Sirmium', *Comptes Rendues de l'Académie des Inscriptions et Belles-Lettres* 1989, 116-22

SCHALLMAYER, E. 1983 'Ausgrabung eines Benfiziarier-Weihebezirkes und römischer Holzbauten in Osterburken, Neckar-Odenwald-Kreis', *Archäologische Ausgrabungen in Baden-Württemberg* 1982 (Stuttgart)

THORNBORROW, J. W. 1959 'Report on the excavations at Beacon Street, South Shields, 1959', *South Shields Archaeological and Historical Society Papers* 1.7, 8-25

WENHAM, L. P. 1939 'Notes on the garrisoning of Maryport', CW^2 39, 19-30

7 The women of Roman Maryport

Lindsay Allason-Jones

Despite the fact that at Maryport there was a well established Roman fort with an extensive *vicus*, the site has produced surprisingly little evidence for the presence of women compared to its contemporary forts on Hadrian's Wall. The reasons for this may well lie in the limited extent of the excavations, but this may not fully explain the situation.

Army officers above and including the rank of centurion were always allowed to marry and able to take their wives and families with them on tours of duty. Anthony Birley has estimated that the average equestrian officer would have had a tenure of three years for each posting;[1] as Maryport was occupied for about 280 years, the implication is that a large number of officers would have been stationed there during its history, each of whom could, legally, have had a wife, and may well have had daughters and other female relatives with them. The *praetoria* of most forts (and there is no reason to think that Maryport was any exception) would have been large enough to house the officers' families in some comfort.

The potential number of women who may have been associated with the centurions on the site is even greater. Such an establishment as Maryport could have had as many as ten centurions at any one time. Centurions were often transferred from legion to legion or province to province, and might marry anywhere en route; their wives, many of whom were of a different ethnic origin to their husbands, would then accompany them on their journeys around the Empire. Centurions lived in a suite of rooms at one end of their barrack block, and there has been some debate as to whether their wives and children shared this accommodation or lodged outside the fort.[2] Some of the more exposed forts had no *vici*, which suggests that provision for centurions' families was made within the walls. The centurion's quarters compare favourably with town houses in southern Britain in size, and would have been adequate for family housing if there were no other reasons for excluding these families from the fort.

The senior officers may also have had female slaves in their households. The *praetorium* would have required a substantial staff in order to ensure its smooth running, and it is known from such examples as M. Cocceius Firmus at Auchendavy that centurions could own female slaves whilst on duty.[3]

Below the rank of centurion, soldiers were forbidden to marry by law whilst still serving in the army. This ban was already in force when the Romans invaded Britain, and continued until the Severan Edict of AD 197 when, according to Herodian, 'to the soldiers he [Septimius Severus] gave a very large sum of money and many other privileges that they had not had before; for he was the first to increase their pay, and he also gave them permission to wear gold rings and to live in wedlock with their wives'.[4] This edict is somewhat ambiguous, and could be taken to mean either that the soldiers were now allowed to marry or that they were finally allowed to cohabit with their existing wives. It has been estimated that 40% of auxiliary *diplomata* recognize an existing relationship with a woman, so the ban may have been more honoured in the breach than in the observance.[5] However, it may be that, as in India under British rule, the soldiers married local girls according to local custom. These marriages would be recognized by the girl and her family but not by the army or by Roman law; whether the man recognized the marriage as legal and binding would have depended on the individual.

Some soldiers may not have confined themselves to one wife. Surviving *diplomata*, such as the example from Malpas in Cheshire, recognize the marriages of the retiring soldiers 'with those who are their wives at the date of this grant, or in the case of the unmarried, any wives they may consequently marry; provided they only have one each'.[6] The implication is not only that most soldiers were already married despite the law but also that, whereas the Romans were monogamous, many of the auxiliaries came from provinces where polygamy was the norm: indeed many of the veterans may well have had several wives before being drafted into the army, or have been looking forward to setting up a modest harem on retirement. The clause did not, of course, hinder multiple marriages in any effective way, but it did ensure that only the children of the first wife were recognized by law, and so were entitled to become Roman citizens.

Wives were not the only female dependents of the soldiers of whatever rank. On the death of a *pater familias* the eldest son was expected to take charge of the unmarried females in his family. Although the state tried on several occasions to secure exemption to this law for serving soldiers, many preferred to honour their obligations to their family. In the military zone several mothers and sisters are recorded by inscriptions, such as Vacia, the sister of a staff clerk at Great Chesters,[7] and Aurelia Lupula, mother of Dionysius Fortunatus at Risingham.[8] It is not clear how the authorities viewed the female dependents who were not wives but who had a legal claim on serving soldiers. It is to be presumed that these women lived in the *vici* of forts, but whether they were housed in official accommodation or were expected to look after themselves is not clear.

Many veterans would have stayed close to their old fort when they retired, living in the *vicus* or establishing farms in the district. Marrying a veteran would have been considered a sensible match for a girl, as the prospective husbands could be expected to be reasonably well off, having earned a good salary for over twenty-five years, and the legitimate children of the match would receive full Roman citizenship. This led to a number of families in the *vici* and towns with young children whose fathers were in their forties and fifties, whilst the mothers were still in their twenties and thirties.

Among the other women present at Roman forts were the wives and daughters of merchants and craftsmen who were attracted by the ready market provided by the army, and the security offered by association with a military installation. The *vicus* at Maryport will have had shops and workshops supplying the needs of the soldiers and the local civilian population. Women would have served in the shops or worked at crafts, either in their own right or as helpmeets for husbands or brothers.

The female dependents of the soldiers mentioned above may have been involved in these pursuits in order to eke out a living: many auxiliaries may have found the support of several female relations a heavy financial burden, so an extra income would have been very welcome.

Vici must have been busy, cosmopolitan places attracting travelling traders, who went from *vicus* to *vicus* selling their wares, as well as the rural population of the area, who might visit the *vicus* on a regular basis to sell their surplus produce. All these people would have had to have been catered for, as would the soldiers in their off-duty hours. Taverns and cafes will have been scattered throughout the *vici* with women serving meals and drinks. Prostitutes, acrobats, singers, dancers and jugglers would also have been found in the *vicus*, providing entertainment for the military and civilian population alike.

All this serves to indicate that the average Roman fort was not a purely male preserve. Many women of all nationalities and walks of life can be expected to have lived at Maryport, either in the fort or in the *vicus* to the north. It is all the more puzzling that only four women are known by name to have lived on the site: [. . .]iana Hermione, Sotera, Maritima and Julia Martina.

[. . .]iana Hermione is known from two large altars dedicated by her: one to the Valour of the Emperor, and one to the goddess Juno.[9] On both altars she refers to herself as 'daughter of Quintus' but does not mention a husband. This is not unusual and can only be taken to imply that she was not married, rather than as positive proof that she was definitely single. Her name is badly damaged on both altars: whilst the name Hermione is clear, all that can be discerned of her *gentilicium* is [. . .]*iana*. Enough survives to indicate that she was a freeborn citizen of Greek extraction. She was not the only Greek to have lived at Maryport; a dedication to Asclepius may indicate that there was a Greek doctor at the fort, A. Egnatius Pastor.[10] Most of the doctors attached to the Roman army were from the Greek provinces and, despite his Latin name, A. Egnatius Pastor's inscription is in Greek.

A third possible member of Maryport's Greek community was a woman called Sotera who was mourned on her tombstone by her husband, Julius Senecianus.[11] The husband's *cognomen* is one which is commonly found in the north-west provinces and is a typical name for a Romanized Celt. The name Sotera, Birley suggests, is also quite common, being the female form of *Soter*, meaning 'saviour'.[12] As Sotera is the only name given to the woman, it is possible that she was not a Greek by birth but was given the name as a slave, there being a fashion for slaves to have Greek names. If she was a slave she would have had to have been freed in order to marry Julius Senecianus so as to comply with Roman law.

Both Sotera and Hermione make their status as either a wife or a daughter quite clear; the third woman from Maryport is more elusive. Maritima is recorded as having set up a tombstone to the centurion Julius Marinus, who died at the age of 40 years, 2(?) months and 20 days.[13] Her single name suggests that she was either of Celtic origin or was not a freeborn citizen, but no clues survive as to whether she was the wife, slave or freedwoman of the centurion: a sister or a mother might be expected to have shared part of Julius Marinus' name.

The fourth woman in the group, Julia Martina, died at the age of 12 years, 3 months and 22 days.[14] Her name suggests a freeborn citizen. The tombstone is rather elaborate, if primitive, but gives no clues as to who set up the memorial nor to her family. Her mother may still have been alive when Julia Martina died, as could the mother of the child Ingenuus who died at Maryport at the age of 10.[15] The fact that neither tombstone mentions a mother cannot be taken as proof that either mother had already died.

The gender of those recorded by name on two other tombstones from Maryport can only be guessed at. One refers to Luca, who died aged 20.[16] The -a suffix might be taken as indicative of a female name, but there was no invariable rule. Rianorix, who is commemorated at a ford over the River Ellen, half a mile south-east of the fort,[17] may be presumed to be male as the -rix suffix normally implies a male name: another example is Morirex, who is also recorded at Maryport.[18] However, it should be remembered that a few miles away, at Old Carlisle, there is the tombstone of Tancorix, who makes it quite clear in her epitaph that she was a woman.[19]

As well as the inscribed tombstones and altars there are two tombstones of women whose epitaphs have been eroded by time. Regrettably, the figures on the memorials have also suffered, and it is difficult to discern the details of dress or hairstyle which the tombstones of such women as Regina at South Shields or Julia Velva at York provide.[20] A female figure on a very battered tombstone, found in 1880,[21] is holding something in her right hand which might be a purse or a mirror, both of which can be seen being held by female figures on tombstones from Chester.[22] The other uninscribed tombstone is now very worn, but a drawing made in the nineteenth century seems to indicate that she wore a hood over her head.[23] This may hint that she was a priestess, as depictions of priestesses invariably show them with their heads covered: an example can be seen on a bronze statuette from South Shields.[24] On the other hand, hooded garments are known from depictions of goddesses in Roman Britain: a stylized mother goddess from Caerwent wears a hood which fits snugly around her head,[25] and it has been suggested that the mother goddess figures from Midlothian are also wearing hoods which cover the neck:[26] a *capitularis* which was lost at Bath may have been a garment of this type.[27] A few details of the Maryport woman's clothing survive around the neck and shoulder: the latter has heavy folds indicating a thick woollen garment or, more likely, a shawl, similar to that worn by a woman from Murrell Hill, Carlisle.[28] She also appears to have a square neckline on her costume; this type of neckline is unusual in Britain and seems to have looked to the eastern Mediterranean for its inspiration rather than the north-west provinces, although her hairstyle of plaits is more in the Celtic tradition.

Of the women known to have lived at Maryport the most interesting is Hermione. Her choice of deities for veneration indicates that she was a follower of mainstream Roman religion. The cult of the Deified Emperor was introduced into Britain at an early stage as a way of welding the new province together: the principle was that if everyone took part in the ceremonies associated with the cult, the process of Romanization would be hastened. Britons may have had some difficulty in believing in the Deified Emperor as a god, but in a multitheistic society few people would have been offended by the concept; most would have gone through the ceremonies in a spirit of civic duty rather than religious fervour. Paying for a large and expensive altar, however, implies a commitment of belief far beyond the lip-service paid by the majority. The worship of the personified virtues of the Deified Emperor – the more philosophical side of the cult – appears to have appealed to women: as well as Hermione's altar to the Emperor's

Virtue, there is also an altar dedicated to the Emperor's Fortune by Aelia Proculina at Risingham.[29]

Hermione's other choice of deity, Juno, was an official state deity of Rome, one of the Capitoline Triad. As the goddess who oversaw the lives of women and offered protection during marriage and childbirth, it might be expected that she would have been a popular choice with the women of the province. However, the Maryport altar is the only one found so far in Britain which is dedicated to Juno by a woman. Several statues have been discovered which have been identified as Juno, such as the lifesize statue from Chesters,[30] but these may be more accurately described as depicting empresses in the guise of Juno, and thus represent an extension of the cult of the Deified Emperor.

The two altars indicate that Hermione was not only a freeborn citizen but one whose roots were firmly in the centre of the Roman Empire, with strong ties of loyalty to the ruling family. They also indicate that she had enough money to commission two expensive altars, and was able to dedicate to the deities in her own right without the involvement of any male members of her family. In this she was unusual but not unique. Female dedicators of altars to Roman, Celtic or Eastern deities in Roman Britain are, however, considerably outnumbered by male dedicators: only 10 per cent of the inscriptions found so far refer to a woman. Most women appear to have relied on the head of their family for the more public demonstrations of faith, confining their own devotions to a domestic setting.[31]

Female deities are more in evidence at Maryport than mortal women. As well as Hermione's dedication to Juno, *RIB* 810 and 811 refer to 'all the gods and goddesses'; *RIB* 812 (Fig. 4.13, p. 83) and 840 are dedicated to Fortune the Homebringer, the latter linking Fortune with the feminine personification of Eternal Rome; whilst *RIB* 841 was dedicated by Labareus, who describes himself as 'a German', to Setlocenia, a Celtic goddess, only attested at Maryport, whose name may mean 'long life'. *RIB* 844 does not mention a goddess but is decorated with two winged Victories. Amongst the uninscribed stones there is a base with the figure of the Celtic goddess Epona in her usual pose, seated sideways on her horse (Fig. 7.1); this is a rare depiction in Britain, as Epona appears to have been more popular in Gaul and Germany.[32]

One relief, often referred to today as 'The Pin-up Girl', which shows a naked female figure standing next to a fort gateway, does not show a mortal woman but

Fig. 7.1 Pedestal with relief sculpture of Epona

Venus in her role of protector of men (Fig. 8.18, p. 125). Her pose, with one hand touching her long hair and with her other hand on her hip, is typical of the pose adopted by the pipeclay statuettes of Venus which are commonly found in the military zone.[33] Another Venus figure is shown in miniature on a small relief holding what may be a garland or a towel across her knees; although very different in scale, this figure resembles one of the nymphs attendant on Venus on the relief from High Rochester.[34] Maryport also had its nymphs in triplicate: a broken relief shows two naked nymphs standing under arches with part of the third still surviving. These are carved in a very stylized way, and although comparable to the relief from High Rochester and another from Coventina's Well, at Carrawburgh, these figures look back to the Celtic tradition rather than to Roman art forms.[35]

The stylized figures of Minerva, goddess of wisdom, the arts and trades, and a seated mother goddess,[36] carved in the round but in a very angular manner, also indicate that the native carving traditions were still strong in Roman Maryport even when it came to depicting Roman deities. The latter figure is seated in a chair, similar to that used by the mother goddesses at Housesteads,[37] but her dress is shown as a one-piece garment which hangs from the shoulders, the folds indicated by deep grooves. This may be intended to suggest the form of dress known as the Gallic coat, seen on the tombstone of an anonymous woman from Murrell Hill, Carlisle,[38] rather than the Mediterranean layered garments worn by the Housesteads *matres*.

In 1732 Horsley described Maryport as having produced more inscriptions than any other Roman fort in Britain to date.[39] The proportion of female deities referred to on these inscriptions is still high compared to similar sites, but the number of ordinary women known at Maryport is low. This may be the result of the excavation methods used on the site over the years, which aimed at the rapid removal of building stone rather than the uncovering of archaeological data. This 'filleting' of the fort and town could account for the lack of small finds which might be attributed to women; there are few small finds of any sort from Maryport, and only one bracelet which can be firmly associated with female use.[40] However, it is known that Colonel Humphrey Senhouse employed a man to make sure that no carved stone left the site before it had been recorded; so we can be reasonably confident that the inscriptions and altars to be seen today are representative of the material from the Roman fort. It is always possible that future investigation of the cemetery might reveal further memorials to women. The few surviving tombstones are very worn, suggesting that they lay on the surface where they were easily visible but open to the elements; the less visible tombstones may not yet have been discovered.

It is possible that another clue to the reasons behind the lack of identifiable women at Roman Maryport is to be found in the very stylized carving on many of the stones. While most of the forts on Hadrian's Wall have some Celtic-inspired sculpture, it is noticeable that at Maryport the number of stones showing Celtic influence is high; even classical deities, such as Minerva and seated *matres*, are depicted in the minimalist style typical of Celtic stone carving. The major group of stones, the altars, were mostly dedicated by the serving unit or its commanding officer, and invariably follow the usual Roman form, as might be expected. It is, therefore, likely that only the military élite and their immediate families were recorded through inscriptions and sculpture, as only this section of Maryport society might have been expected to favour the Roman traditions. It is possible that the rest of the population looked to their Celtic origins and felt no need to express themselves in stone. Whatever the cause of the lack of evidence, there is no reason to see this gap as proof that there were no women at Roman Maryport. Indeed, the evidence from contemporary forts in the military zone would seem to suggest that Maryport's population over the years would have included a high proportion of women of all ages from all over the Roman Empire.

Notes
1. Birley 1979, 60
2. Allason-Jones 1989, 58
3. Justinian, *Digest* XLIX.17.13
4. Herodian, *Histories* 3.8.4-5
5. Birley, A., pers. comm.
6. *CIL* XVI, 48
7. *RIB* 1742
8. *RIB* 1250
9. *RIB* 845; *RIB* 813
10. *RIB* 808
11. Jarrett 1976, 42-5
12. Birley 1979, 111
13. *RIB* 858
14. *RIB* 866
15. *RIB* 860
16. *RIB* 867
17. *RIB* 862
18. *RIB* 861
19. *RIB* 908
20. *RIB* 1065 (*CSIR* I.1.247); *RIB* 688 (*CSIR* I.3.42)
21. Robinson 1881, 243
22. Wright and Richmond 1955, nos. 118 and 120
23. *LS* 890; Bailey 1915, 49
24. Allason-Jones 1989, pl. 56
25. *CSIR* I.5.14
26. MacDonald 1917-18, 38-48 (*CSIR* I.4.61)
27. Tomlin 1988, 185, no. 55
28. *CSIR* I. 6.228
29. *RIB* 1211
30. *CSIR* I.6.117
31. Allason-Jones 1989, 142-63
32. Webster, G. 1986, 70-2; Ross 1967
33. Jenkins 1958, 60-76
34. The Maryport figure is unpublished; High Rochester: *CSIR* I.1.218
35. Maryport Nymphs: *LS* 896; Coventina's Well: Allason-Jones and McKay 1985
36. Bailey 1915, pl. VI, no. 37
37. *CSIR* I.6.166-71
38. *CSIR* I.6.497
39. Horsley 1732, 279
40. Webster, J. 1986, no. 38

References
ALLASON-JONES, L. 1989 *Women in Roman Britain* (London)
ALLASON-JONES, L. and MCKAY, B. 1985 *Coventina's Well: a shrine on Hadrian's Wall* (Chollerford)
BAILEY, J. B. 1915 'A catalogue of the Roman inscribed and sculptured stones, coins, earthenware, etc., discovered in and near the Roman fort at Maryport and preserved at Netherhall', *CW²* 15, 135-72
BIRLEY, A. 1979 *The People of Roman Britain* (London)
HORSLEY, J. 1732 *Britannia Romana* (London)
JARRETT, M. G. 1976 *Maryport, Cumbria: a Roman fort and its garrison* (Kendal)
JENKINS, F. 1958 'The cult of the pseudo-Venus in Kent', *Archaeologia Cantiana* 72, 60-76
MACDONALD, G. 1917-18 'A sculptured relief of the Roman period at Colinton', *PSAS* 52, 38-48
ROBINSON, J. 1881 'Notes on the excavations of 1880 at Maryport', *CW¹* 5, 253-7
ROSS, A. 1967 *Pagan Celtic Britain* (London)
TOMLIN, R. S. O. 1988 'The curse tablets', in B. Cunliffe (ed.), *The Temple of Sulis Minerva at Bath. Volume II. The Finds from the Sacred Spring* (Oxford), 59-277
WEBSTER, G. 1986 *The British Celts and their gods under Rome* (London)
WEBSTER, J. 1986 'Roman bronzes from Maryport in the Netherhall Collection', *CW²* 86, 49-69
WRIGHT, R. P. and RICHMOND, I. A. 1955 *Catalogue of the Roman inscribed and sculptured stones in the Grosvenor Museum, Chester* (Chester)

8 The stone sculptures

J. C. N. Coulston

Introduction: the collection

The collection and preservation of Roman stone sculptures found in the area of the Roman fort at Maryport have been conducted since the Elizabethan period. Indeed, the Senhouses of Maryport/Ellenborough started as Renaissance collectors of Roman antiquities. William Camden (as well as other early antiquaries) had thus occasion to visit the site, and in 1599 he found that

'. . . many altars, stones with inscriptions and statues, here are gotten out of the ground, which J. Sinous, a very honest man, in whose grounds they are digged up, keepeth charily, and hath placed orderly about his house.'[1]

Unsurprisingly enough, one of the most weathered pieces in the present collection is also one of the earliest finds, a wreathed building inscription supported by two very worn Victories (Fig. 8.1).[2] Lost detail and an assured reading of the inscription are provided by Camden's publication. Overall, however, the stones are remarkably well preserved, both as individual pieces and as a whole collection, despite the vicissitudes of weather, damage and housing over time. The body of sculptures has continued to grow through single finds and group discoveries. The years 1870 and 1880 saw the most spectacular accessions, namely the dedicatory altars dealt with elsewhere in this volume (Chapters 4-6), and the 'Serpent Stone' discussed in detail below (pp. 121-3). The findspots of these outstanding pieces were well recorded, but items discovered before 1870 in many cases have no associated information about the date and the context of their discovery, and others were just strays, surface finds or stones which accidentally came to light during quarrying.[3] Often all that can be said is that a piece is from Maryport. Subsequent to their discovery some pieces have unfortunately been lost,[4] whilst others have left Maryport and then later been reunited with the collection. Only a couple of major pieces now remain away from the Senhouse Roman Museum.[5]

Overall, there have been more than ninety items of Roman sculpture found, a figure which makes Maryport in this respect amongst one of the most productive Roman sites in Britain.[6] Various reasons may be put forward to explain this, such as the ready availability of red sandstone for carving, the lack of modern occupation over the site of the fort and of much of its environs, and the pattern of archaeological work. However, there are certainly also historical and cultural factors involved. The site was a military installation occupied through the second and third centuries AD, just like the sites along Hadrian's Wall with which it, and the collection, are most closely comparable. The sculptural requirements and the patronage

Fig. 8.1 Sculptured slab showing Victories holding up a wreath (RIB 844)

Fig. 8.2 Fragment of inscribed slab showing a running wild boar (RIB 854)

of individual units, unit commanders, soldiers and associated civilians were at their greatest over this period and in northern Britain. The specific activities of individual regiments in garrison at any one time may also have played a part.[7] Moreover, the body of sculptures is not merely marked by quantity, but is also outstanding for both the quality of some pieces and the rarity of others.

Most of the classes of work which might be expected from a fort, its extramural facilities, its *vicus* and its cemeteries are present in the Maryport collection. It is not the purpose of this paper to provide a catalogue of the sculptures, but it will review the classes of finds, and discuss the more important and outstanding pieces.

Architectural Sculpture

There is a small number of ornamented stones which were originally part of buildings. Two record the building activities of legionary troops. The first (Fig. 8.2) depicts a wild boar running to the left, tusks carefully outlined, above a fragmentary inscription which reads [. . .]ORD.[8] If a restoration such as *leg(io) XX VV [G]ord(iana)* is correct, then this is one of the latest datable sculptures of that legion's boar emblem to survive. There is also an ashlar from Maryport inscribed simply LEG XX with no ornament.[9] The second piece is a decorated inscribed panel recording work by *vexillationes* of both the *II Augusta* and *XX Valeria Victrix* legions (Fig. 8.3).[10] A *tabula ansata* bears a cable mould-

Fig. 8.3 Inscribed panel recording Legiones II Aug(usta) *and* XX V(aleria) V(ictrix) *(RIB 852)*

ing, and six-petalled rosettes decorate the *ansae* and the background. Pairing of detachments drawn from these two *legiones* is well attested in northern Britain during the second and third centuries. They were away from their fortresses at Caerleon and Chester performing construction and garrison duties on both Walls, in the Wall hinterland, and in Scotland.[11] Evidence of continental service of paired II and XX *vexillationes* is provided by a copper-alloy *phalera* found in France.[12] This artefact, which is datable by its decoration to the third century, provides not only the names of the units but also their capricorn and boar emblems; it may even be roughly contemporary with the Maryport boar.

Of the small number of auxiliary building inscriptions from Maryport, only one, set up by *cohors I Hispanorum*, is ornamented.[13] This has a die flanked and surrounded by plain-terminal *peltae*, ivy-leaf tendrils and roundels. The latter match others carved on Hadrianic altars from the site,[14] and this might perhaps be taken as a comparatively early inscription recording building by auxiliaries.[15]

The badly weathered panel recorded by Camden and mentioned above (Fig. 8.1) employs the common motif of an inscription supported by a pair of Victories.[16] As such it takes the tradition of architectural epigraphy and expresses a triumphalist celebration of building achievement in the military context.

Two key-stones bearing representations of deities are discussed below as religious sculptures. One last architectural piece deserves mention here, however, a capital with stylised acanthus leaves on two adjoining sides. It served to cap either an engaged pier or a pair of corner pilasters. The size of the block[17] suggests that it came from a substantial structure incorporating a pier colonnade, an order of pilasters or a framed feature, such as a major doorway or apse (perhaps in the *principia* or a temple). There should be at least one companion capital to be found in future.

Religious Sculpture

One dedication to Jupiter not taking the form of an *I.O.M.* altar is an inscribed stone found in 1873 near the 1870 altar group. Although broken into three pieces, it is in good condition with the loss of only the upper right-hand corner (Fig. 4.11 on p. 80).[18] The inscribed panel is supported by a very richly decorated pair of griffin-headed *peltae*. Two seven-petalled rosettes (only one survives) are positioned in the spaces between the upper *pelta* arms and the panel, but no rosettes appear in the lower corresponding positions. The panel itself is surrounded by a triple moulding, on only the upper margin of which a line of *squamae* has been incised. Overall the effect is rich and would have been impressive with paint, but a closer look reveals that the mouldings are not drafted exactly, and the inscription is poorly cut with letters of varying heights and slightly diagonal lines. The sculptor did not complete the moulding decoration, and he seems to have miscalculated the available space for the lower arms of the *peltae*; thus there is only one pair of rosettes.

Clearly the stone was attached to a building, perhaps a temple or similar structure. The dedicatee was Postumius Acilianus, *praefectus* of *cohors I Delmatarum*, and the piece thus forms a group with that officer's five (?) other dedications, one of which also bears rosettes.[19] Even without the inclusion of Pius' name in the inscription, the griffin-*peltae* would have suggested an Antonine date.[20]

Asklepios is honoured with a *pelta*-decorated Greek inscription by A. Egnatius Pastor.[21] Perhaps the dedicant was a Greek doctor in military service.

A wide range of images of Graeco-Roman deities is represented in the collection. Amongst the gods is a depiction of Hercules on the side of an altar with his club, lion-skin and the Apples of the Hesperides (Fig. 8.4).[22] He is twinned with Mars on the other side of the shaft, who rests on spear and shield, and wears a Roman type of Corinthian helmet.[23] Both deities, the labouring-in-adversity Her-

Fig. 8.4 Figure of Hercules, on right side of altar (RIB 810)

Fig. 8.5 Key-stone with incised figure of Hercules

cules and the god of war, were appropriately symbolic patrons for the army, and they are combined elsewhere in sculpture.[24] Hercules also appears on a keystone from a voussoir arch, executed in incised outline and shown with club upraised (Fig. 8.5).[25] This is a fitting load-bearing position for the strongest of the gods, and one about which the Romans were sensitive; elsewhere ox-heads or apotropaic symbols decorate key-stones.[26]

A broken and unfinished piece (see below) appears to be part of a statue of the god Vulcan. He wears a tunic and boots, and rests his hammer on top of an altar by his side (Fig. 8.6).[27] An altar of unknown date dedicated by the *praefectus* of *I Hispanorum*, Helstrius Novellus, also attests to the worship of Vulcan at Maryport.[28]

A statuette of a Genius from Maryport depicts the deity in familiar form holding a cornucopia and a *patera*.[29] More difficult to identify are two heads, one in the round, the other in relief. The first (Fig. 8.7) is life-size and shows a man with thickly-curled hair, moustache and full beard. He might be Jupiter, but a river god or, perhaps most likely, Neptune might also be suggested.[30] The relief head (Fig. 8.8) is crudely modelled on the front of an ashlar.[31] Its face is round with incised features. Six projections of varied proportions radiate out from the head, and at least three exhibit surviving terminal detail. Even taking into consideration the crudity of execution, the projections are too irregular to be a radiate crown, and the details clearly depict the *glandes*. Therefore, it is possible that we have a Mercury wearing an unusual, mul-

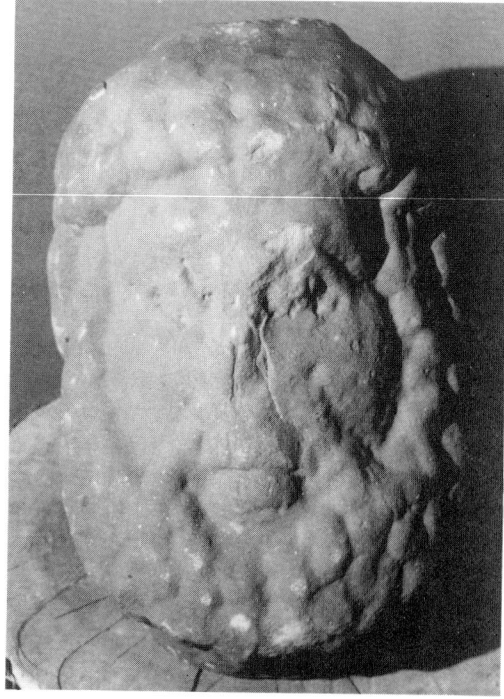

Fig. 8.6 Unfinished statue of Vulcan (?)

Fig. 8.7 Bearded head carved in the round

Fig. 8.8 Ithyphallic head of Mercury (?)

tiple ithyphallic *petasos* of a type seen on a statuette from Pompeii.[32] If this is right an apotropaic function may be ascribed to the piece.

Of the Graeco-Roman goddesses, Minerva is represented by a low relief which shows the goddess in typical pose leaning on spear and shield (Fig. 8.9).[33] A very crudely incised set of facial features defines the *aegis* on her chest. As the goddess of war and wisdom she was the perfect patroness of soldiers, particularly clerks. A second sculpture depicts a seated goddess (Fig. 8.10).[34] The carving is very basic with the drapery incised rather than cut in relief, and the stone is 'stepped' to indicate the lap. The sides of the chair are merely outlined, and the only element really in the round is the (lost) head. Identification as a Celtic Mother Goddess (*Mater*) has been favoured, of the type which appears in threes on reliefs, and cut singly (to make up a set of three) as statues in the round.[35] However, some care has been taken with the figure's hands, and the one on the right is grasping what appears to be a cornucopia. This would make the goddess Fortuna, rather than one of three Matres, and there are direct seated parallels for this goddess from other sites in northern Britain.[36]

There is in fact one example of a triad of deities from Maryport. This is a much weathered relief of three niched figures; two survive full-length, whilst the third is now reduced to part of the head alone (Fig. 8.11).[37] They are naked, and, although damaged over the chest areas, it is clear from the peculiar emphasis of the genitalia that they are female. The outermost two figures clasp their hands below their breasts, whilst the middle one gestures with her right arm. These figures are most unlikely to be Mother Goddesses, because Matres were not depicted naked. It is possible that Venus and two Nymph attendants were intended, but each occupies a separate niche and there is no distinction in status between them.[38] That the figures depict (Sea?) Nymphs is the most likely explanation, although these too usually have some drapery around their lower parts.[39]

Fig. 8.9 Relief of Minerva

The oriental gods are represented in the collection by a single relief of Sol (Fig. 8.12). A key-stone bears a full-length male figure wearing only a cloak.[40] His right hand is upraised to hold a spear or staff, and his left hand holds an orb. Around his head is a nimbus of thirteen rays.[41]

Dedications to the Celtic horse-goddess Epona are rare in Britain.[42] However, at Maryport a relief of the goddess appears on one face of a socketed base, the only complete representation of the goddess from the province (Fig. 7.1, p. 109).[43] She is shown frontally, mounted side-saddle on a horse which walks right. Her arms come in

Fig. 8.10 Statue of Fortuna (above)

Fig. 8.11 Female triad relief (below)

Fig. 8.12 Key-stone carved with the figure of Sol (right)

Fig. 8.13 Relief depicting a horned warrior god (right)

Fig. 8.14 Picked-out sketch of an armed god (below)

towards her lap and the worn relief may originally have shown her holding the basket which figures on continental reliefs of this goddess.[44] The block may have taken a stone shaft or a structural timber. Epona was claimed as a patroness by some soldiers who worked with horses and other pack animals.[45] Perhaps the relief belongs to the period when *cohors I Hispanorum equitata* was in residence at Maryport.

The deities Belatucadrus and Setlocenia are mentioned in inscriptions but are without any accompanying anthropomorphic representations.[46] However, there is one Celtic horned god which, within its own genre, is well represented, and is perhaps the most engaging piece in the collection (Fig. 8.13).[47] A full-length, naked male figure stands frontally with a square body, short legs and feet in profile. The head is round with incised features: round eyes, a straight mouth and a long rectilinear nose. It is topped by a pair of horns. The god carries a spear, held vertically, which has a delineated butt and a triangular head. No attempt has been made to depict any detail on the hand. His left arm disappears behind a rectangular shield which exhibits a round boss. This form of shield is well-attested in religious iconography and in Romano-British triumphal representations of British barbarians (both official and private).[48] Interestingly, the arm is in direct line with the boss which would have protected the single, central hand-grip used in Roman and Celtic shield traditions. A rectangular native shield from Clonoura (Republic of Ireland) provides direct artefactual support for the type.[49] Horned-god representations are plentiful in northern Britain, largely because of the Roman army's presence and soldiers' patronage of local cults. Some deities are hunter-gods with links to game-animals, whilst others are war-gods associated with Mars.[50]

Fig. 8.15 Serpent Stone, both sides [(a) and (b), left], and [(c), opposite] as first found, before damage to the snakes and fishes around the face. The stone stands 1.24m (4ft 1in) high

In contrast a second armed-god sculpture from Maryport lacks horns (Fig. 8.14).[51] He is roughly incised, has a rectangular body and a round head with simple features. He holds up a round shield and a sword. Sword-armed gods also find British parallels, as does the circular shield.[52] It is clear from Roman gravestones alone that a variety of round, rectangular and oval shield-board forms were in native use during the first and second centuries.[53] Unarmed, and even more crudely incised deities appear on two miniature altars: one figure has a rectangular body with diagonal lines across it, and incised facial features; the second is long and narrow with hardly a suggestion of a face.[54]

Funerary Sculpture

The Serpent Stone is perhaps the most striking item in the Maryport collection (Fig. 8.15).[55] It consists of a tapering, octagonal shaft rising from a rectangular base which has triple mouldings on its sides, but not on its two faces. On one face the shaft is topped by a broad oval human visage. Facial features consist of lentoid eyes and a triangular nose, with lines projecting down to the corners of an open, slightly down-turned mouth. A pair of confronting snakes, broken away since discovery (Fig. 8.15c, p. 121), met over the forehead, their tongues extended. Each may have worn a neck-torque. Below the chin is a pair of confronting, scaley fish. On the back of the human head, the stone is smoothed around to form a truncated, pear-shaped protrusion. Up to this writhes a crested snake with flicking tongue, its head seen in profile with a lentoid eye, and its body extending down the length of shaft and base. It too appears to wear a torque. A socket cut in the top of the stone contains an iron peg set in lead.

To judge from the mouldings, this was originally a very substantial altar which has been recut. The two faces of the base have been chiselled back, very crudely in the case of the head face, flush in the case of the other. The corners of shaft and capital have been reduced to form new hexagonal and ovoid sections respectively, but both are still predominantly rectilinear. Elements of the altar's *focus* still define the top, but the nature and function of the iron attachment is unknown. Sufficient stone was removed from the altar to produce an object which, when seen from the snake face, is unmistakably phalliform.

The stone was found in a roadside cemetery surrounded by burials and other monuments (including a pine-cone and a conical finial). Immediately in front of it was a flagged pavement (3.9 m by 1.8 m), directly beneath which were found four cremation burials.[56] Whilst the Serpent Stone thus seems to have had a funerary function, its further interpretation is problematic. There are essentially three elements involved: the head, the serpent(s) and the giant phallus.

The stone has been related to the Celtic 'cult' of the severed head, and the presence of the torque immediately suggests a native element.[57] Numerous stone heads in relief or in the round have been found on Roman sites in Britain, and these appear to have fulfilled an apotropaic function.[58] Few are directly linked with funerary practice, but those which are seem to bear a more Roman significance. For example, the sculpture group from the Burrow Heights mausoleum at Lancaster (Lancashire) includes two lions and four heads representing the Four Winds.[59] The upstanding crest of the large snake on the Serpent Stone is commonly seen in Roman representations.[60] The association of the smaller snakes with the human head and hair recalls elements of the Sulis/Gorgon head at the centre of the temple pediment at Bath.[61] Snakes appear in association with Celtic deities.[62] In Roman contexts they represent the benevolent *genius loci* and are seen attacking the Evil Eye.[63] An overt funerary connection is made with the appearance of snakes wound around pine-cones from Kirkby Thore and Carlisle (Cumbria).[64]

Giant *phalli* did have a long lineage in Greek and Roman usage, having been employed in fertility rites and festivals.[65] There is some suggestion of an apotropaic Celtic combination of severed head and phallus,[66] and three small, human-headed *phalli* come from the Cotswolds region (varying in length from 0.085 m to 0.28 m).[67] Given Maryport's position on the coast facing the Isle of Man and Ireland, it is tempting to make an analogy between the Serpent Stone and Irish phalliform standing stones, such as the Turoe Stone or the Lia Fáil at Tara.[68] Phallic imagery is comparatively rare in Roman funerary practice, although attention may be drawn to a substantial phallic sculpture from York, and a polygonal shaft topped by a pine-cone from South Shields (Tyne and Wear).[69] Both are likely to come from mausolea or to have acted as grave-markers in

Fig. 8.16 Gravestone of a horseman

uneven ground and is foreshortened to fit it into the space (a common practice). Its rump is simply delineated by punching. Faint, incised lines represent rein, and tack on the head. Eye and mouth are not clearly shown. The rider's left calf and small foot are outlined, and he turns to face the viewer. An oval head with prominent ears has no surviving facial features. He wears a cloak which billows out behind him. No shield seems to be present, there is no falling barbarian below the horse, and the latter's pose is relatively sedate, suggesting that the stone is part of the unarmoured cavalry gravestone genre. From the second century onwards the latter rather took over from the more energetic type, representing a cavalryman riding down the hapless enemy, although even this form continued as a British insular tradition later than it did on the continent.[71]

A number of female gravestones from Maryport depict the deceased as full-length figures. All, unfortunately are badly eroded and damaged. The torso of a woman alone survives from what must once have been an impressive *stela* (Fig. 8.17), but it is so worn that the objects she holds across her front are unidentifiable.[72] A second girl or woman stands in an arcuated niche half-turned towards the front, but the lower two-thirds of the stone's surface has layer-eroded away.[73]

Another *stela* is not so much weathered as smashed.[74] A blow has been delivered to the area of the deceased's upper torso and head, shattering the stone. The unfortunate result is that parts of the sculpture are tantalisingly lost. A full-length figure stands within a shell-headed *aedicula* wearing a cloak and one or two tunics, the lower of which seems to come down well below the knee. A rectangular object is held in its left hand, and a square object with a vertical shaft above sits down to its right.

their own right. Thus, the Maryport Serpent Stone combines elements of Celtic and Roman symbolism in a funerary, apotropaic function, presumably in order to protect the graves associated with it, if not also to ward the spirits of the departed.

The cemeteries of Maryport have produced a series of more conventional funerary monuments. The most impressive is a gravestone which bears a full-length representation of horse and rider (Fig. 8.16).[70] It is unfortunately very eroded, and it is also evidently unfinished. The figure is outlined within a recessed panel, the background of which is coarsely punch-dressed without any further chisel-smoothing. The high-stepping horse moves left over an

Fig. 8.17 Female torso, funerary relief

is a number of plain, pine-cone finials, most (?) presumably coming from funerary monuments, but there are no funerary statues of lions in the collection.[79]

Other Sculpture

The last group of sculptures to be discussed concerns those pieces which do not fit neatly into any of the categories above.

On the front of a large rectangular block is the representation of what is presumed to be a Roman fort-gate structure (Fig. 8.18).[80] Despite weathering the detail is convincing. There are two gate portals made up of piers supporting arches of slightly more than semicircular profile. Each opening has a pair of impost blocks which project both into the openings and out towards the viewer. The wall above the portals has two horizontally-incised lines, and in turn there are five, arched window openings above these. The windows are not symmetrically placed over the piers below; each has a pair of imposts and an arch of similar profile to the portals. The wall continues above these without further detail. To the left of the whole structure is an arcuated niche, flanked by two engaged semi-columns to the right and one to the left. Some detail of torus mouldings is preserved below the capitals. Within the niche is a full-length, naked female figure. Details of facial features have been completely lost, but an overhanging projection suggests breasts. One hand is raised to the head, the other seems to rest on one hip.

One interpretation is that the deceased wears a belted tunic and carries a 'book' of writing tablets, suggesting that we have here the gravestone of a soldier.[75] Alternatively, a box or bag may be carried, two tunics may be worn, and the lower left object may be identified as a chest or jewellery box with a lock-plate. Thus a deceased woman may be represented. Girls sometimes have a calf-length under-tunic, and the cloak/mantle would not be out of place.[76] The vertical object is mysterious. It does not project far enough upwards to be a staff, spear or standard, and it may be associated with the figure's right hand.[77]

Other gravestones include one bearing an incised bust of a female (to judge from the inscription);[78] and some, more fragmentary items have simple geometric decoration and wheel or rosette motifs. There

The double gateway is characteristic of second- to third-century stone forts, and the projecting imposts are mirrored by standing remains at High Rochester in Redesdale, and at Birdoswald, Housesteads, Chesters and at Milecastle 37 (Northumberland) on Hadrian's Wall. The multiple windows recall finds of window arches at Wall forts, and are directly paralleled by a terracotta gate-model from

Fig. 8.18 Relief of Venus standing within a gateway structure

Fig. 8.19 Incised phallus with evil eye (?) (RIB 872)

Intercisa (Hungary), as well as by the surviving upper structures of some continental town gates.[81] The gender, nudity and pose of the niched figure suggest that she is Venus. Victory, Mars, Hercules, Fortuna or Roma might seem more appropriate figures in this setting, but a building inscription from Croy Hill (Strathclyde) on the Antonine Wall provides a useful parallel.[82] On this piece Venus stands in a very similar, if more elegantly rendered, pose between two columns. The latter support an architectural structure which 'shelters' an inscribed wreath. The inscription is of course the centre of attention, and in comparison the Maryport relief seems unbalanced. It seems likely that on a block to the right of it was another figure within a columnar niche. Mars would be an obvious pendent candidate. The Maryport gate sculpture is unique, but the substantial block on which it is carved may itself have formed part of a gate structure. The link might be made between representing a gate flanked by figures and the practice of decorating a real gate with figural reliefs, such as at the east gate at Housesteads.[83]

Other miscellaneous Maryport sculptures include the usual phalli carved on ashlars which are to be expected from a military site. There are three in all, one in high relief, and two incised. One of the incised stones also bears an inscription (Fig. 8.19), and its phallus points at an elliptical shape.[84] The latter is either an evil eye or a vulva, but the exact identification is a recurrent problem with such pieces.[85] Apotropaic phalli appear on buildings, fort walls, kilns and ovens, quarry-faces and bridges, wherever people felt threatened and in need of protection or good luck.[86]

Lastly, there is a small incised human figure on a naturally-shaped stone with the inscription SIG(*nifer?*). This is part of a class of 'doodles' on stones from Roman sites which often shows hunters and game.[87]

Discussion

Nearly all the sculptures are cut from Cumbrian red sandstone. A few buff sandstone examples very likely come from the same sources, given the colour range present in local complexes (dark red, pink, buff, yellow, grey etc.). The stone weathers grey, and a few pieces still bear their black legacy of exposure to Industrial Revolution pollution.[88] Sandstones for architecture and sculpture are relatively ubiquitous in northern England, and there is little evidence for the transport of stone for sculpture over any great distance. Nor is there much indication for the circulation of either 'quarry-state' or finished sandstone sculptures from one region to another, or even between sites.[89] There was probably no 'trade' in altars, for example, between forts or units.[90] Thus it is fairly certain that everything in the Maryport collection was carved at or near the fort, as and when it was required. Pieces for architectural use, such as decorated building inscriptions, were sculpted on site, if not *in situ*, then on the building itself. Altars were presumably shaped and decorated specifically for the occasions of their use.

The worked surfaces of the sculptures exhibit employment of the normal tools – punch, drill and a range of bladed chisels. As usual there is no evidence for use of the claw-chisels.[91] Faces of secondary importance, for example the backs of some altars, and unfinished pieces, like the rider gravestone, are especially informative about sculpting techniques. The unfinished Vulcan statue (Fig. 8.6) is shaped with a punch, and has had the basic outline of legs and tunic drapery very roughly worked. The line of the top of the boots has been taken across between the legs. The sculptor has set to work on the deity's left leg with a bladed chisel, so that the knee, shin and boot (notably its sole and five toes) are much further advanced than the rest. This is a common feature of unfinished ancient sculpture: the shape of the piece was blocked out and then discrete portions were worked on, sometimes virtually to completion. The whole sculpture was not worked all over, stage-by-stage. The same may be said of the unfinished statue of Hercules from Carlisle, which is roughly shaped overall with a chisel, but which has completed work on the head, left shoulder and left chest.[92]

There is no evidence for a 'civilian' service-industry providing sculpture to the army in northern Britain, and there is good reason to suppose that nearly everything was produced by soldiers (including, perhaps, some active veterans). This was keenly appreciated by Bruce. Impressed by the quality of work on the Maryport altars he was moved to observe:

'As they must have been the work of soldiers, and not of professional sculptors, we must suppose that even the auxiliaries of the Roman army possessed an unusual amount of artistic taste and skill.'[93]

Of course, there are also many pieces discussed above which were executed with much less skill than enthusiasm, but this is to be expected from a body of sculpture which was produced over a long period of time for a great variety of functions.

Any distinction which might be drawn in a modern context between 'masons' and 'sculptors' or 'artists' does not really hold true in the ancient world, where demarcations between skill-areas were less clear-cut. Training and experience were the important variants. In a civilian, urban context the sculptor worked through, potentially from apprentice to master, within a workshop context, learning a variety of skills and working on a range of classes of product. The city or region, as well as the patronage of the workshop, created and provided the cultural/artistic milieu.[94] Military sculptors learnt and developed their skills within the army as part of the normal development of personal *immunitas*; the legion or auxiliary regiment was the workshop context.[95] Particular practices, for example the erection of figural military gravestones in Britain, and specific motifs, for instance Antonine griffin-head *pelta*-terminals (see above, pp. 114-5), might have a regional/provincial army currency. Beyond these elements it is possible to detect the 'hands' of individual sculptors through the isolation of specific working practices on more than one product. The modelling of cult figures and the depiction of drapery on gravestones at Housesteads, and the appearance of four-spoked wheels on altars from Castlesteads (Cumbria), suggest the work of three different sculptors.[96] Obviously there needs to be a large enough sample from a given site to draw such inferences, and this is where the employment of specific decorative motifs on the numerous Maryport altars comes into play. Recessed lunettes and circles, bands of chip-carved ornament, rosettes, wheels, dot-in-circle motifs and moulding combinations can suggest an approximate temporal association between altars. They can also provide a perspective on the varying skills and predilections of the individual sculptors or workshops of a series of auxiliary regiments in residence at Maryport.[97]

Acknowledgements

The writer is very grateful to Ms L. Allason-Jones and Mr F. O'Súilleabháin for their great assistance with studying the Senhouse Roman Museum collection, and for advice offered on specific points by Mr P. T. Bidwell, Dr H. Dodge, Mr J. N. Dore, Ms C. Parker and Mr M. Humphries. Dr D. J. Breeze very kindly made a copy of his paper in this volume available to the writer before publication.

Notes

N.B. Throughout these notes, the designation *Cat.* (a) refers to Bailey 1915, *Cat.* (b) to Haverfield 1916.

1. Camden 1789, 171; *Cat.* (a) 135.
2. *Cat.* pl. VIII.7; *LS* No. 866; *Cat.* (a) 1; *RIB* 844.
3. Bruce 1874; *LS*, 29; Robinson 1881; Bellhouse 1992, 35-50; *Cat.*, throughout.
4. An incised figure (*Cat.* (a) 59; *RIB* 871; Bellhouse 1992, pl. XIV, mid-bottom row), various stone heads (ibid., 48, pl. XV, top row; *Cat.* (b) 9-14), a deer relief (*Cat.* (b) 56), pine-cones (*Cat.* (b) 57-8) and the figure of a Genius (*LS* No. 900; *Cat.* (b) 15) were not located by the writer at the museum in June 1996. *RIB* 856 and 877 are long lost.
5. *RIB* 812 (British Museum), 831 (Museo della Civiltà Romana, EUR, Rome).
6. Defining 'sculpture' in *CSIR* terms.
7. See the comments by David Breeze in this volume (pp. 67-70) about the pattern of altar dedications.
8. H. 0.18 m, W. 0.195 m, D. 0.06 m. *LS* No. 892; *Cat.* (a) 6; *RIB* 854. The boar has been

adopted as the emblem of the Senhouse Roman Museum.
9 RIB 853.
10 H. 0.355 m, W. 0.61 m, D. 0.11 m. LS No. 891; Cat. (a) 13; RIB 852.
11 Breeze 1989; Casey 1991, 5-8.
12 Casey 1991, 6; Bishop and Coulston 1993, pl. 3b.
13 Cat. (b) 35; RIB 855; cf. 850. If the horizontal axis of the surviving right *pelta* is taken as the middle of the stone as a whole, this gives a height of *c*. 0.6 m, and insufficient room for the third line postulated in RIB.
14 Notably RIB 824. See Breeze in this volume, p. 71. A predilection for ivy leaves is seen on two Hadrianic altars (RIB 815, 817).
15 The Carvoran *Hamii* may have been unusual in having eastern stone building traditions (RIB 1816, 1818, 1820, with 1778).
16 H. 0.495 m, W. 0.69 m, D. 0.155 m. LS No. 866; Cat. (a) 1; RIB 844. Cf. RIB 783, 1093; CSIR, I.1, No. 46, 94-6, 294; I.4, Nos. 26-7, 150, 156.
17 H. 0.28 m, W. 0.61 m, D. 0.57 m. Cat. (a) 17.
18 H. 0.61 m, W. 0.775 m, D. 0.75 m. Cat. (a) 56; RIB 832. The loss of the top right-hand corner is recent: it was still intact when Collingwood drew it in 1928.
19 RIB 810, 833, 840 (?), 847, 850. 840 may be included on stylistic grounds.
20 Cf. CSIR, I.1, No. 215; I.4, Nos. 68, 114, 122, 138, 145, 152, 154, 158 (although see No. 171); I.6, No. 276.
21 H. 0.23 m, W. 0.43 m, D. 0.125 m. Cat. (a) 15; RIB 808.
22 H. 1.14 m, W. 0.57 m, D. 0.49 m. LS No. 876; Cat. (a) 9; RIB 810. Cf. CSIR, I.1, Nos. 189, 297; I.6, Nos. 31-2, 35, 317, 477.
23 That is to say, a Corinthian helmet made as though permanently pushed up and back on the head (as in the iconography of Athena) and with the addition of cheek-pieces and/or a vertical crest-mount (Robinson 1975, pl. 413, 468; this is also an element of pl. 376-82). Cf. CSIR, I.6, No. 69.
24 CSIR, I.1, No. 297.
25 H. 0.375 m, W. 0.18 m, D. 0.24 m. Cat. (b) 65; Bellhouse 1992, 48-9, Pl. XV, mid-right. Cf. CSIR, I.1, No. 6.
26 CSIR, I.1, No. 326; I.6, No. 391, 448.
27 H. 0.59 m, W. 0.42 m, D. 0.17 m. Cat. (a) 20. Cf. CSIR, I.6, No. 23b; Espérandieu 1931, Nos. 99, 158, 239, 382.
28 RIB 846. See Breeze in this volume, p. 77.
29 Approximately H. 0.26 m, W. 0.15 m. LS No. 900; Cat. (b) 15. Cf. CSIR, I.1, No. 5; I.6, Nos. 21-2, 23d, 25-7, 468-70; I.7, Nos. 32-41.
30 H. 0.38 m, W. 0.24 m, D. 0.28 m. Cat. (a) 11. Cf. CSIR, I.6, No. 88, 94, 510; I.7, No. 89. Would the River Ellen have warranted such a scale of deity as the Tyne, or even the Eden?
31 H. 0.275 m, W. 0.255 m, D. 0.75 m.
32 Johns 1982, 54, fig. 39.
33 H. 0.345 m, W. 0.33 m, D. 0.14 m. Cat. (b) 42. Cf. CSIR, I.2, No. 25; I.7, No. 88; I.8, No. 10a.
34 H. 0.335 m, W. 0.23 m, D. 0.2 m. Cat. (b) 37; Bellhouse 1992, pl. XV, upper right.
35 Ross 1974, 265-71. Cf. CSIR, I.1, Nos. 62-3, 235-6, 240, 243; I.2, No. 38; I.6, Nos. 166-77, 180; I.7, Nos. 117-22; I.8, Nos. 15-17.
36 CSIR, I.6, Nos. 14-17.
37 H. 0.53 m, W. 0.56 m, D. 0.65 m. LS No. 896; Cat. (a) 4; Ross 1974, 275-6, fig. 142. When drawn for LS less of the stone was lost, so that the left-most figure retained its upper half and more of its head. This still seems to have been the case in 1914 (Cat.).
38 This is very different from CSIR, I.1, No. 218.
39 Cf. CSIR, I.6, Nos. 88, 93, 150.
40 H. 0.32 m, W. 0.13 m, D. 0.21 m. LS No. 899; Cat. (b) 40.
41 Cf. CSIR, I.1, No. 56; I.6, Nos. 130-1. According to RIB 856, a lost altar from Maryport bore an incised chi-rho symbol. This is an extremely unlikely context for Christian usage, and perhaps is the product of the antiquarian wishful thinking which has so bedevilled Early Christian studies (see Mawer 1995, 141-2).
42 RIB 1777, 2177.
43 H. 0.65 m, W. 0.42 m, D. 0.4 m. Cat. (a) 20.
44 There are scores of votive Epona reliefs from the continental Celtic Roman provinces (cf. Espérandieu 1931, Nos. 131, 333, 363, 369, 372, 379, 392, 711). In Britain, apart from the Maryport example, there is a fragmentary statuette of Epona mounted (of unknown provenance, CSIR, I.8, No.

45 14), and a wooden statuette of Epona (?) on foot (from Winchester: *CSIR*, I.2, No. 115).
45 *RE*, *s.v.* 'Epona'; Magnen and Thevenot 1953; Ross 1974, 286-8; Birley 1976, 98.
46 *RIB* 809 (lost), 841.
47 H. 0.34 m, W. 0.335 m, D. 0.11 m. *Cat.* (b) 39.
48 *CSIR*, I.1, No. 259; I.4, No. 68, 137; I.6, No. 162; I.7, No. 130; Ross 1974, fig. 15, pl. 38; Schleiermacher 1984, Nos. 73, 82.
49 Stead 1985, pl. XI.
50 *CSIR*, I.1, Nos. 232, 324-5, 351; I.6, Nos. 326, 363, 373, 377.
51 H. 0.245 m, W. 0.255 m, D. 0.075 m. *Cat.* (b) 61.
52 Cf. *CSIR*, I.5, No. 15; I.6, No. 360; I.7, Nos. 48-52, 58-9, 123, 131-2.
53 E.g. *CSIR*, I.1, No. 68; I.7, No. 137; I.8, No. 48; *RIB* 291.
54 H. 0.25 m, W. 0.13 m, D. 0.105 m; H. 0.29 m, W. 0.15 m, D. 0.11 m. *Cat.* (b) 22, 41. Cf. *CSIR*, I.3, No. 37; I.7, Nos. 126-7, 129.
55 H. 1.24 m, W. 0.44 m, D. 0.32 m. Robinson 1881, 241-2, 254-6, pl. opposite 255; *Cat.* (a) 55.
56 Robinson 1881, 241, 243, 255.
57 Ross 1974, 126-7. For the 'cult' in general, see ibid. 94-171.
58 Especially *CSIR*, I.5, No. 55; I.6, Nos. 339, 351, 354, 405; Ross 1974, 107-24.
59 Shotter and White 1990, pl. 3.
60 Toynbee 1973, pl. 112; Jashemski 1979, figs. 100, 186, 209, 247, 318; Coulston 1991, 109.
61 *CSIR*, I.2, Nos. 32-7; see Ross 1974, 124-7.
62 Ross 1974, 430-4.
63 Toynbee 1973, 223-6, 233-6. Attack: mosaic from Antioch-on-the-Orontes, sculpture from Lepcis Magna (Bianchi Bandinelli 1966, pl. 196).
64 *LS* No. 757; *CSIR*, I.6, No. 504.
65 Johns 1982, figs. 1, 27, 120.
66 Ross 1974, 127-8. Ross' main piece of evidence is the Maryport Serpent Stone, so there is a danger of circularity here.
67 *CSIR*, I.7, Nos. 156-8.
68 Harbison 1988, 158 (cf. 160); Bhreathnach 1995, 136-7. Maryport fort does not of course just command excellent views across the Solway and up to Burnswark, but the Isle of Man is frequently visible, and, under rare conditions, so is Ireland.

69 *CSIR*, I.3 (H. 0.63 m, incomplete); I.1, No. 251. Pinecones and *glandes* might in any case be easily confused.
70 H. 1.34 m, W. 0.88 m, D. 0.195 m. *LS* No. 14; *Cat.* (a) 5.
71 *LS* Nos. 754-6; *CSIR*, I.1, No. 259; I.6, Nos. 191, 231; Schleiermacher 1984, Nos. 68, 71-3, 80, 82-3. The same could be said about full-figure standing soldier gravestones in Britain which close the temporal gap between the first-century Rhineland and third-century Danubian practices.
72 H. 0.51 m, W. 0.34 m, D. 0.15 m. Robinson 1881, 243; Bellhouse 1992, pl. XVI, left; *Cat.* (b) 1. Deceased females may hold a bird, a vessel, fruit and/or a spindle, partly depending on the subject's age (cf. Wright and Richmond 1955, Nos. 37, 89, 117-20; *CSIR*, I.1, Nos. 77, 247; I.3, No. 41; I.6, Nos. 211, 228, 233, 493, 495, 497).
73 H. 1.13 m., W. 0.64 m., D. 0.11 m. *LS* No. 890; *Cat.* (a) 49.
74 H. 0.89 m, W. 0.8 m, D. 0.15 m. *LS* No. 895; *Cat.* (a) 8.
75 Tablets: Wright and Richmond 1955, No. 38; *CSIR*, I.1, No. 272; I.3, No. 44; I.4, No. 111; I.6, No. 227.
76 Bag/basket: I.3, No. 99; I.4, No. 61. Caskets etc. *CSIR*, I.1, Nos. 77, 247; I.2, No. 116. Shorter tunics: I.1, Nos. 71, 273; I.3, No. 39; I.6, Nos. 211, 216, 493.
77 Cf. I.1, No. 115; I.2, No. 116.
78 H. 1.15 m, W. 0.825 m, D. 0.135 m. Camden 1789, pl. IX.2; *LS* No. 879; *Cat.* (a) 2; *RIB* 866. Cf. *CSIR*, I.1, Nos. 66, 267, 271; I.6, Nos. 209, 213; I.8, No. 59.
79 Geometric: *Cat.* (b) 57; *RIB* 868. Pine-cones: Bellhouse 1992, pl. XVI; *Cat.* (b) 43, 57-8.
80 H. 0.34 m, W. 0.465 m, D. 0.43 m. *LS* No. 901; *Cat.* (a) 12.
81 For example Trier, Autun, Susa, Torino, Verona, Roma, Fano (Ward-Perkins, 1981, figs. 103, 108, 135, 279, 303). For discussion of fort-gateway features, see Bidwell et al. 1988, 155-211. Intercisa model: ibid., fig. 7.14 (cf. Fig. 5.5). The Maryport gate relief has played its part in the full-size reconstruction of the south-west gate at South Shields (Tyne and Wear).
82 *CSIR*, I.4, No. 91.

83 *CSIR*, I.6, No. 99; Crow 1995, figs. 5, 17. A decorative motif very similar to the Maryport relief portals is occasionally seen on other sculptures (*LS* No. 840; *CSIR*, I.6, No. 431).
84 *Cat.* (b) 86 (H. 0.16 m, W. 0.35 m, D. 0.22 m); *RIB* 872.
85 Johns 1982, 73; cf. *CSIR*, I.6, Nos. 404, 407. A definite eye is shown with a nasally ithyphallic head from Vindolanda (I.6, No. 448).
86 *CSIR*, I.1, Nos. 175-6; I.3, No. 124; I.4, No. 28, 82; I.5, No. 98; I.6, Nos. 404-7, 434, 442-9, 457-9, 461, 465-6, 529; I.7, end section Nos. 6-9; I.8, Nos. 86-9. For phallic votives, see I.1, No. 341; I.4, No. 85. Turnbull 1978; Johns 1982, 62-75; Henig 1984, 185-6.
87 Approximate H. 0.075 m, W. 0.1 m. *Cat.* (b) 59; *RIB* 871; cf. 1001, 1008; *CSIR*, I.6, Nos. 386, 389, 401-3.
88 *RIB* 814, 834.
89 Milling stones of Mayen lava and Millstone Grit are of course a different matter. Thus ancient imports of marble sculptures really stand out (*RIB* 1-4; *CSIR*, I.7, Nos. 1-16).
90 *Contra* Kewley 1974.
91 Blagg 1976. Contrast claw-chisel marks on *CSIR*, I.1, No. 315 (if it is genuinely Roman). The circumferences of circles decorating some altars (*RIB* 815, 819, 822, 824-6) would have been cut using compasses (cf. Claridge 1983, figs. 3-4, 6-7), and the central hole may have been further drilled.
92 *CSIR*, I.6, No. 477. Cf. I.1, Nos. 102, 125; I.6, Nos. 106, 170, 534-5 (Phillips 1976a).
93 Bruce 1874, 186.
94 Burford 1972, 38-9, 78-80, 91, 97; Henig 1995, 109-18.
95 For *immunes*, see *Digest* 50.6.7. In recent work artefacts such as sculpture, military equipment and ceramics are increasingly being identified with specific army formations (Henig 1995, 50; Bishop and Coulston 1993, 196-8; Swan and Monaghan 1993).
96 *CSIR*, I.6, Nos. 200-1; 202-3; 55, 133, 320. Cf. Phillips 1976b.
97 See the contributions by Breeze and Hill in this volume, above Chapters 4 and 6. In addition to the altars with inscriptions, the collection includes a detached altar capital with deeply recessed lunettes and triangles, and a fragmentary capital with two registers of large, shallow lunettes.

References

BAILEY, J. B. 1915 'Catalogue of Roman inscribed and sculptured stones, coins, earthenware, etc., discovered in and near the Roman fort at Maryport, and preserved at Netherhall', CW^2 15, 135-72

BIANCHI BANDINELLI, R. 1966 *The Buried City* (London)

BELLHOUSE, R. 1992 *Joseph Robinson of Maryport: archaeologist extraordinary* (privately printed)

BIDWELL, P., MIKET, R. and FORD, W. 1988 *Portae cum turribus. Studies of Roman fort gates* [BAR British Series No. 206] (Oxford)

BIRLEY, E. 1976 *Roman Britain and the Roman Army* (Kendal)

BHREATHNACH, E. 1995 *Tara* (Dublin)

BISHOP, M. C. and COULSTON, J. C. N. 1993 *Roman Military Equipment from the Punic Wars to the Fall of Rome* (London)

BLAGG, T. F. C. 1976 'Tools and techniques of the Roman stonemason in Britain', *Britannia* 7, 152-72

BREEZE, D. J. 1989 *The Second Augustan Legion in North Britain* (Cardiff)

BRUCE, J. C. 1874 'Altars recently found in the Roman camp at Maryport', CW^1 1, 175-88

BURFORD, A. 1972 *Craftsmen in Greek and Roman Society* (London)

CAMDEN, W. 1789 *Britannia: or, a Chronographical Description of the Flourishing Kingdoms of England, Scotland and Ireland and the Islands Adjacent from the Earliest Antiquity*, translated from the 1607 edition by R. Gough, vol. III (London)

CASEY, J. 1991 *The Legions in the Later Roman Empire* (Cardiff)

CLARIDGE, A. 1983 'Roman methods of fluting Corinthian columns and pilasters', *Città e architettura nella Roma imperiale* [Analecta Romana Instituti Danici, Supplement 10] (Odense), 119-28

COULSTON, J. C. N. 1991 'The "draco" standard', *Journal of Roman Military Equipment Studies* 2, 101-14

CROW, J. 1995 *Housesteads* (London)

ESPÉRANDIEU, É. 1931 *Recueil général des bas-reliefs, statues et bustes de la Germanie romaine* (Paris)
HARBISON, P. 1988 *Pre-Christian Ireland. From the first settlers to the Early Celts* (London)
HAVERFIELD, F. J. 1916 'Roman notes', CW^2 16, 282-6
HENIG, M. 1984 *Religion in Roman Britain* (London)
HENIG, M. 1995 *The art of Roman Britain* (London)
JASHEMSKI, W. F. 1979 *The Gardens of Pompeii, Herculaneum and the Villas Destroyed by Vesuvius* (New York)
JOHNS, C. 1982 *Sex or Symbol? Erotic images of Greece and Rome* (London)
KEWLEY, J. 1974 'A Roman stone-masons' workshop at Chester-le-Street and Lanchester', *Antiquaries Journal* 54, 53-65
MAGNEN, R. and THEVENOT, E. 1953 *Épona, déesse gauloise* (Paris)
MAWER, F. 1995 *Evidence for Christianity in Roman Britain* [BAR British Series No. 243] (Oxford)
PHILLIPS, E. J. 1976a 'Unfinished Roman sculpture in North Britain', *Archaeological Journal* 133, 50-6
PHILLIPS, E. J. 1976b 'A workshop of Roman sculptors at Carlisle', *Britannia* 7, 101-8
ROBINSON, H. R. 1975 *The Armour of Imperial Rome* (London)
ROBINSON, J. 1881 'Notes on the excavations near the Roman camp, Maryport, during the year 1880', CW^1 5, 237-57
ROSS, A. 1974 *Pagan Celtic Britain* (London)
SCHLEIERMACHER, M. 1984 *Römische Reitergrabsteine. Die kaiserzeitlichen Reliefs des triumphierenden Reiters* (Bonn)
SHOTTER, D. and WHITE, A. 1990 *The Roman Fort and Town of Lancaster* (Lancaster)
STEAD, I. M. 1985 *The Battersea Shield* (London)
SWAN, V. and MONAGHAN, J. 1993 'Head pots: a North African tradition in Roman York', *Yorkshire Archaeological Journal* 65, 21-38
TOYNBEE, J. M. C. 1973 *Animals in Roman Life and Art* (London)
TURNBULL, P. 1978 'The phallus in the art of Roman Britain', *Bulletin of the Institute of Archaeology* 15, 199-206
WARD-PERKINS, J. B. 1981 *Roman Imperial Architecture* (Harmondsworth)
WRIGHT, R. P. and RICHMOND, I. A. 1955 *Catalogue of the Roman inscribed and sculptured stones in the Grosvenor Museum, Chester* (Chester)

9 Roman coins from Maryport

David Shotter

The record of Roman coin-finds at Maryport, whilst a good deal more detailed and substantial than those from many sites, contains deficiencies and confusions. The majority of coins that are known to have been found at the site are those which were at one time part of the Senhouse Collection at Netherhall. These are, however, not available for study now, and do not appear to have been seen by anyone since the Second World War.

According to J. C. Bruce (1867, 370), a list of them was made by 'the late Mr Senhouse', although this list appears to have consisted simply of an allocation of coins to their issuing authorities, with no note made either of the denominations of the coins or, more importantly, of their reverse types. Bruce does, however, indicate that the majority of the coins were denarii, and (along with other commentators) noted the presence in the Collection of 'a great many forged denarii of Trajan and Hadrian', although there is some dispute amongst the authorities as to whether these forged coins were of bronze or of lead (Birley 1961, 220). Their purpose also remains unclear (Casey 1976, 47); they may have constituted a forger's hoard, or they may have been manufactured for votive purposes. Alternatively, it is possible that they were copies made for the Senhouse family of the whole or part of a hoard that had been found locally.

Little is known of the precise find-spots of the coins in the Collection, nor when they were acquired; Stukeley, however, who in 1725 was entertained by Humphrey Senhouse (d. 1738) on a visit to the Roman site at Maryport and to other sites in the area (including Papcastle), notes that 'coins innumerable have been found formerly, now but seldom'. Stukeley indeed was the source of information concerning the only two coins in the Collection for which any information survives concerning the circumstances of discovery (*Surtees Society Publications* 76 [1883], 112 and 245).

One of these refers to an aes-issue of Trajan (rev. SPQR OPTIMO PRINCIPI SC), which was found in *c.* 1740, whilst the other cites the discovery of a 'denarius of Nero' (rev. AVGVSTVS AVGVSTA), which was found in *c.* 1741. It is clear that in fact the Neronian coin was an aureus (*RIC* I^2, 44, of AD 64-5), for its discovery is mentioned in a letter to Roger Gale from Thomas Routh of Carlisle (dated 30th May 1742, and quoted in Hutchinson 1794, 280); here the coin is said to have been found 'upon the sea shore, within flood mark'. It had, however, been lost before the publication of the most authoritative list of the coins in the Netherhall Collection (Bailey 1915, 170f).

Bruce (1867, 370) produced the following list of 115 coins:

Marcus Antonius	1
Nero	3
Vespasian	3
Titus	1
Domitian	2
Nerva	4
Trajan	18
Plotina	1
Hadrian	6
Sabina	2
Antoninus Pius	6
Faustina	1
Marcus Aurelius	11
Pertinax	1
Julia Domna	1
Geta	1
Julia Mamaea	1
Philip	1
Postumus	1
Victorinus	5
Gallienus	5
Claudius II	2
Tetricus	7
Carausius	1
Licinius	4
Constantine I	13
Fausta	1
Crispus	5
Constantine II	3
Magnentius	7
Constantius II	4
Valentinian II	1
Theodosius	1
Honorius	1

He noted that this list included the seventeen 'forged denarii' (Nerva 3, Trajan 7, Hadrian 1, Sabina 2, Antoninus Pius 4). As we have seen, this list will also have included the aureus of Nero and the aes of Trajan to which Stukeley had referred.

The next authoritative list was that published by Bailey in 1915, to which a few corrections were published by him eleven years later (CW^2 26 [1926] 422). The 1915 list was of 134 coins (of which 125 were in the Netherhall Collection and nine were other privately-owned coins); with the corrections of 1926, Bailey's list was of 129 coins:

Republic	1
Marcus Antonius	1
Nero (including the aureus, which had been lost)	3
Vespasian	4
Titus	1
Domitian	2
Nerva (including 3 forgeries)	4
Trajan (including 7 forgeries)	18
Plotina	1
Hadrian (including 1 forgery)	8
Sabina (both forgeries)	2
Antoninus Pius (including 4 forgeries)	9
Faustina I	1
Marcus Aurelius	4
Pertinax	1
Julia Domna	1
Geta	1
Julia Mamaea	1
Philip	1
Gallus	1
Gallienus	5
Postumus	1
Victorinus	6
Tetricus (I and II)	7
Claudius II	2
Carausius	1
Licinius	4
Constantine I	15
Fausta	1
Crispus	5
Constantine II	3
Magnentius	7
Constantius II	4
Valentinian II	1
Theodosius	1
Honorius	1

At first sight, Bailey included the Republican denarius found on the shore in 1893

(CW^1 16 [1900] 145; *RRC* 141, 1), but excluded four other privately-owned coins which he himself had published in 1912 (CW^2 12 [1912] 432); these consisted of an as of Hadrian (*RIC* 617), found on the shore in 1911, an antoninianus of Gallus (*RIC* 79), found at the Empire Theatre in 1911, a radiate of Victorinus (*RIC* 57), found on the shore in 1911, and an aes-issue of Constantius II as Caesar (*LRBC* I.530), found at the Queen's Head Inn in 1911. The descriptions of these, together with a comparison of Bruce's and Bailey's lists, makes it likely that these four coins were in fact included in Bailey's list of 1915, and have thus been 'double-counted' subsequently (Shotter 1990, 85; corrected in Shotter 1995).

The other group of coins to be recorded from Maryport consists of the thirteen from the excavations of 1966, which were identified and published in full detail by P. J. Casey (1976):

Republican	1 (AR)
Domitian	1 (AR)
Trajan	2 (AE)
Faustina II	1 (AE)
Lucilla	1 (AE)
Julia Domna	1 (AR)
Unassignable radiate copies	2 (AE)
Constantinian (AD 330-41)	2 (AE)
Valentinianic	1 (AE)
Theodosian	1 (AE)

A few other coins have been recorded – one of Hadrian (CW^2 86 [1986] 256), one of Maximian (*Carlisle Journal*, 2nd August 1935), and a radiate copy (CW^2 91 [1991] 272); it should be noted that the coin of Trajan Decius recorded in CW^2 91 (1991) 272 in fact came from Mote Hill, Bellhouse's presumed site of Milefortlet 25 on the coastal fortifications (Bellhouse 1989, 56: marked as Tower 24A on Fig. 1.4). In addition, the Senhouse Roman Museum has recently been shown three further coins – one each of Domitian (*RIC* 166), Antoninus Pius (*RIC* 655), and Septimius Severus (CW^2 94 [1994], 294).

As we have seen, one of the problems regarding the coins from Maryport is the lack of denominational information; the other is that the nature of the recording leaves it as virtually impossible to break down the 42 coins of the House of Constantine (AD 294-364) into shorter issue-periods. Fourteen of these coins can be securely allocated on the information provided:

AD	294-324	4
	324-330	1
	330-346	2
	346-364	7

The rest are left 'spanning' more than one issue-period:

AD	294-324	}6			
	324-330		}3		}15
	330-346			}4	
	346-364				

A notional distribution of all forty-two can be attempted, taking into account the distribution of such coins at other Cumbrian sites, although clearly care needs to be exercised in using these coins in any assessment of the length of occupation:

AD	294-324	10
	324-330	2
	330-346	19
	346-364	11

We can now produce a revised list of Roman coins from Maryport:

Republic (*RRC* 141, 1; 385, 1)	2 AR
Marcus Antonius (*RRC* 544)	1 AR
Nero including 1 AV (*RIC* I^2. 44)	3
Vespasian	4

Titus		1
Domitian including 2 AR (RIC 85, 166)		4
Nerva		1
Trajan including 3 AE		13
Plotina		1
Hadrian including 1 AE (RIC 617)		9
Antoninus Pius including 1 AE (RIC 655)		10
Faustina I		1
Marcus Aurelius		4
Faustina II AE (RIC [Marcus], 1625)		1
Lucilla		1 AE
Pertinax		1
Septimius Severus		1 AE
Julia Domna (including 1 AR RIC 560)		2
Geta		1
Julia Mamaea		1
Philip		1
Gallus		1
Gallienus		5
Claudius II		2
Postumus		1
Victorinus (including RIC 57)		6
Tetricus (I and II)		7
Unassigned radiate copies		3
Maximian (RIC V. 621)		1 AE
Carausius		1
Licinius		4
Constantine I		15
Crispus		5
Fausta		1
Constantine II		3
Constantius II		5
Constantinian		2
Magnentius		7
Valentinianic		1
Valentinian II		1 AE
Theodosius		1 AE
Honorius		1 AE
Theodosian		1 AE

This provides a site-total of 137 coins, distributed as in the table below and in the histogram (Fig. 9.1).

The use to which coin-loss statistics may be put has been shown elsewhere (Shotter 1993), although in the case of the Maryport coins we have to bear in mind that in the majority of cases we can make no allowance for wear. Clearly, we should expect such a sample to offer some indication of the date of earliest activity. However, the relevant coins (I-IV) are not overly helpful; all of those from period I are Republican issues or belonging to Marcus Antonius. The three coins are certainly denarii; Reece (1988) has demonstrated that whilst Trajan recalled old (that is, pre-Neronian) silver for melting down, such coins continued in Britain to circulate

TABLE: Coin finds from Maryport distributed by coin-period

		%			%			%
I	3	2.19	VIII	6	4.38	XV	10*	
II	–	–	IX	–	–	XVI	2*	
III	3	2.19	X	5	3.65	XVII	19*	42 30.66
IV	9	6.57	XI	1	0.73	XVIII	11*	
V	15	10.95	XII	2	1.46	XIX	1	0.73
VI	9	6.57	XIII	24	17.50	XX	–	–
VII	11	8.03	XIV	2	1.46	XXI	4	2.91

at least into the Hadrianic period, whilst those of Marcus Antonius survived in circulation into the third century AD.

No coins (legitimate or copied) of Claudius are recorded from the site, whilst those of Nero (of which one was an aureus), could be losses of any period into the early third century; none is specified as an aes-issue, the shortest-circulating of Nero's coins. The absence of aes-coins of Claudius or Nero makes it very difficult to give any support to a proposition of pre-Flavian activity at Maryport. However, the fact that nearby Papcastle has produced two Claudian copies (in the excavations of 1984) does suggest that there may have been pre-Flavian or other early activity in the area, though not necessarily at the known site. Furthermore, the discovery in field-sampling at Blennerhasset of Neronian/early Flavian pottery (Evans and Scull 1990) itself suggests that the Solway Plain may have been separated from the interior, at least as early as the governorship of Cerialis, by a road running from Carlisle to the coast – though one terminating presumably at a location other than Maryport itself (Shotter 1994a).

Nor does the Flavian period show up much more impressively: nine coins are recorded, of which two were of Domitian and one of Titus. Information regarding denominations or dates-of-issue for the coins of Vespasian is not available. However, on statistical grounds it is hard to propose an early, or even a middle, Flavian commencement for a site where Flavian coins as a whole make up only 6.5 per cent of the sample. Indeed, the closest parallel in Cumbria to the picture at Maryport is that provided by Watercrook (Potter 1979), where occupation before the late Flavian period (that is, after *c.* AD 90) was regarded as very unlikely. Indeed, on present evidence, the creation of a fort at Maryport would appear to fit best with the post-Agricolan abandonment of Scotland (Hobley 1989), and the establishment of the Stanegate *limes* (Breeze 1988; Jones 1991). This was the period during which the full occupation and consolidation of Cumbria appears to have been undertaken, with establishments at Ambleside, Hardknott and Ravenglass in the very latest years of the first century and the first quarter of the second century.

In the case of Maryport, the high showing of Trajanic issues – fifteen coins or eleven per cent of the sample – suggests that this site too should be regarded as having been established in *c.* AD 90-110, although again care has to be exercised, since the two Trajanic aes-issues recorded in the excavations of 1966 appear to have demonstrated a considerable residuality. The size of the Trajanic group of coins would, however, suggest that there is no compelling reason to view the building-records of Hadrianic date (*RIB* 851 and 855) as representing building *ab initio* (Jarrett 1976, 12).

The number of Hadrianic coins found as casual losses at Maryport (period VI) represents a slight 'trough' between the Trajanic and Antonine periods, offering a profile which is a little unusual; normally, coin-loss in the second century shows a steady decline from a peak in the Trajanic period. A number of sites in north-west England share this phenomenon with Maryport, including Lancaster and two sites on Hadrian's Wall, Castlesteads and Birdoswald. At all three sites, a plausible case can be made that they saw a period of abandonment or reduced activity coinciding with the re-occupation of southern Scotland, as garrisons were wholly or partly redeployed (Hartley 1972). Epigraphic evidence (e.g. *RIB* 832) indicates that there was building-work at Maryport in the Antonine period, although this could have occurred before AD 142 or in the later 150s, following the end of Antonine Wall I. We should remember that the installations of the Cumberland coast display three phases of activity which were punctuated by the occupations of the Antonine Wall (Potter 1977). Although Maryport may not have commenced occupation as part of the Hadrianic coastal system (and thus akin to Hadrian's Wall itself), this evidence may suggest that it came to be viewed as if it were. There can be little doubt, in view of the strength in the sample of coins of Antoninus Pius and Marcus Aurelius (periods VII and VIII), that even if occupation at Maryport was affected by the Antonine advance into Scotland, the effect was temporary only, and that full occupation was resumed after the abandonment of Scotland in *c*. AD 163, if not before.

Statistics of coin-loss become harder to discuss after the middle of the second century AD; deteriorating economic conditions in the Empire had a visible effect on the coinage, in the progressive loss from circulation of the lower denominations. By the end of the century little was left in general circulation besides the denarius and the sestertius, with a consequent effect on the coin-population and on coin-loss; inevitably, the loss of higher denominations such as these was followed by a more vigorous search (Casey 1988). In any case, if ground-surfaces were changing from earth to stone, then loss will presumably have been more easily detectable.

In view of these considerations, it is normal to find a steady decline in coin-loss through the Antonine and into the Severan periods. This indeed happens at Maryport, although the Severan period (period X) holds firmer than it does at some other sites. Notably, the closest parallel in the north-west for the pattern of coin-loss detected in the second century at Maryport is that provided by nearby Papcastle,

where the bulk of the coin-sample derives from the excavations of 1984 (Shotter 1990, 91-5), although these were largely concerned with *vicus*-locations. There is a hint too, from a much smaller (and casually-acquired) sample from Old Carlisle, that that fort may have been behaving in a similar fashion (Shotter 1996). Unfortunately, other coastal forts in north-west Cumbria have not produced samples sufficiently large to allow discussion.

We may, therefore, assume unbroken activity at Maryport from the late second into the early third centuries. Nor is there any reason to propose any deviation from this pattern during the first half of the third century: again, it is rare to encounter many coins from the reigns of Alexander Severus and his immediate successors, and a few coins are generally sufficient to demonstrate continued activity. In the mid-third century, the Empire experienced severe disruption both politically and economically. The effect upon the coinage was dramatic, and the coin population through the 260s and 270s (and beyond) was dominated by copper radiates of legitimate and rebel emperors; many of these were produced by local copying to a standard that can only be described as execrable. It is likely that at least one major centre for such copying was located in north Cumbria, at Carlisle (McCarthy 1990, 102), with another possibly at Brougham (Casey 1978).

In the present instance, it is to be regretted that the majority of the coins of period XIII are noted only in terms of their issuers, with no information surviving on the size or quality of individual coins. However, the fact that 17.5% of the whole Maryport sample derives from this period makes it closely comparable to other sites in the north-west which were occupied at this time. Individual issuers may have enjoyed an extended survival for political reasons –

for example, Constantine's spurious claim to have been descended from Claudius II – but the zenith of circulation of these coins probably tailed away from the 280s, when coins of the rebel, Carausius, became relatively abundant.

As we have seen, it is possible to recreate an approximate distribution of coins of the Constantinian periods, but it would be unwise to argue for too much from such an exercise. It would, however, seem to be uncontentious to suggest continuing and unbroken activity down to at least c. AD 350. We might, however, speculate as to whether importance should be attached to the absence of coins of Constans, and to the relative scarcity of those of his brother, Constantius II. In view of the very poor representation of coins of the House of Valentinian (period XIX), there might be a case for suggesting a disturbance between the mid-350s and c. AD 370. At the same time, the strong showing of coins of the rebel, Magnentius (AD 351-3), is striking, and perhaps finds an echo in the recently-discovered hoard from Hackthorpe near Penrith (Shotter 1994b). Possibly, Maryport temporarily lost its garrison in the aftermath of the rebellion.

As noticed above, the virtual absence of Valentinianic coins is notable, although one was recorded in the excavations of 1966. Few sites in north-west England share this feature with Maryport, particularly in view of the presence in the sample of later coins (period XXI); only Ravenglass, with a much smaller sample, shows a steep decline from periods XVIII to XIX. Whilst we may not be able to provide a precise context for this, it is intelligible in the broad terms of the reorganisation and redeployment that will have affected the west coast in the second half of the fourth century. The building of the new bastioned forts at Caer Gybi and Lancaster indicates the radical nature of the new planning.

The scarcity of coins of period XIX is the more remarkable in view of the fact that, with the generally dwindling coin-sup-

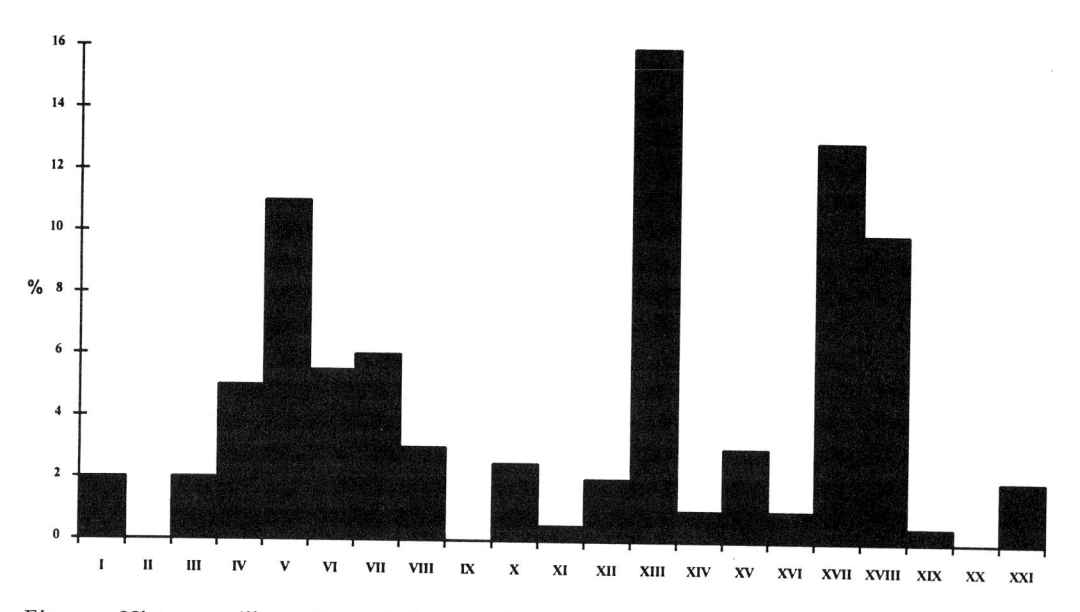

Fig. 9.1 Histogram illustrating coin-loss at Maryport

plies to Britain in the final quarter of the fourth century, coins of the House of Valentinian must normally have formed a significant part of the coin-population of that period. By contrast, the sample shows a remarkable 'recovery' in period XXI, with no fewer than four coins of the period, including one from the excavations of 1966. Of course, with no information available on the state of any of these coins, it is impossible to estimate their 'loss-dates', although these might have been well into the fifth century. The extended use of coins of the late fourth century can be paralleled at Carlisle and elsewhere (Keevil, McCarthy and Shotter 1989; McCarthy 1990, 103; Kent 1951). Furthermore, Lancaster provides a parallel on the west coast for a similar relative strength of coins of period XXI (Shotter 1990, 17).

It is clear that the west coast was militarily active in the last years of the fourth century; we have already noted the new forts at Caer Gybi and Lancaster; major reconstruction, presumably after AD 367, has been noted at Ravenglass and Bowness-on-Solway (Potter 1979). Evidence of activity in the fourth century is available from Beckfoot, Burrow Walls and Moresby. In addition, the discovery in c. 1800 of a solidus of Theodosius I beneath Muncaster Castle, and of other late coins in Furness and Cartmel, including an issue of Magnus Maximus from Broughton-in-Cartmel (Shotter 1990, 239), serves to emphasize the apparently crucial nature of the defences of the west coast in the last years of Roman occupation. It is reasonable to suppose that, as at earlier times, Maryport played a key role in the defence of the west.

Thus we can see that, although it would be inappropriate to claim certainty for the suggestions made in this paper, the coin evidence is nonetheless capable of making a positive contribution to a discussion of the history of Maryport.

Postscript

A few other coin-finds from the area are worth noting; two milefortlets of the coastal system to the north and south of Maryport have produced coins, MF 21 (Swarthy Hill) where one of Galba and two of Trajan were found; and Bellhouse's 'MF 25' (Mote Hill: contrast Fig. 1.4), which yielded three of Hadrian and one of Trajan Decius (Shotter 1995; Bellhouse 1989, 48 and 56). From Mote Hill also, it appears, came in c. 1920 a hoard of aes-issues, including coins of Hadrian.

References

BAILEY, J. B. 1915 'Catalogue of the Roman inscribed and sculptured stones, coins, earthernware etc, discovered in and near the Roman fort at Maryport, and preserved at Netherhall', CW^2 15, 135-72

BELLHOUSE, R. L. 1989 *Roman Sites on the Cumberland Coast. A new schedule of coastal sites* (Kendal)

BIRLEY, E. B. 1961 *Research on Hadrian's Wall* (Kendal)

BREEZE, D. J. 1988 'The Roman army in Cumbria', CW^2 88, 9-22

BRUCE, J. C. 1867 *The Roman Wall*, 3rd. ed. (London)

CASEY, P. J. 1976 'The coins', in Jarrett 1976, 46-8

CASEY, P. J. 1978 'The Ninekirks (Brougham) Hoard: a reconsideration', CW^2 78, 23-8

CASEY, P. J. 1988 'The interpretation of Romano-British site-finds', in Casey and Reece 1988, 39-56

CASEY, P. J. and REECE, R. (eds.) 1988 *Coins and the Archaeologist* (London)

EVANS, J. and SCULL, C. 1990 'Fieldwork on the Roman fort site of Blennerhasset, Cumbria', CW^2 90, 127-37

HARTLEY, B. R. 1972 'The Roman occupations of Scotland: the evidence of Samian ware', *Britannia* 3, 1-55

HOBLEY, A. S. 1989 'The numismatic evidence for the post-Agricolan abandonment of the Roman frontier in northern Scotland', *Britannia* 20, 69-74

HUTCHINSON, W. 1794 *The History of the*

County of Cumberland, volume II (Carlisle)

JARRETT, M. G. 1976 *Maryport, Cumbria: a Roman fort and its garrison* (Kendal)

JONES, G. D. B. 1991 'The emergence of the Tyne-Solway frontier', in Maxfield and Dobson 1991, 98-107

KEEVIL, G. D., MCCARTHY, M. R. and SHOTTER, D. C. A. 1989 'A solidus of Valentinian II from Scotch Street, Carlisle', *Britannia* 20, 254-5

KENT, J. P. C. 1951 'Coin evidence and the evacuation of Hadrian's Wall', *CW*² 51, 4-15

MCCARTHY, M. R. 1990 *A Roman, Anglian and Medieval Site at Blackfriars Street* (Kendal)

MAXFIELD, V. A. and DOBSON, M. J. (eds.) 1991 *Roman Frontier Studies 1989* (Exeter)

POTTER, T. W. 1977 'The Biglands Milefortlet and the Cumberland coast defences', *Britannia* 8, 149-83

POTTER, T. W. 1979 *Romans in North-west England* (Kendal)

REECE, R. 1988 'Numerical aspects of Roman coin-hoards in Britain', in Casey and Reece 1988, 86-100

SHOTTER, D. C. A. 1990 *Roman Coins from North-West England* (Lancaster)

SHOTTER, D. C. A. 1993 'Coin-loss and the Roman occupation of North-west England', *British Numismatic Journal* 63, 1-19

SHOTTER, D. C. A. 1994a 'Rome and the Brigantes: early hostilities', *CW*² 94, 21-34

SHOTTER, D. C. A. 1994b 'Recent finds of Roman coins in Cumbria', *CW*² 94, 291-4

SHOTTER, D. C. A. 1995 *Roman Coins from North-West England: First Supplement* (Lancaster)

SHOTTER, D. C. A. 1996 'Recent finds of Roman coins in Cumbria', *CW*² 96, 27-33

10 Senhouse of Netherhall – 1726 Achievement of Arms: recovery of an eighteenth-century masterwork

Brian Ashmore

Nine years after completing the purchases of the Manor of Alneburgh (or Ellenborough) from his six nieces, Humphrey Senhouse of Netherhall, first of four successive Lords of the Manor of that name, began modernising, extending and embellishing the old Mansion and its grounds. On 25th October 1726, he entered in his Cash Book:

Cash paid Mr Smith the stonecarver in full for himselfe and his son Thomas cutting the Caesar's pillar in the flower garding, the Shiels with the several matches of our family put up on the South East side of the Tower, two Pineapples, two Accorns, and the two litle Piramids with a Parrot on the topp of each being 26 days in doeing them at 2s 6d a day and meat for both £3 - 5s - 0
Given Thomas the son to himselfe more 2s - 0

and, belatedly, 3rd February 1727:

Cash paid John Lowson in full for sharpning the Stonecarver's tools when he cut the Caesar's pillar 1s - 0

Later views of the Hall show the 'Pineapples', the 'Accorns' and the 'two litle Piramids with a Parrot on the topp of each' as finials to the posts of three handsome gateways set in the new boundary wall, each with a straight path to the centre of the garden before the Mansion. The 'Caesar's pillar' was set in that garden – an imposing tall plinth with impressive statue of an Imperial Roman mounted upon it; so appropriate, for Humphrey possessed the incomparable collection of Roman inscriptions and sculptures from the ruins of Alauna on his land, begun 150 years earlier by his ancestor John.

In this same year he also records in his Cash Book the forwarding address for Alexander Gordon on leaving his hospitality, after inspecting and drawing those items for publication in his *Itinerarium Septentrionale*; and within four years similar hospitality was enjoyed by Horsley, likewise engaged upon his *Britannia Romana*. Both remembered their visits with gratitude, as had Camden in 1599, but also with the material contribution of a copy of their books to Humphrey's growing library.

The 'Pineapples and Accorns' did not survive later extensive alterations. The Parrots were re-located on the gate-posts for the nineteenth-century great carriage entrance off the Carlisle Road. The posts remain; but the Parrots have flown. A question remains over the fate of 'Caesar's pillar'. A sketch (no earlier than 1750) of the Netherhall front and its gardens shows an impressive statue on a plinth, set to the right of the principal drive leading straight to the front door, and also on line with the ornamental gates in the new boundary walls, thus forming the central view from

Fig. 10.1 The 1726 'Achievement' of Arms, in store before conservation

the front door and all three approaches. The statue is shown as a man in full Roman imperial military dress with helmet. This is surely the 'Caesar's pillar' of Humphrey's Day Book. Its fate has until now remained unknown.[1] Group photographs around 1890 and 1910 show no sign whatever of any 'pillar'. Recently, however, behind the south-east corner of the buildings of Netherhall School (which stands on lands originally part of the Mansion's 'pleasance'), a hitherto unnoticed sandstone 'pillar' has been found, 8 feet 7 inches tall (2.62 m), which has good claim to be identified with 'Caesar's pillar'. Its four faces depict in bas relief Julius Caesar, a 'Roman', 'a Britain' (sic) and Antoninus Pius,[2] each between 35 inches (0.89 m) and 42 inches (1.07 m) tall; they are set within panels of slightly differing dimensions, above a plinth taking up 5 feet 7 inches (1.70 m) of the full height. The entablature above one panel, however, bears the date 1718, the year after Humphrey completed his purchases of Netherhall from his six nieces and began his major refurbishment – eight years before the entry in his Day Book.[3] Despite this discrepancy of date, and despite the inferior workmanship when contrasted with the 'Achievement',[4] the present writer concludes that this is indeed the missing 'Caesar's pillar'[5] carved by Smith along with the 'Achievement'.[6]

All efforts to trace Mr Smith have been fruitless, but on the evidence of the 'Achievement' alone he was no ordinary stonecarver. The delicacy and accuracy of his detailed workmanship are equal to the best of that notable period. The 'Achievement' (Fig. 10.1) is 4 feet (1.22 m) high by 32 inches (0.91 m) maximum breadth; it is carved in solid local red sandstone, and weighs just over 4 cwts (203 kgs). The first eight cantons, set in two lines, being the major heritage, are arranged across a convex face at its broadest. The last four –

'Several matches of our family' – occupy a re-entrant curved frame below. The whole is garlanded in the florid early-eighteenth-century style, with a pensive, cherubic head and bust to either side, one male, one female, set proud from the scroll work and foliage. Centrally at the top is the Senhouse 'Popinjay' crest, matched at the base with the mask of a fearsome lion. The relevance of the lion still eludes identification, although it is not conventional decoration. It was also executed on wooden bosses around the cornice of the hall of the Mansion. Several of these have survived as a gift to the writer from Roger Senhouse (died 1970), the last Lord of the Manor to bear the Senhouse name.

R. S. Boumphrey and C. R. Hudleston faithfully note, in their indispensable encyclopedia *Cumberland Families and Heraldry*, that within the Senhouse family the Crest is sometimes recorded as a 'Popinjay' and sometimes a Parrot, the latter always being used when the bird appears in the Arms. The distinction merits enquiry. Parrots are not indigenous to the old Norman kingdoms, and may not have been known when first adopted in the Senhouse Arms; whereas 'Popinjay' is the rural name for the native green woodpecker, certainly from the fifteenth century onwards. Significantly, the Senhouse Crest was 'Vert', and minuscule flakes of green paint have been detected on the Crest atop the 'Achievement'. Yet in the Arms, the Parrot is always registered as 'Or'. It may be surmised that the colloquial adoption of 'Popinjay' by Elizabethan times, for an overdressed fop of little brain, stimulated re-designation of the bird as a Parrot from the time when systematic registration of the Arms of families of gentry status began. Roger Senhouse referred to his Crest as a 'Popinjay', and his Arms as a 'Parrot'. The superbly accurate workmanship on the 'Achievement' lends credence to the interpretation that the slight distinctions in representation of the two birds are intentional. Beneath the lion mask, a label carries the motto *Vae victis* ('Let the vanquished beware') and the date 1726.

The south-east side of the Tower selected by Humphrey for mounting his prestigious sculpture has undergone major alterations, being first pierced for large windows at the first and second floors, perhaps by Humphrey himself, but certainly in the eighteenth century. In the next century, following the Pocklington marriage, a very large library and music room were built across its full width up to and including the second floor, with access provided by converting those windows to doors. Until the 1950s this tower wall belonging to the fourteenth century was thus wholly invisible within the building and its heavy interior wall plaster, returning to view only after demolition of this grand extension, brought on by structural unsoundness aggravated by lack of maintenance. The eighteenth-century stone window frames were revealed, and the openings built up with rough sandstone masonry. Exposure of the original external wall, however, has also revealed the earlier infill of a cavity with random undressed sandstone pieces.

The cavity was in the centre of the wall face, extending for about 4 feet (1.20 m), at a height between approximately 10 feet (3 m) and 14 feet (4.25 m) above ground level, mid-way between the eighteenth-century window frames, with its top slightly above their stone sills. From its peculiar shape roughly conforming with the outline of the 'Achievement', it may now be concluded that this cavity in the massive thickness of the Tower wall was made for the setting of Mr Smith's work; and very imposing it must have been there.

Three years after the payment to Smith, Humphrey's Cash book records, under the date 15th November 1729:

Paid 28th of October cash to Mr Read, Painter, in full for his painting (see note on file) –
£9 5s - 0
Cash given him more to his nephew Hynde –
4s - 0
Lent Mr Christian which I pd Mr Read for painting his Coat of Arms and Crest on his Chaise –
5s - 0
(marginal note) – 'pd me'

Mr Christian was Humphrey's neighbour, Lord of the Manor of Ewanrigg. This entry suffices to identify the painter of the 'Achievement' as Matthias Read (1669-1747), a Londoner who came with his master, Jan Wyck, via Ireland, to the honey-pot of Whitehaven. Here the enterprises of the redoubtable Sir John Lowther were creating abundant wealth, with the accompanying growth in artistic and cultural aspirations which characterised the 'Age of Enlightenment'. Read soon found a patron in William Gilpin of Scaleby Castle, Steward to Sir John Lowther, probably the richest and most influential employment in the County, and secured the post of tutor in art to Gilpin's children, and indeed to Gilpin himself. Thereafter, his fortune was made, enabling him to acquire a most desirable plot in the new development in Whitehaven; to build thereon an elegant and substantial mansion; and to marry into local 'society'; 'the nephew Hynde' to whom Humphrey gave 'extra 4s - 0' was the son of his wife's brother.

Amongst his many commissions for landscapes, altar-pieces, and the copying of Dutch old masters for the rising middle class (who could not afford 'originals' to embellish the walls of their fine new town houses), Read undertook interior decorating. One of his Gilpin pupils, the Reverend William, records that

'... hardly a house in Whitehaven whose master could afford it had not a picture or two painted in panels over doors or windows by his hand.'

Humphrey Senhouse was amongst those smaller landowners who deemed it prudent to express alliance with the rising, and ruthless, ambition of Lowther and his faction, encouraged no doubt by his cousins in Whitehaven. As the Curwens at Workington were discovering, it was perilous to resist the Lowther intention to bring under their control, directly or indirectly, all the coal and sea-port resources of West Cumberland. Since no marital alliances had ever been contemplated, there is a strong whiff of 'protection money' about the gift by Humphrey's predecessor, John, of the prize of his Roman collection, the great *Volanti Vivas* altar celebrated by Camden (*RIB* 812: Fig. 4.13 above, p. 83), to Sir John Lowther in 1683, to increase the prestige of the Lowther Whitehaven residence. Read's engagement at Netherhall will certainly not have displeased the Lowther faction.

Regrettably, the 'note on the file' cannot now be traced. There is no record of exactly what Read undertook, beyond the armorial work for Mr Christian, which at least strongly suggests that his commission from Humphrey included the painting of the 'Achievement', probably observed by Christian and admired before adding his chaise to the work to be done for his neighbour. It is nonetheless instructive in the light of Read's wealthy life-style to compare his remuneration at £9 5s with that of the stonecarver Smith, at least as creative and accomplished in his art, at a mere £3 5s plus meat for his 26 days' hard labour. Smith was clearly not a Lowther protegé: but for the survival of the 'Achievement' (and, it seems, the Pillar as well) he has passed from this earth as though he had never been.

Exposed to fierce elements, Read's work deteriorated while Smith's endured. At some time the 'Achievement' was coated overall in heavy black paint. This may have happened before the post-1835 period, when removal from the tower wall became unavoidable to permit the building of the great library. It was then set in a protected position within the eastern wall of the long classical portico, built at that time across the front entrance of the Mansion, following Pocklington's marriage with the heiress Elizabeth Senhouse. Within this portico were arranged the major items of the Roman collection, down to the last days of Netherhall. Being effectively an inside wall, the east wall of the portico was lightly constructed, the 'Achievement' being set in a cunningly-disguised heavy plaster panel, where, if observed at all across the Roman sculptures, it presented itself as a ponderous, black and ugly object.

The portico 'improvement' also involved the nice conceit of building into the house wall itself, alongside the entrance door, the stone from the Roman fort (*RIB* 852: Fig. 8.3 above, p. 114) recording that 'vexillations of the II Augusta and XX Valeria Victrix legions built this', and the sculptured tombstone to a Roman officer or cavalryman, brought to Netherhall in the eighteenth century from Stanwix (*RIB* 2030), and now displayed in Tullie House Museum, Carlisle. Retrieval of those two stones was essential before the crumbling portico collapsed, with the Mansion following shortly after.

The personal interest of their Manager, and the generosity of Seymour Plant Hire, provided masons of outstanding skill who addressed this task on 1st June 1973. The Roman stones were removed without damage. As there was time in hand, we tackled the 'Achievement' although it lay outside our remit. It was an anti-climax to find that it was only set in heavy plaster, from which it came away easily. Not so fortunate was the discovery that, at over 4 cwts, it weighed twice as much as the other stones combined; the task of getting it into store with them, where it remained until 1992, was considerable.

As owner of the Collection and Lord of the Manor through his Senhouse descent, Mr P. J. Scott Plummer at first planned to retain the 'Achievement' somewhere within the Netherhall grounds. Once the impracticability of this project was fully realised, he asked the Trustees of the Senhouse Roman Museum to accept it for mounting in the reception area of the Museum, created two years earlier for the bulk of the Collection. The 'Achievement' was added to a selection of major Roman items for immediate conservation, under the hands of Sue and Lawrence Kelland of Street, Somerset, well known for their experience of sandstone and armorial church statuary. After several weeks of delicate and painstaking attention in the bleak environment of the store, the black paint was wholly removed, revealing, unexpectedly, the remains of the colouring applied by Matthias Read.

Mounting at the Museum was undertaken by the architect to the Senhouse Museum, Cyril Winskell, MBE, FRIBA, of Newcastle upon Tyne, and the young Maryport builder Kevin Pattinson. The massive structure of the Museum building, a former Naval Gun Battery (constructed in 1885), was clearly capable of supporting the weight of the 'Achievement' on the wall of the reception area, but neither the original method of fixing it in the tower wall, nor its nineteenth-century insertion in a new wall, could be adopted. The solution found was a central, concealed, steel hanger, with constraining side brackets. The problem of raising it some thirteen feet (4 m) above floor-level into a position over the entrance doors to the Exhibition Hall was resolved, thanks to the strength and courage of three men, as lifting gear proved impracticable.

Conservation, deliberately eschewing any element of restoration, has transformed the 'Achievement'. With its off-white garlanding and surround, and the discreet remains of its originally brilliant colours, it seems to float in air. Visitors have echoed the view expressed by Pattinson and his two assistants, on recovering from their task: 'everyone will think it is a polystyrene or plaster cast'! It is hard to match in Cumbria this outstanding tribute to eighteenth-century stonecarving and painting, coupled with its twentieth-century conservation and mounting.

Acknowledgements
The 'Achievement' has been rescued, conserved, and mounted at no cost to the Senhouse Museum Trustees through the generosity of Seymour Plant Hire; of Cyril Winskell; of Kevin Pattinson; and especially of the Lord of the Manor, P. J. Scott Plummer, Esq., to all of whom the writer, as instigator and manager of the project, wishes to record his deepest appreciation.

Notes
1. Roger Senhouse spoke of it as overthrown and vandalized shortly before 1950, but his recollection may have been confused by memory of a nineteenth-century plinth (and urn, or small female statue?), in the turning circle of Joseph Pocklington's extended drive across the front of the Mansion, some 20 yards east of the position indicated in Humphrey's 'flower garding'.
2. The choice of the two 'imperial' figures points strongly to Humphrey's selection: Julius Caesar is self-evident as a symbol of Rome, and Antoninus Pius is the only emperor recorded by name in the Netherhall Collection of Humphrey's time (*RIB 850*).
3. On the other hand Humphrey's Day Books are otherwise wholly silent over commissioning, or paying for, this monument, and there are no other references to it, whether in 1718 or at any other date.

4   There is a marked contrast for an eighteenth-century stone-carver between the layout, content and surroundings of an armorial presentation and an attempt to present four wholly imagined figures from remote antiquity, whose delineation by notable antiquarians in that century can only be regarded as crude.

5   There may well be a strong element of artistic license in the post-1750 sketch, which clearly shows a statue rather than a pillar.

6   Its removal from the 'flower garding' to its present position on the line of the Roman road from the fort, through the Mansion grounds, on its approach to the river crossing (if we accept that it occurred), is consistent with Pockington's dedication to antiquities. He was not averse, indeed, to creating them, as shown by his creation of pastiche follies on his island in Derwentwater, and the building of Netherhall's long classical portico to display the largest items in the Collection. On balance, however, I believe this 1718 Pillar to be genuine. Removal to its present site, where happily it has remained *in situ*, is consistent with Pockington's reshaping of the drive and frontage.

Armorial bearings

The Armorial bearings on the Achievement are:

Cantons 1 & 6: SENHOUSE: *Or a parrot proper with sable canton* (John Senhouse, ?1534-1604; first sole Senhouse, Lord of the Manor of Alneburgh; he succeeded his elder brother Peter who died young and unmarried)

Cantons 2 & 5: EAGLESFIELD: *Gules 3 Eagles displayed Or* (Elizabeth Eaglesfield, elder daughter of Gawen; mother of Peter and John above; last Eaglesfield Lord of the Manor)

Cantons 3 & 8: PONSONBY of HAILE: *Gules a chevron between 3 combs Argent* (Anne, 6th daughter of John Ponsonby, wife of John Senhouse, ?1547-1609)

Cantons 4 & 7: BLENNERHASSET of FLIMBY: *Gules a chevron Ermine between 3 Dolphins embowed Argent* (husband of John's eldest daughter Jane, born c. 1576)

Canton 9: SKELTON of ARMATHWAITE: *Azure a Fess between 3 Fleurs-de-lys Or* (Frances, daughter of Lancelot Skelton, wife of John's son and heir Peter, ?1569-1654)

Canton 10: WHARTON of GILLINGWOOD, Yorkshire: *Sable a Maunch Argent* (Elizabeth Wharton, 3rd daughter of Humphrey; wife of Peter Senhouse's son and heir John, d. 1667: from this marriage the name Humphrey entered the Senhouse family for the next three centuries)

Canton 11: HUDLESTON of HUTTON JOHN: *Gules Fretty Argent* (Mary, daughter of Andrew Hudleston, 2nd wife of John, ?1648-1677, 2nd son and heir of John Senhouse and Elizabeth Wharton)

Canton 12: KIRKBY of ASHLACK, Lancashire: *Argent 2 bars Gules, on a canton of the last a Cross Moline Or* (Eleanor, daughter of William Kirkby, wife of Humphrey Senhouse, 1669-1738, who bought the manor from his six nieces, and commissioned the Achievement)

Crest: *A Popinjay Vert*, for Senhouse

11 George Senhouse of Maryport 1739-1793

Mary E. Burkett

Netherhall was the home of the Senhouse family and Humphrey was the favoured name. The second Humphrey (1706-1770: Fig. 11.1) and his wife Mary (1713-1790: Fig. 11.2), eldest daughter and co-heir of Sir George Fleming, Bishop of Carlisle, were married in 1731. Humphrey was High Sheriff in 1742. Their first son, Humphrey (Fig. 11.3), was born the year following their marriage, and he was later to be Mayor of Cockermouth, in 1786. George, the second son to live, was born in 1739. His brothers Joseph and William came next, and there were also three daughters who survived.

If it were not for the many letters written by Humphrey to various people concerning his son, and luckily kept, we should not know the tragic story of George's life. The letters are lodged at the County Record Office in Carlisle; some were published in 1965.[1] In them we have a fairly full story of his early promise, and then of his sad decline and humiliating fall. Alas, there are no pictures definitely attributable to him, although recently a photograph of one of his drawings has been discovered (p. 155 below). All we know is that his artistic reputation as a young teenager was extremely promising. So good did he appear to friends and family at art, at the age of eleven or twelve, that it was recommended that he go to no less a famous artist than Hogarth, for tuition and as an apprentice. His parents encouraged and indulged him, and were delighted with his talents.

It is clear from correspondence between George's father and Captain William Thynne, of London, beginning in 1751, how seriously the family took George's talents. Hogarth declined to take him, although he was sympathetic. After all, William Hogarth's father had been a Cumbrian. He, however, recommended Mr Knapton, 'who is chiefly a Portrait Painter, and who is at present employed in Drawing the Princess of Wales and all her children in one grand picture'.[2] Both Hogarth and Knapton thought the boy too young, so other names were put forward – Mr Stratfield of Lombard Street, Arthur Devis, William Hoare, and Thomas Hudson; the last had trained with Joshua Reynolds. From this distinguished list, Arthur Devis was chosen, understanding him to be a 'Boy of Genius'. Dr John Brown, essayist, poet and another friend of Humphrey Senhouse, described Devis as having 'the appearance of a good-natured, sensible and sober man'.[3] George was to serve his apprenticeship with Devis for a sum of a hundred and fifty guineas for a period of seven years. He would lodge and eat with the Devis family, but pay for his own washing.

It was with great hope that in 1751 arrangements were finalised for George to develop his artistic leanings, '. . . to which the turn of his Genius is adapted and for which Nature seems to have designed him . . .' George had to take an example of his work to the various prospective teachers to prove his genius. He chose a picture entitled 'The gentleman that walks on his Heel & Toe', and it was said that this picture 'showed his extreme talent more than any copy'. Its present whereabouts are alas unknown. Some people had thought that an engraver's training would be too practical for him. Thynne was full of praise for George's creative talents, and did not wish to restrict him in any way. So with great excitement the long journey was made to London.

After a short while Devis certainly seemed to be very pleased with the boy's progress and talent. George, in his letters, was thrilled at being with Devis. A letter soon after his arrival in 1752 from George to his mother reads:

'Dear Mama, Mr Devis's Brother (who is a very good man) took me with him last Sunday to see the King's palace at Kensington, which tho' the Gardens are very fine, yet the Palace did not at all answer my expectation. For I thought it would have more grandeur in it than any thing I had seen before . . .'[4]

Another undated letter reads:

'Mr Devis's Brother (who is a very good Landscape Painter) says he will carry me to Whitehall with him to see the seven Cartoons of Raphael which I fancy will be something far grander than anything I have seen yet.'

Then on June 4th George wrote:

'Dear Papa. Cousin Kirkby's Clerk went with me this afternoon to St Pauls, which tho' it be a very Grand building, yet I think it not quite so uniform as the minster at York. Mrs Kirkby went with me the other day to see the foundling hospital where I was very agreeably entertain'd with some very fine History paintings done by the most celebrated hands this age can afford. I have seen Aunt Flemming who was very kind to me and took me with her into the Park to take a walk. I have not seen any of the Royal family yet but I fancy I shall very soon. All my very good friends at London give their services to you. I am (Dear Pappa) your most ob't son, George Senhouse. P.S. Please give my Duty to Mamma and love to Brothers and Sisters.'[5]

William C. Kirkby, a cousin of the Senhouses, and a delightful and sensitive character, was also looking after the affairs of George, and constantly keeping in touch with his father. At the time Devis himself was having difficulties in selling his own work; so perhaps the thought of employing a 'genius' for the relatively low sum of one hundred and fifty guineas for seven years seemed to be a good investment.

By the end of the summer of 1752 all still seemed happy in the apprenticeship. A letter to Humphrey from Cousin William Kirkby, dated 12th July 1752, reads 'Mr Devis says he thinks he will not only prove a good painter but a great one'. George's own letters were positive, and express happiness with his placement. His descriptions of the splendid sights and architecture of London showed plenty of confidence, such as his comparing St Paul's unfavourably with York Minster. Here his northern loyalty came to the fore in rather naive fashion; yet he was only twelve. His anticipation of the next 'grand sight' showed his youthful zest for life.

In 1753, aged fourteen, he had however a bad attack of smallpox, which may help to account for his later problems. 'George contracted smallpox in one of the epidemics which periodically swept through the Capital. By all accounts he was very ill and delirious at the peak of the attack. Many years afterwards people were wondering if it had permanently affected his brain, but the probability is that his delirium was due to the high fever in the gener-

Fig. 11.1 Portrait of Humphrey Senhouse II (1706-1770), artist unknown (private collection)

al systemic infection, rather than actual inflammation of his brain tissue causing long-lasting damage; otherwise it is more likely that he would have died there and then. But he recovered.

'Whether this serious illness and his long subsequent convalescence from smallpox was the cause of his losing interest in painting is questionable. At fourteen to fifteen years old it was dawning upon George that there was more to do in London than could be seen from the window of Arthur Devis' studio, and more to the Arts than simply drawing and painting.

'He widened his artistic horizons into literature and drama. He started to spend much of his time reading novels and plays, spending what money he had on going to the theatre, and the pleasures of the town,

Fig. 11.2 Portrait of Mary Senhouse (1713-1790), after whom 'Mary['s] Port' is named, artist unknown (Maryport Maritime Museum)

and dallying with dress and the fashions of the day, all rather limited by his inexperience and his purse. His scant pocket money and family allowance simply showed how differently Maryport and London looked at the cost of living, and what sort of living. George was developing a chip on his shoulder about it.'[6]

The letters begin again in December 1754 on a much less happy note. Problems were arising of an almost petty nature. William Kirkby reported that George complained that his father should pay for his washing, and William almost pleaded his case, saying that it was a trifling cost, and that George's allowance was small enough. William himself added: 'have also disbursed some other small sums'. Apparently George was staying in bed late, 'sometimes till mid-morning', overspend-

Fig. 11.3 Portrait of Humphrey Senhouse III (1732-1814), artist unknown (Maryport Maritime Museum)

ing and going to play-houses – innocent enough for any teenager then or now, one might say. But in a letter of 20th February 1755, Mr Devis complained about George's behaviour, saying that it had been unsatisfactory for the last twelve months. Despite the advice of friends who had tried to make him reform he had got worse, and Devis said also he had become lazy.

'... his whole thoughts is took up with Dress, Pleasure and reading of plays and novels, and painting ... is now quite disagreeable to him.'

Similar complaints came from Dr Brown, a

family friend, and from Kirkby, who strongly suggested a meeting between George and his father.

'... the boy is of a very obstinate temper and whatever he determines upon is to be done at all hazards.'

Kirkby was not completely damning the boy, as he suggested in a subsequent letter that it was 'youth to blame', and that George had no serious vices. Then Brown reported that George had serious desires to join the army. He and George travelled north together, back to Netherhall. Alas, George's self-will led to arguments, but even Dr Brown said to his father that despite the misunderstandings George was 'good company upon the road'.

Back in Maryport, his father and he must have come to an agreement, and by the autumn of 1755 Humphrey had got the help of influential friends to get him into Colonel Hengwood's regiment at Canterbury with an ensign commission in the 20th Regiment of Foot; the General was Wolfe. His wish to enter the army fitted in with his image of being a dashing young man. His father hoped that the break from art would make him, in the end, return to it, and encouraged him to enlist

'... in the hope that his eccentricities and odd behaviour might not be too noticeable amid the far-flung duties of the Army, trying to keep the Highlands of Scotland and the North American continent under English control'.[7]

Once again full of promise and with all his new kit, he travelled south. Alas, Mr Kirkby said he was 'as profligate as before', going 'to plays', which Kirkby excused him for, as he said it proved 'a soldier's spirit', and thought 'it was rather sowing wild oats than the seeds of schizophrenia'.

But by January he seemed to have become antagonistic, and was 'in a scrape' with another ensign. In March he wrote home and apologised for not writing earlier, explaining, bluntly but truthfully, that he was too idle. He asked his father for money, and did not even pay for the postage on his own letter.

But also in that month, friends of his father told him that his son stood a good chance of military preferment if he behaved himself. His temperament went from 'highs' to 'lows'. When in a 'high' he was 'intolerably arrogant' with his seniors and his equals, while his 'lows' brought forth the deepest contrition. Finally, these moods became so bad that in the spring of 1757 his own will became paralysed, and his letters ceased until the autumn of 1757.

He had lasted twenty months in the army before he walked out. In the next letter, on 1st November 1757, George wrote that he had deserted all his possessions, and in his rage walked the 170 miles from Exeter to London. He wrote in the tones of one who is persecuted, and described an 'unlucky' step he had made, allowing his 'enemies' to have a 'handle' against him. The reason he gave for leaving was that four officers junior to him had received promotion before he had. If he had stayed in the army, he would undoubtedly have risked a court martial.

'What was drying up was George's ability to cope with his personal relationships inside the Regiment, and with it his self-control. He did not take kindly to being told curtly that if he could not afford to buy a camp bed he would have to sleep on the ground when his unit moved to Dorchester. He grumbled and quarrelled, resented instruction and guidance, and started to complain of persecution by conspiracies fostered against him. The shadow of schizophrenia was creeping up on him with paranoid stealth.'[8]

Dishevelled and distraught, he arrived on the doorstep of Mr Kirkby, in London, not making himself very popular. His father was trying to find him another military post, but this time none of his influential friends would support him. In the meantime George's spirits rose and fell to depressions in which he thought a plot had been made to get him out of the army in favour of someone else. He was indignant in his letters when his father did not quite believe in the plot. Then he would be sorry and apologise for being such a disappointment to his parents. 'But of course he really had not got away with it so lightly. He was left to come to terms with himself. The Senhouse family were appalled as the ripples of the scandal spread around Maryport and Carlisle. In everyone's eyes it was one thing to emulate the Rake's Progress in London, but quite another for a young officer to desert from the Army'.[9]

At last even Kirkby's patience ran out and George moved into a coffee house, pawning all his belongings. He lied to his father about where he had got the money. He tried to explain his failure with Devis in quite contrary terms to those he had expressed before, now saying that Devis had treated him badly as an apprentice, and made him 'sit with the servant'.

Humphrey was by now really worried about George, and sent for him in December 1757, to come home to Maryport. 'Although firmly entrenched with those paranoid feelings about people conspiring to persecute him, and trick him, and quarrel with him, George does not seem to have lost entirely all touch with reality. He did not claim to hear voices in his brain, or to have too disjointed a pattern of thought. He did not withdraw into silence or immobility. In fact he made the journey north unescorted, so his behaviour en route must have been tolerable to his fellow passengers. Perhaps his ability to keep in touch with reality ebbed and flowed capriciously from time to time'.[10] For a while he stayed at Carlisle with Humphrey's brother-in-law, Mr J. Thompson, who said George was again abject for his misdeeds, but seemed 'rather dull'. He stayed on with Mr Thompson until March 1759; the latter seemed to have a good effect on George, who was still repentant. But then even Mr Thompson wrote to his father, saying that George's temper was even more unpredictable, and that he had begun to go for very long walks of up to twenty-four hours, by himself. At this time George wrote a letter to his father with the cryptic message that James Lowther was the 'greatest villain in the world' and that he (George) was not 'disposed to see anyone'.

In April 1759 correspondence between Mr Senhouse and Dr Carlisle showed that George had finally lost all control over himself. He had been quiet, after a visit from his father, spending two days in his room combing and dressing his hair, but finally chopping it all off and wrapping a napkin round his head. 'Vincent van Gogh, one hundred and fifty years later, made much the same sort of gesture in cutting off his ear in a similar frenzy, and maybe with a similar disease.'[11] George was now having a full-blown mental breakdown.

As a last resort his father made arrangements, through his Carlisle doctor Dr Carlisle, with a Dr Chew of Billington, near Preston, for George to go to the latter's home for mental patients (later this institution was referred to as 'Mad House Farm'). It is curious that he was not sent, like most other mentally sick people from northern Cumbria, to 'The Creighton' on the Solway. Perhaps this was to distance him from the family. He had to be controlled round the clock on the journey down to Preston.

'Once admitted into Billington asylum, things were not so bad for George. He was locked in a reasonably comfortable room, for fifteen shillings a week, inclusive of meals and a servant to attend him. Medicines were to be charged extra, and Dr Chew struck a pretty bargain that his professional fee would be one guinea per week if serviceable to George's case, or dropped to five shillings a week if the treatment was not effective. Linen, clothes and shaving extra. The Senhouses thought that the terms were on the high side, but at least twenty-year-old George was in safe hands at long last'.[12]

Dr Chew's asylum was a very respectable place, and by May 1759 Dr Chew reported that there were fewer 'oddities of temper' in George, although no major improvement took place until October. In November he wrote to his father saying that he felt better, and that he would like a flute; also that he had been doing some drawing. On one occasion Dr Dixon of Whitehaven was sent down to see him.[13]

The faithful steward Philip Nelson visited him every year to pay the annual fee of £50. This ended in 1774 when George received an annuity from an Aunt.[14] It may have been at this time or later that he drew a portrait of Philip Nelson. Just as this article was about to go to press, Miss C. Dixon, a descendant of Philip Nelson, very unexpectedly after thirty years of searching showed me a photograph of a drawing by George (Fig. 11.4). It was presumably done on one of Nelson's visits to Billington, and the picture itself used to hang at Netherhall, but alas no trace of it exists now. Nelson was born in 1730 and died in 1806. The drawing shows him in profile against a carefully shaded background. His age appears to be no more than about thirty-eight, and he is wearing jacket, waistcoat, shirt and necktie. His face is serious and he looks intently forwards. Depiction of the shoulder-length hair shows considerable skill in draughtsmanship, and the technique of the hatching lines is particularly confident. Despite the fact that George had been so ill and was in the Asylum, the

Fig. 11.4 Drawing of Philip Nelson by George Senhouse

drawing illustrates his considerable artistic ability. The dimensions of this work are however unknown: it was probably only quite a small drawing.

'George had enough insight to realise the Mercy of it all. He knew that he could not cope with the outside world; nor could the outside world cope with him. From time to time he could not cope with himself. In the best sense of the word, 'asylum', he had found refuge. Whether he was then labelled as having some species of maniacal disorder, or what a couple of centuries later would have been called some sort of schizophrenia, really did not matter to George. Some days he felt muddled and poorly, some days he saw life with the clarity of an artist's eye, and felt well. Most mental diseases have their ups and downs, their remissions and their relapses'.[15]

'Dr Chew explained about these ups and downs. Sometimes George was looking better, with less oddities of temper, more muscular and fleshy; sometimes he was emaciated when the disorder became violent. Sometimes he had to be locked up and restrained; sometimes he was allowed to stroll free in the gardens.

'Sometimes he took an intelligent interest in the outside world. He was much moved by the newspaper report of the death of General James Wolfe storming the Heights of Abraham at Quebec, and reminisced about his days in the Regiment and that he might have been sent to Quebec with Wolfe. He enquired very sensibly about his father's progress in building a new chapel in Maryport. At other times he wrote home in contrite mood to ask for forgiveness for all he had brought down on the heads and hearts of the Senhouse family. Above all he had time to think: when he could.

'Better than that. Something re-kindled his artistic urge and talent. He had last laid down his pencils and paint-brushes five years earlier in Arthur Devis' studio in London. In those five turbulent years he had forsworn all further contact with drawing and painting. Now in the peace of Billington Asylum the repressions of the outside world were lifted from his mind, and all the whisperings of his early youth were heard again, the eager eye of the artist, the guiding of his hand on the drawing paper.'[16] One can do no better than quote the words from one of his letters to his father:

'You would be extremely diverted if you were to see some drawings that I have made of the people here, which I peg up against the wall and entertain myself with looking at 'em. I have drawn some little landscapes and heads besides. When I return home I shall probably bring some of them with me.'[17]

But he never came out of Billington, and as his condition improved, he lived a sedentary and uneventful life, spending thirty-five years in all there. We know that he sat next to Dr Chew for some of his meals, and with Dr Chew's son who was also to become a doctor there. So George wasted his life of 54 years, until he died, still at Billington, in 1793. All through his stay he had sent letters to his father, and when Humphrey had died in 1770 George continued to write affectionate letters to his mother. She in turn, as she got older, used to worry about him, and was obviously deeply sad that he had not achieved their early hopes. She died in 1790, three years before George. They had corresponded closely, and on 4th May 1789 she had sent a Mrs Wigglesworth down to see that he was being cared for properly, and to report back.

What was the cause of George's illness? Because of the availability of George's letters, several well-qualified modern doctors have been persuaded to examine them, both for their content and their graphological details. Dr Chew had thought that the trouble might be mercury poisoning, but one expert I consulted, Dr Frank Madge, has discounted that, feeling that the increased depressions would have been described today as a nervous breakdown. It could also, he felt, be a viral infection which developed after his smallpox attack, and which would have manifested itself later. Infection of the endocrine glands can lead to manic depressive psychosis, which would cause the patient to experience exaggerated elevation followed by lowness. Another physician, Dr David Sloss, feels that today his condition could per-

Fig. 11.5 Billington near Preston, 'Mad House Farm', front elevation

Fig. 11.6 Billington near Preston, 'Mad House Farm', rear elevation

haps have been rectified: 'maybe it was a sort of schizophrenia which a simple pill could have balanced'. George's writing varies from being neat and tidy to a terrible scrawl, crossed out and covered by blots of ink.

The location of the hospital at Billington at first eluded us. Dr Madge and I searched for records at Preston; but there was no sign of any. Then one day, on the steps of the Royal Academy, Dr Madge was talking by chance with the next person in the queue. He asked where she lived, and when she replied 'near Preston', he asked if she had ever heard of Billington Asylum. "Yes, of course", replied Mrs Sylvia Hopwood. "It was known as Mytton Fold Farmhouse, and later as Mad-House Farm, but it's a restaurant now." By a stroke of luck we had found it!

When I visited the house, in 1985, the owner said that he had tried not to tell people of its former use, as knowledge of it might have mitigated against the success of the new restaurant. The house is well constructed, in its own grounds (Figs. 11.5-6). One very interesting fact in the life of this building is that, when it had ceased to be a mental home in the late nineteenth century, after both Dr Chews had died and gone, the main staircases to the first and second floors had been taken out, leaving only the ground floor in use for nearly a hundred years. As a result absolutely no-one could see the cells, which remained inaccessible on the second floor. Just before my visit new stairs had been put back, prior to transforming the house into a restaurant: the former bedrooms were still intact, with narrow slit-holes and bars in the doors of some, through which the inmates took their food. One room has a painted dado and a good view: might this room even have been the one George occupied? The visit was an emotional experience. Legend still hung around the place.

Apparently the locals said that their grandfathers' generation had gone on Sundays to visit Dr Chew's establishment to look at art exhibitions there, and had paid a shilling per head for the visit. Could that have been referring back even to George's day?

There is no gravestone for George: Dr Chew's and his son's graves can be seen in the little churchyard of Langho, one mile away; but neither there nor in Cross Canonby has it been possible to trace a headstone for George Senhouse. He was buried on 28th July 1793 at Langho, according to the register. More humiliating still, some genealogical books, such as *Burke's Peerage*, have actually cut out all reference to his birth or life: such was the shame our ancestors felt about any mental illness. 'The disease' was just deleted from existence. Until more works definitely attributable to George Senhouse turn up, either painted during his apprenticeship with Devis, or when he was at Billington (he often told his mother in letters that he had been doing a lot of sketches, and we now know what one looked like: do any originals survive?), we may never have enough evidence to put him on the artistic map of Cumbria and indeed of Britain.

For a long time I have questioned the attributions of some paintings ascribed to Devis. In the exhibition of his work in Preston and London in 1983/84, it was obvious that there was great unevenness in some of the works.[18] Could some have been completed by his pupil? In my survey of Cumbrian portraits, conducted in 1986/7, I searched the northern counties for evidence of work by George Senhouse; but until one has seen a picture definitely by him it is difficult to attribute a work to him on stylistic grounds alone without a signature. From the title of the picture which he took to his possible teachers, 'A Gentleman that walks on Heel & Toe', one visualises a lively person walking with verve. Could this painting still exist, and be recognised by its title? Unless new evidence turns up one day in Devis' papers, we may never know.

Acknowledgements

I am most grateful to Sylvia Hopwood, who was instrumental in locating the site of the asylum at Billington, and who conducted much independent research on its progress as an asylum. She followed up local press-cuttings and parish registers, and provided the much-needed connection between George Senhouse and his time at Preston. The late Dr Frank Madge threw much light on George's medical condition on the basis of the letters available, as did Dr David Sloss. I am also grateful to the owner of the asylum building today for granting me access to the interior. The Cumbrian portraits survey mentioned in the last paragraph was made possible by my tenure of a Leverhulme Fellowship, and I am grateful to the Leverhulme Trust for that award. Mr C. L. Randall kindly supplied Figs. 11.5-6 and prepared the master copy of the Senhouse Family Tree, a condensed version of which appears on page 160.

Notes

1 Hughes 1965, passim.
2 Hughes 1965, 90
3 Hughes 1965, 92
4 Hughes 1965, 96
5 Hughes 1965, 98
6 Dr Frank Madge, pers. comm.
7 ibid.
8 ibid.
9 ibid.
10 ibid.
11 ibid.
12 ibid.
13 Miss C. Dixon, pers. comm.
14 ibid.
15 Dr Frank Madge, pers. comm.
16 ibid.
17 George Senhouse, letter
18 Harris, Cross and Sartin 1983

References

HUGHES, E. 1965 *North Country life in the eighteenth century*, Volume 2 (Durham)

HARRIS, J., CROSS, M. and SARTIN, S. 1983 *Polite Society by Arthur Devis* [Catalogue for the Exhibition held at Harris Gallery and Museum, Preston, 1st October – 12th November 1983, and National Portrait Gallery, London, 25th November 1983 – 29th January 1984] (Preston)

THE SENHOUSE FAMILY OF NETHERHALL, MARYPORT

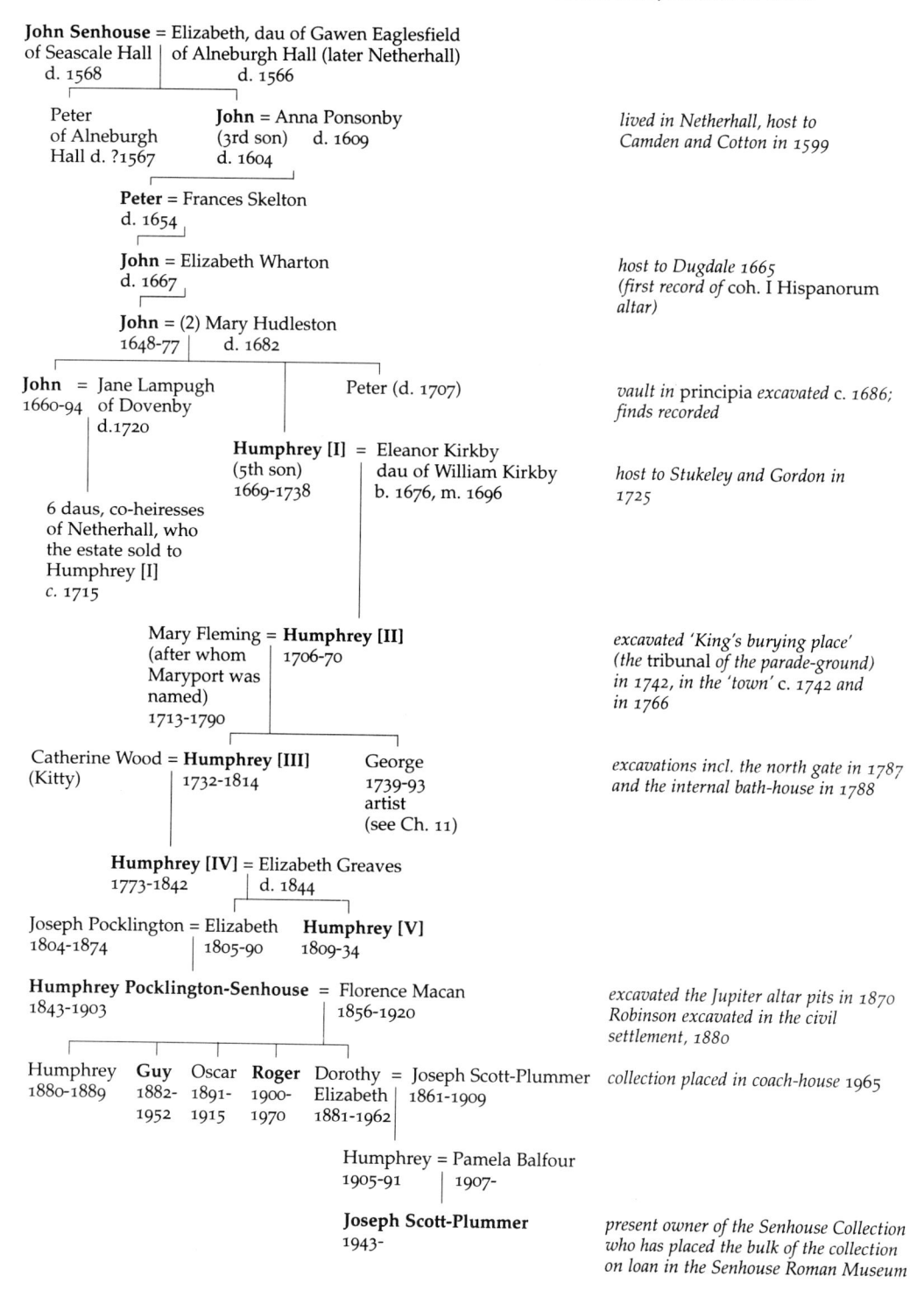

John Senhouse = Elizabeth, dau of Gawen Eaglesfield
of Seascale Hall | of Alneburgh Hall (later Netherhall)
d. 1568 | d. 1566

Peter   **John** = Anna Ponsonby   *lived in Netherhall, host to*
of Alneburgh   (3rd son)   d. 1609   *Camden and Cotton in 1599*
Hall d. ?1567   d. 1604

Peter = Frances Skelton
d. 1654

John = Elizabeth Wharton   *host to Dugdale 1665*
d. 1667   *(first record of coh. I Hispanorum altar)*

John = (2) Mary Hudleston
1648-77 | d. 1682

John = Jane Lampugh   Peter (d. 1707)   *vault in principia excavated c. 1686;*
1660-94   of Dovenby   *finds recorded*
    d.1720

               Humphrey [I] = Eleanor Kirkby
               (5th son)   dau of William Kirkby   *host to Stukeley and Gordon in*
               1669-1738   b. 1676, m. 1696   *1725*

6 daus, co-heiresses
of Netherhall, who
the estate sold to
Humphrey [I]
c. 1715

Mary Fleming = **Humphrey [II]**   *excavated 'King's burying place'*
(after whom   1706-70   *(the tribunal of the parade-ground)*
Maryport was   *in 1742, in the 'town' c. 1742 and*
named)   *in 1766*
1713-1790

Catherine Wood = **Humphrey [III]**   George   *excavations incl. the north gate in 1787*
(Kitty)   1732-1814   1739-93   *and the internal bath-house in 1788*
                           artist
                           (see Ch. 11)

Humphrey [IV] = Elizabeth Greaves
1773-1842 | d. 1844

Joseph Pocklington = Elizabeth   **Humphrey [V]**
1804-1874   1805-90   1809-34

Humphrey Pocklington-Senhouse = Florence Macan   *excavated the Jupiter altar pits in 1870*
1843-1903   1856-1920   *Robinson excavated in the civil*
                                  settlement, 1880

Humphrey   **Guy**   Oscar   **Roger**   Dorothy = Joseph Scott-Plummer   *collection placed in coach-house 1965*
1880-1889   1882-   1891-   1900-   Elizabeth   1861-1909
               1952   1915   1970   1881-1962

                         Humphrey = Pamela Balfour
                         1905-91   1907-

                         Joseph Scott-Plummer   *present owner of the Senhouse Collection*
                         1943-   *who has placed the bulk of the collection*
                                       on loan in the Senhouse Roman Museum

LIST OF CONTRIBUTORS

Ms Lindsay Allason-Jones, BA, MLitt, FSA, FSA (Scot.), MIFA, FMA
Archaeological Museums Officer, University of Newcastle upon Tyne; Trustee of the Senhouse Roman Museum
    Museum of Antiquities,
    University of Newcastle upon Tyne,
    Newcastle upon Tyne NE1 7RU.

Lt Cdr Brian G. Ashmore, MBE, RD, JP, MA, FSA
Formerly Honorary Curator, Netherhall Collection
    Waterside,
    Bladnoch,
    By Newton Stewart,
    Wigtownshire DG8 9AB.

Mr Keith Blood
Investigator, Royal Commission on the Historical Monuments of England
    Shelley House,
    Acomb Road,
    York YO2 4HB.

Dr David J. Breeze, BA, PhD, FSA, FSA (Scot.)
Chief Inspector, Historic Scotland; Visiting Professor of Roman Archaeology, University of Durham; Trustee of the Senhouse Roman Museum
    Longmore House,
    Salisbury Place,
    Edinburgh EH9 1SH.

Miss Mary E. Burkett, OBE, BA, FMA, FRGS
Formerly Director of the Lake Art Gallery and Museum and the Abbot Hall Museum, Kendal; Trustee of the Senhouse Roman Museum
    Isel Hall,
    Cockermouth,
    Cumbria CA13 0QG.

Mr Ian D. Caruana, MA
Honorary Treasurer, Trustees of the Senhouse Roman Museum
    10 Peter Street,
    Carlisle CA3 8QP.

Dr J. C. N. Coulston, MA, PhD
Lecturer in Roman Archaeology, School of Greek, Latin and Ancient History, University of St Andrews
    St Salvator's College,
    St Andrews,
    Fife KY16 9AL.

Mr P. R. Hill
Stone and Historic Building Consultant
    25 Webb Street,
    Lincoln LN5 8DL.

Ms Amy Lax, BA
Investigator, Royal Commission on the Historical Monuments of England
    Shelley House,
    Acomb Road,
    York YO2 4HB.

Professor J. C. Mann, BA, PhD, FSA
Emeritus Professor of Romano-British History and Archaeology, University of Durham
    28 St Catherine's Avenue,
    Bletchley,
    Milton Keynes MK3 5EE.

Dr David Shotter, BA, PhD, FSA
Senior Lecturer in Roman History, University of Lancaster
    Department of History,
    Lancaster University,
    Lancaster LA1 4YG.

Professor R. J. A. Wilson, MA, DPhil, FSA
(Editor)
Professor of Archaeology, University of Nottingham; Trustee of the Senhouse Roman Museum
    Department of Archaeology,
    University of Nottingham,
    Nottingham NG7 2RD.

LIST OF ILLUSTRATIONS

Half-title: Altar dedicated by Labareus to the goddess Setlocenia (*RIB* 841); ht: 74 cm (2 ft 5 in)

Frontispiece: Portrait of Michael Jarrett

1.1 Map of principal Roman sites in north-west Cumbria (all periods)
1.2 Aerial photograph of Maryport Roman fort, from the south-west
1.3 Tower 2B, Campfield, plan of excavated structures
1.4 Map showing the known and conjectured locations of milefortlets and towers near Maryport
1.5 Milefortlet 21, Swarthy Hill, plan
1.6 General plan of fort, showing the location of the parade ground and of the *vicus* structures excavated in 1880, and the find-spots of some of the inscribed and sculptured stones
1.7 Plan of the two temples uncovered in 1880 in the *vicus*
1.8 Joseph Robinson's photograph of rectangular temple under excavation, 1880
2.1 Map indicating certain and possible forts and marching camps built during the governorship of Petillius Cerialis
3.1 RCHME topographical survey: plan of the earthworks of the Roman fort
3.2 RCHME topographical survey: plan of crop-marks and other features in the fields north of the Roman fort
4.1 Dedication to Jupiter by *cohors I Hispanorum* while C. Caballius Priscus was its tribune (*RIB* 817); ht: 99 cm (3 ft 3 in)
4.2 Detail of decoration on the top of the altar dedicated by *cohors I Hispanorum* under the command of Maenius Agrippa (*RIB* 826)
4.3 Detail of decoration on the top of the altar dedicated by *cohors I Hispanorum* under the command of Helstrius Novellus (*RIB* 822)
4.4 Detail of decoration on the top of the altar dedicated by *cohors I Hispanorum* under the command of Antistius Lupus Verianus (*RIB* 816)
4.5 Detail of decoration on the top of the altar dedicated by *cohors I Hispanorum* under the command of Cammius Maximus (*RIB* 828)
4.6 Dedication to Jupiter by *cohors I Hispanorum* while Marcus Maenius Agrippa was its tribune (*RIB* 823); ht: 1.09 m (3 ft 7 in)
4.7 Dedication to Jupiter and the Divine Power of the Emperor by *cohors I Hispanorum* while Marcus Maenius Agrippa was its tribune (*RIB* 824); ht: 84 cm (2 ft 9 in)
4.8 Dedication to Jupiter, badly damaged but still legible, by Marcus Censorius Cornelianus, commanding officer of *cohors I Hispanorum* (*RIB* 814); ht: 1.07 m (3 ft 6 in)
4.9 Dedication to Jupiter by L. Cammius Maximus, prefect of *cohors I Hispanorum*, revealing his promotion to be tribune of the *cohors I Voluntariorum* (*RIB* 827); ht: 1.12 m (3 ft 8 in)
4.10 Dedications to Jupiter by *cohors I Hispanorum* while (a) L. Antistius Lupus Verianus was prefect (*RIB* 816), ht: 1.09 m (3 ft 7 in); and (b) while the prefect was Helstrius Novellus (*RIB* 822), ht: 1.12 m (3 ft 8 in)
4.11 Dedication to Jupiter on behalf of the emperor's safety by Paulus Postumius Acilianus, prefect of *cohors I Delmatarum* (*RIB* 832); width: 77 cm (2 ft 6 in)
4.12 Dedication to the Victory of the Emperor by *cohors I Baetasiorum* while its prefect was Titus Attius Tutor (*RIB* 842); ht: 94 cm (3 ft 1 in)
4.13 Dedication to the *genius loci*, to Fortune the Home-Bringer, to Eternal Rome and to Good Fate by C. Cornelius Peregrinus, tribune (*RIB* 812); ht: 1.52 m (5 ft)
6.1 Osterburken (Baden-Württemberg, Germany), reconstruction sketch of the altars dedicated by *beneficarii* as they may have appeared in a sanctuary outside the fort
6.2 Altars dedicated by *cohors I Baetasiorum* while T. Attius Tutor was its prefect: (a) to Jupiter (*RIB* 830); and (b) to Military Mars (*RIB* 837); height of both altars: 94 cm (3 ft 1 in)
6.3 Altars dedicated by *cohors I Baetasiorum* while Ulpius Titianus was its prefect: (a) to Military Mars (*RIB* 838), ht: 86 cm (2 ft 10 in); and (b) to the Emperor's Victory (*RIB* 843), ht: 94 cm (3 ft 1 in)
6.4 Detail of decoration on the top of the altar dedicated by *cohors I Hispanorum* while Lucius Cammius Maximus was its prefect (*RIB* 827); cf. Fig. 4.9
7.1 Pedestal with relief sculpture of Epona; ht: 65 cm (2 ft 2 in)

LIST OF ILLUSTRATIONS

8.1 Sculptured panel showing Victories holding up a wreath (*RIB* 844); width: 69 cm (2 ft 3 in)
8.2 Fragment of inscribed relief showing a running wild boar (*RIB* 854); width: 19.5 cm (8 in)
8.3 Inscribed panel recording *Legiones II Aug(usta)* and *XX V(aleria) V(ictix)* (*RIB* 852); width: 61 cm (2 ft)
8.4 Figure of Hercules, on the right side of an altar (*RIB* 810)
8.5 Key-stone with incised figure of Hercules; ht: 37.5 cm (1 ft 3 in)
8.6 Unfinished statue of Vulcan (?); ht: 59 cm (1 ft 11 in)
8.7 Bearded head carved in the round; ht: 38cm (1 ft 3 in)
8.8 Ithyphallic head of Mercury (?); ht: 27.5 cm (11 in)
8.9 Relief of Minerva; ht: 34.5 cm (1 ft 2 in)
8.10 Statue of Fortuna; ht: 33.5 cm (1 ft 1 in)
8.11 Female triad relief; width: 56 cm (1 ft 10 in)
8.12 Key-stone with the figure of Sol; ht: 32 cm (1 ft 1 in)
8.13 Relief depicting a horned warrior god; ht: 34 cm (1 ft 2 in)
8.14 Picked-out sketch of an armed god (ht: 24.5 cm (10 in)
8.15 Serpent Stone, both sides (a) and (b); and (c) as first found, before damage to the snakes and fishes around the face; ht: 1.24 m (4 ft. 1 in)
8.16 Gravestone of a horseman; ht: 1.34 m (4 ft 5 in)
8.17 Female torso, funerary relief; ht: 51 cm (1 ft 8 in)
8.18 Relief of Venus standing within a gate way structure; width: 46.5 cm (1 ft 6 in)
8.19 Incised phallus with evil eye (?) (*RIB* 872); width: 36 cm (1 ft 2 in)
9.1 Histogram illustrating coin-loss at Maryport
10.1 1726 Achievement of Arms, in store before conservation; ht: 1.22 m (4 ft)
11.1 Portrait of Humphrey Senhouse II (1706-1770), artist unknown (private collection)
11.2 Portrait of Mary Senhouse (1713-1790), after whom 'Mary['s] Port' is named, artist unknown (Maryport Maritime Museum)
11.3 Portrait of Humphrey Senhouse III (1732-1814), artist unknown (Maryport Maritime Museum)
11.4 Drawing of Philip Nelson by George Senhouse
11.5 Billington near Preston, 'Mad House Farm', front elevation
11.6 Billington near Preston, 'Mad House Farm', rear elevation

Photographic credits
Courtesy of Lt Cdr Brian Ashmore: Fig. 1.8; Robert Bewley: front cover aerial photograph and Fig. 1.2; Dr D. J. Breeze: Figs. 4.1, 4.9, 4.12; Dr J. C. N. Coulston: Figs. 4.2-5, 6.4, 7.1, 8.1-13, 8.17, 8.19; courtesy of Miss C. Dixon: Fig. 11.4; English Heritage: Figs. 4.6-7, 8.14, 8.15a-b, 8.16, 8.18; Lane Art Gallery: Figs. 11.1-3; courtesy of Professor W. H. Manning: frontispiece; C. L. Randall: Figs. 11.5-6; Trustees of the British Museum: Fig. 4.13; Trustees of the Senhouse Roman Museum: Figs. 4.8, 10.1; courtesy of the Board of Trinity College Dublin (photo: Brendan Dempsey): back cover photograph

Line-drawings
Fig. 1.1: David Taylor; Fig. 1.3: after *Manchester Archaeological Bulletin* 8 (1993), 35, fig. 2 (by courtesy of Professor G. B. D. Jones); Fig. 1.4: drawn by David Taylor after *Britannia* 21 (1990) 404, fig. 1; Fig. 1.5: drawn by David Taylor after *Britannia* 23 (1992) 271, fig. 9; Fig. 1.6: drawn by David Taylor after CW^1 5 (1881), plan between 236 and 237, and CW^2 15 (1915), plan facing 135; Fig. 1.7: drawn by David Taylor after R. L. Bellhouse, *Joseph Robinson of Maryport: archaeologist extraordinary* (n.d.), 47, fig. 9; Fig. 2.1: Ian Caruana; Figs. 3.1-2: Royal Commission on the Historical Monuments of England; Figs. 4.10, 4.11, 6.2-3 and half-title page (and *passim*): by courtesy of the Administrators of the Haverfield Bequest, Oxford, and their Chairman, Dr A. Bowman; Fig. 6.1: Dr E. Schallmayer (by courtesy of Dr J. Ronke); Fig. 8.15c: after Bellhouse, *Joseph Robinson of Maryport*, 41, fig. 8; Fig. 9.1: Dr David Shotter

INDEX

Only text or caption references are indexed. References therefore to specific inscriptions in *RIB* are only given here where the *RIB* numbers are cited in the text; more (unindexed) references to them will be found in the notes. *RIB* and *AE* inscription numbers are listed below in bold type to distinguish them from page reference numbers. References to the illustrations and their captions are shown in italics.

Achievement of Arms, of the Senhouses 141-6, *Fig. 10.1*
Acilianus, Paulus Postumius 68, 79-80, 93, 115, *Fig. 4.11*
AE 1922, **116** 91
aedicula, tombstone of woman set in 123
Aelia, see Proculina
Africa, north 77, 85
Agricola, Cn. Julius 40, 42, 43, 44, 46, 47, 48, 49
Agricola of Tacitus 40, 47-8, 49
Agricolan, alleged date of fort at Maryport 22, 40
Agrippa, Maenius 67, 68, 71, 72, 77, 84, 85, 92, *Figs. 4.2, 4.6-7*
ala Gallorum et Pannoniorum cataphractariorum 72
ala I Batavorum 81
ala I Tungrorum Frontoniana 81
Alauna, ancient river- and place-name 17, 26
Albinus, Clodius 102
Aldborough, probable fort at 45
Allonby Bay 52
Alneburgh (see also Ellenborough) 160
Ambleside, fort at 22, 136
Antistius Lupus Verianus, see Verianus
Antonine Wall 25, 80, 81, 83, 114, 125, 137
Antoninus Pius, see Pius
Aquincum (Budapest) 81
Ardoch, fort at 70
Asclepius (Aesculapius) 84, 107, 115
Ashmore, Lt Cdr B. G. 8, 12, 100
Attius Tutor, see Tutor

Auchendavy 105
Aurelia, see Lupula
Axelodunum 70

Baatz, D. 94
Baginton, see Lunt
Bailey, J. B. 29, 30, 48, 63, 101, 133, 134
Bar Hill, fort at 80, 83
barracks (see also Maryport, barracks) 46, 95, 105
Bath 108, 122
Battery, The, at Maryport 12, 61, 62, 63, 146, *Fig. 1.2*
Beckfoot, fort at 29, 48, 139
Belatucadrus 32, 84, 119
Bellhouse, Richard 17, 21, 134, 139, *Fig. 1.4*
beneficiarii 32, 94, 95
Biglands, milefortlet 26
Binchester, fort at 46
Birdoswald, fort at 84, 102, 136
Birley, Anthony 53, 57, 105, 107
Birley, Eric 11, 22, 43, 61, 70, 102
Billington, near Preston 154-8, *Fig. 11.5-6*
Blennerhasset, fort at 22-3, 40, 41, 48, 49, 136
boar, as emblem of *Leg. XX* 113-4, *Fig. 8.2*
Bolanus, Vettius 42, 43
Bootham Stray 44
Bordeaux 91
Bothwellhaugh, fort at 47
Boudiga, goddess 91
Boumphrey, R. S. 143
Bowes, fort at 45
Bowness, fort at 19, 139
Breeze, David 7, 24, 90, 92
Brigantes, Brigantia 42, 44, 45, 47, 49, 94
British Museum 28, *Fig. 4.13*
brooch types 41
Broomholm, fort at 46
Brougham, fort at 45, 137
Broughton-in-Cartmel 139
Brough-under-Stainmore, fort at 45
Brown, Dr John 148, 152-3
Bruce, J. Collingwood 30, 57, 60, 100-1, 126, 132, 134
Burrow Heights (Lancaster), mausoleum 122
Burrow-in-Lonsdale 45

Burrow Walls, fort at 139

Caballius, see Priscus
Caecilius, see Vegetus
Caer Gybi (Holyhead), fort at 29, 138, 139
Caerleon 70, 114
Caernarfon, fort at 29, 47
'Caesar's Pillar', at Netherhall 141-3, 145
Caerwent 108
Caledonians 43
Camden, William 17, 28, 53, 61, 112, 114, 141, 145
Camelon, fort at 46
Camerinum (Italy) 72
Cammius, see Maximus
Campfield, tower at 20-1, 26, *Fig. 1.3*
camps, see marching camps
Candida, Dea 94
Canterbury, George Senhouse posted to 153
capitularis, garment 108
Cardurnock, milefortlet at 26
Carkin Moor, possible fort at 45
Carlisle 17, 22, 40-1, 44, 45, 47, 48, 49, 108, 110, 122, 126, 137, 139, 145, 148, 154
Carrawburgh, Coventina's well at 110; mithraeum at 31
Cartimandua 42
Caruana, Ian 7, 22-3
Carvoran, fort at 21
Casey, John 42, 134
Castledykes, fort at 46, 47
Castlesteads, fort at 127, 136
Catterick 44, 45
Censorius, see Cornelianus
centurion, auxiliary 105, 107; legionary 73-4, 77, 82, 85
Cerialis, Petillius 22-3, 40-1, 42, 43, 44, 46, 136, *Fig. 2.1*
Chester 70, 108, 114
Chesters, fort at 79, 109, 124
Chesterholm (Vindolanda) 46
Chew, Dr, of Billington, and son 154-8
Christian, Mr of Ewanrigg 144, 145
Christians 90
Civilis, Julius 42, 84, 85
clothing, at Maryport 108
Clodius, see Albinus

INDEX

Clonoura (Ireland) 120
coastal defences, Cumbrian 17-23, 26, 52, 137, 139, *Fig. 1.1*
Cocceius, see Firmus
cohors I Aelia Hispanorum 70, 77
cohors I Asturum 94
cohors I Baetasiorum 67, 68, 80-1, 84, 86, 101, *Fig. 6.2-3*
cohors I Delmatarum 25, 67, 77, 79-80, 84, 115
cohors I Hispanorum 24-5, 31, 67, 68, 70-9, 82, 84-6, 101, 114, 119, *Fig. 6.4*
cohors II Flavia Brittonum 72
cohors III Bracaraugustanorum 74
cohors III Nerviorum 26, 27
cohors XVIII Voluntariorum 76, 84, *Fig. 4.9*
coins, see numismatic evidence
Colchester 41
Collingwood, R. G. 30, 53, 62, 63, 102
Corbridge (see also Red House) 46
Cordova (Cordoba) 80
Cornelianus, M. Censorius 68, 71, 73-5, 77, 78, 85, *Fig. 4.8*
Cornelius, see Gaius
Cornelius, see Peregrinus
Crackenthorpe 44
Crawford, fort at 46, 47
cremation burials, at Maryport 122
Cross Canonby 79, 158
Crosscanonby, church of St. John at 53
Croy Hill 125
Curwens, Workington family 145

Dacia 81, 85
Dalswinton, fort at 46
Daniels, Charles 21
Danube, river 29, 72, 76, 85
dendrochronology 22, 40
Dere Street, Roman road 45
Devis, Arthur, painter 148-52, 154, 156, 158-9
Dionysius, see Fortunatus
diplomas, evidence from 70, 79, 106
Dixon, Dr, of Whitehaven 155
Dixon, Miss C. 155
doctor, possible 84, 107
Dorchester, proposed move to by George Senhouse 153

Dura Europos 68

Easter Happrew, fort at 47
Eden, river valley 45
Egnatius, see Pastor
Elginhaugh, fort at 47
Ellen, river 17, 23, 29, 41, 48, 108
Ellenborough, early name for Maryport 141
Emperor, dedications to 68-9, 72, 81, 84, 93; deified, cult of 108-9
Epona 109, 118-9, *Fig. 7.1*
Euphrates, river 68
evil eye 122, *Fig. 8.19*
Exalbiovix, epithet of Mars 94
Exeter, George Senhouse walks to London from 153

Fate, Good, dedication to 27, 81, *Fig. 4.13*
Feriale Duranum 68, 84, 91
Firmus, M. Cocceius 105
Fortunatus, Dionysius, at Risingham 106
Fortune, dedication to 27, 81, 109, *Fig. 4.13*; possible representation of 117, 125, *Fig. 8.10*
Frere, S. S. 45
Frontinus, C. Julius 43, 47
Furness 139

Gaius, P. Cornelius 67, 82-3
Gale, Roger 132
Galloway 48, 52
gateway, representation of 124-5, *Fig. 8.18*
Gaul 109
Genius 116
Genius Loci, dedication to 27, 81, 94, 122, *Fig. 4.13*
German, a, at Maryport 109
Germany, frontier in (see also Mainhardt, Osterburken, Stockstadt, Taunus) 20, 29, 80, 94, 109
Gilpin, William, of Scaleby Castle 144
Goessler, P. 95
Gordian III, emperor 26, 83
Gordon, Alexander 57, 141
gravestone, see tombstone
Great Chesters 106
Greek, use of at Maryport 84, 107; of Greek extraction, people at Maryport 107, 115

Hackthorpe (Cumbria), coin hoard at 138
Hadrian, emperor 22, 72, 76, 77
Hadrianic, frontier system 17-19, 21
Hadrian's Wall 19, 21, 25, 41, 70, 79, 82, 84, 85, 105, 110, 112, 114, 124, 136
Haltonchesters 57
Hanson, W. 47
harbour facilities 22, 24, 29, 48
Hardknott, fort at 136; parade ground at 33
head, cult of 122
hearth 26, *Fig. 1.5*
Helstrius, see Novellus
Hen Waliau 29
Hengwood, Colonel 153
Hercules 115-6, 125, 126, *Fig. 8.4-5*
Hermione, dedication by 32, 97, 107, 108-9
Herodian, historian 105
Hesperides, Apples of 115
High Rochester, fort at 79, 110, 124
Hill, Peter 69, 71, 83
Hoare, William, artist 148
Hod Hill, fort at 41
Hogarth, William, artist 148
Holyhead, see Caer Gybi
Hopwood, Mrs Sylvia 158
horned god 33, 119-21, *Fig. 8.13-14*
Horsley, J. 99, 110, 141
Housesteads 110, 124, 125, 127
Hudleston, C. R. 143
Hudson, Thomas, artist 148

Ingenuus 108
Intercisa (Hungary) 125
Italy 72, 85

Jarrett, Michael 11-12, 13-16, 22, 23, 24, 29, 40, 41, 49, 53, 57, 61, 102
Jewish rebellion 74-5, 77
Jones, Barri 7, 17, 19-21, 26
Judaea 73, 74, 75, 77
Juno, dedications to 32-3, 90, 94, 107, 109
Jupiter Optimus Maximus, dedications to 32, 67-9, 70, 71, 72, 74, 77, 90, 92, 93, 94, 101, 114, *Figs. 4.1, 4.6-11, 6.2a*; representation of (?) 116, *Fig. 8.7*

INDEX

Kef, Le (Tunisia), see Sicca
Kelland, Sue and Lawrence 146
Kirkby Thore 45, 122
Kirkbride, fort at 49
Kirkby, William 149, 151, 152, 153-4
Knapton, Mr, painter 148

Labareus, a German 109
Lancaster (see also Burrow Heights) 46, 55, 122, 136, 138, 139
Langho 158
legio II Adiutrix 42, 81, 84
legio II Augusta 70, 71, 83, 113, 114, 145, *Fig. 8.3*
legio X Fretensis 73, 75, 77, 85
legio XIV 42
legio XX [Valeria Victrix] 42, 70, 71, 83, 113, 114, 145, *Fig. 8.2-3*
lettering, style of, on Maryport altars 96-8
Lewis, M. J. T. 30
lions, representations of 122, 124
Loudoun Hill, fort at 46
Low Borrow Bridge, fort at 45
Low Mire, milefortlet at 26
Lowson, John 141
Lowther Castle 28
Lowther, James 154
Lowther, Sir John 28, 144, 145, *Fig. 4.13*
Luca 108
Lunt, Baginton, fort at 41
Lupula, Aurelia 106
Lupus, Antistius, see Verianus
Lyon ware pottery 46

McIntyre, J. 44
Madge, Dr Frank 156, 158
'Mad House Farm', Billington 158, *Fig. 11.5-6*
Maeatae 102
Maenius, see Agrippa
Mainhardt (Germany) 94, 98
Malpas (Cheshire), diploma from 106
Man, Isle of 52
Manchester 45
marching camps 44-5, 48
Marcomannic War 95, 102
Marinus, Julius 107
Maritima 107
marriage, of soldiers 105-6
Mars, dedications to 67, 81, 94, 101, 120, 125, *Fig. 6.2b-3a*
Martina, Julia 107
Maryport (see also clothing; cremation burials; German, a, at; Greek, use of; lettering, style of; numismatic evidence; quarry; roads; sculptors; streets; strip buildings)
 altars 24, 27, 31-2, 52, 62, 67-86, 90-1, 92-103, 112, 114-5, 122, 126; degree of weathering of 98-100, 102; sculptural decoration on 31, 68, 71, 72, 73, 74, 77, 83, 85, 95-6, 99, 127; stone used in 98-9
 barracks 24, 60
 bastion on defences, possible 55
 baths, external 33, 64
 baths, internal 24, 60
 burials, see cemeteries
 cemeteries at 27, 33, 52, 62, 110, 113, 122, 123
 civilian settlement, see *vicus*
 commanding officer's house, see *praetorium*
 date of foundation 22-3, 48-9, 136
 defences (see also Maryport, *vicus*) 23, 49, 52, 53-9, *Fig. 3.1*
 ditches 53, 57-8
 fort gates 23, 29, 30, 52, 53, 55, 58-9, 61, 62, 63, 64, 99
 granary 60
 harbour facilities at 22-3, 48
 headquarters' building 23, 33, 59-60, 114
 in fourth century 24, 26, 33, 55
 in third century 24, 26, 30, 33, 63, 81-3
 latrine, possible location of 56
 length of occupation at 24
 mansio (?) 64
 mithraeum, alleged 31
 modern, Curzon Street in 99; Midland Bank at 99; Queen's Head Inn 134; Senhouse Street in 99
 position of Hadrianic fort 17, 52, *Fig. 1.2*
 praetentura 57, 60, 61
 praetorium (commanding officer's house) 24, 53, 59, 61
 pre-Hadrianic fort, possible site of 22-3, 48-9
 principia, see headquarters' building
 reduction in size of garrison, possible 24-5, 70, 73-4
 relationship to Cumbrian coastal defences 21
 retentura 57, 60, 61
 river fortification (?) 28-9
 sculpture (see also Maryport, altars, sculptural decoration on) 32, 62, 101, 110, 112-31, 144, 145; stone used in 126
 size of Hadrianic fort 17, 24-5, 53, 70-1
 storebuilding (?) 24
 strong-room 23-4, 59-60
 temples 30-2, 62-3, 69, 114, *Fig. 1.7-8, Fig. 3.2*
 via principalis 59, 60
 via praetoria 60
 vicus (civilian settlement) 17, 29-33, 52, 62-4, 103, 105, 106, 107, 113, *fig. 1.6*; defences of (?) 30, 63; temples in, see Maryport, temples
 well 23, 33, 60
 women at 105-111
 workshop (?) 60
Matres, see mother goddesses
Mauretania Caesariensis 81
mausolea 122
Maximus, L. Cammius 24, 68, 70, 71, 74, 76-7, 78, 83, 84, 99, *Figs. 4.5, 4.9, 6.4*
Mercury (?) 116-7, *Fig. 8.8*
Midlothian 108
milefortlets, on Cumbrian defences 19, 21, 23, 134, *Fig. 1.5*
Minerva 110, 117, *Fig. 8.9*
mithraeum, at Carrawburgh 31; at Maryport, alleged 31
Moesia 72, 85
Moresby, fort at 21-2, 139
Morirex 108
Mote Hill, milefortlet at 134, 139
mother-goddess, reliefs of 32, 94, 108, 110, 117
Muncaster Castle 139
Mytton Fold Farm, see 'Mad House Farm'

Nelson, Philip, steward to Senhouses 155, *Fig. 11.4*

INDEX

Nemausus (Gaul) 73
Neptune (?) 116, *Fig. 8.7*
Netherby 70
Netherhall 8, 12, 99, 101, 132, 141-5, 160
Newstead, fort at 46, 47
Nîmes, see Nemausus
Noricum 77, 81, 85
Notitia Dignitatum 26, 80, 82
Novellus, Helstrius 67, 68, 71, 77, *Figs. 4.3, 4.10b*
numismatic evidence, at Maryport 22, 24, 26, 27, 42, 132-9; elsewhere 41, 45-6
Nymphs 117, *Fig. 8.11*

officers, commanding, average length of service in post 79, 85
Ogilvie, R. M. 46
Old Carlisle, fort at 29, 41, 62, 63, 108, 137
Old Kilpatrick, fort at 80
Old Penrith, fort at 45, 46, 48
optio, at Maryport 85
Osterburken (Germany) 32, 69, 93-4, 98, *Fig. 6.1*
oven 26

palisade, as part of defences 19
Pannonia 76, 85
Papcastle, fort at 41, 132, 136, 137
parade ground 32, 33, 52, 69, 70, 93, 94, 95, 98, 102, 103, *Fig. 1.6*
Paret, O. 95
Pastor, A. Egnatius 107, 115
Pattinson, Kevin 146
Pen Llystyn, fort at 47
Peregrinus, C. Cornelius 81-2, 85
Petillius Cerealis, see Cerialis
phalera, of copper 114
phallus 122, 126, *Fig. 8.19*
pine-cone, sculpture of 122, 124
Pius, Antoninus, emperor 25, 70, 79, 80, 86 93, 94, 143
Pliny (the Elder), author of *Naturalis Historia* 43
Pliny (the Younger), governor of Bithynia 69
Plummer, Joseph Scott 8, 12, 146
Plumpton Head 44
Pompeii 117
Postumius, see Acilianus
Potter, T. W. 7, 22, 46
praetoria, in forts (see also Maryport, *praetorium*) 105

prefect (*praefectus*), as title of commanding officer 25, 67, 68, 70, 72, 73-4, 75, 77, 82, 84, 85, 95, 101, 114, *Figs. 4.9-12, 6.2-4*
Priscus, C. Caballius 31, 67, 68, 71, 72-3, 74, 77, 92, 97, *Fig. 4.1*
Proculina, Aelia 109
procurator 80, 82, 85
procuratorship of Britain, held by Maenius Agrippa 72
Provence (see also Nemausus) 85
Pudding Pie Hill (see also *tribunal*) 33

quarry, at Maryport, ancient (?) 52, 102; modern 33, 52, 62, 64, 112
Quebec (Canada) 156
Quintus, father of Hermione 97, 107

Raeburnfoot, fortlet at 47
Ravenglass, fort at 136, 138, 139
Read, Matthias, painter 144, 145, 146
Reculver, fort at 80
Red House, near Corbridge, fort at 46
Reece, Richard 135
Reed, N. 48
Regiment of Foot, 20th 153, 156
Regina, at South Shields 108
Rey Cross 44
Reynolds, Sir Joshua, painter 148
Rhine, river 29, 42
Rianorix 108
RIB 810 109; **811** 109; **812** 27-8, 109, 145, *Fig. 4.13*; **813** 32, 97; **814** *Fig. 4.8*; **815** 91; **816** *Figs. 4.4, 4.10a*; **817** 72, 92, *Fig. 4.1*; **819** 92, 97; **820** 31; **822** *Figs. 4.3, 4.10b*; **823** 99, *Fig. 4.6*; **824** 101, 102, *Fig. 4.7*; **825** 92; **826** 101, 102, *Fig. 4.2*; **827** 76, 99, 101, 102, *Figs. 4.9, 6.4*; **828** 99, *Fig. 4.5*; **830** 95, 96, 97, *Fig. 6.2a*; **832** 136, *Fig. 4.11*; **834** 99; **836** 31; **837** 95, 96, 99, *Fig. 6.2b*; **838** 97, *Fig. 6.3a*; **840** 109; **841** 109; **842** 95, 96, 97, *Fig. 4.12*; **843** 97, 101, *Fig. 6.3b*; **844** 109; **845** 97; **852** 145, *Fig. 8.3*; **853** 42; **854** 26; **859** 41; **872** *Fig. 8.19*; **2030** 145
Ribchester 45, 46

Richborough 46
Richmond, Sir Ian 12, 44, 46
Rise How, tower 21, *Fig. 1.4*
Risehow, tower *Fig. 1.4*
Risingham 106, 109
roads (see also Dere Street; Maryport, *via principalis, via praetoria*; streets) 29-30, 41, 47, 52, 60, 62, 63-4, *Fig. 1.6*
robber trenches, see stone-robbing
Robinson, Joseph 29, 30, 32, 62, *Fig. 1.7-8*
Roma, representation of 125
Rome, Eternal, dedication to 27, 81, 109, *Fig. 4.13*
Rooke, Hayman 58
Routh, Thomas 132

St Bees Head 19, 99
St Joseph, Kenneth 29
St Paul's Cathedral (London), George Senhouse at 149
Saldae (Bejaia, Algeria) 81
Salway, Peter 29, 30
samian pottery 40-1, 45, 46, 47
sculptors, stonemasons 68, 97-8, 114-5, 126-7
Senecianus, Julius, husband of Sotera 107
Senhouses 11-12, 17, 53, 59, 62, 99, 112, 132, 160; Achievement of Arms 141-6, *Fig. 10.1*
Senhouse, Elizabeth 145, 160
Senhouse, George 148-59, 160
Senhouse, Humphrey (1669-1738) 132, 160
Senhouse, Humphrey (1706-1770) 53, 141-5, 148, 149, 153, 154, 160, *Fig. 11.1*
Senhouse, Humphrey (1732-1814) 58, 60, 61, 110, 148, 160, *Fig. 11.3*
Senhouse, Humphrey Pocklington 32, 67, 100, 144, 145, 160
Senhouse, John 28, 53, 112, 160, *Fig. 4.13*
Senhouse, Mary 148, 160, *Fig. 11.2*
Senhouse, Roger 8, 11, 143, 160
Serpent Stone 33, 62, 112, 121-3, *Fig. 8.15*
Setlocenia 32, 109, 119, *Fig.* on half-title and chapter heads

168 INDEX

Severus, Iulius, governor of Britain 74-5, 77, 85
Severus, Septimius, emperor 105
shield-type 120-1
shoes 41
Shotter, David 22, 26
Sicca (Le Kef, Tunisia) 77
sig(nifer), stone inscribed 30, 84, 126
signum (personal name) 81-2
Silloth 63
Sirmium (Serbia) 32, 69, 95, 98, 102
Sloss, Dr David 156-8
Smith, father and son, stonecarvers 141, 143, 144, 145
snakes, representation of 122
Sol 118, *Fig. 8.12*
Solva (Noricum), *origo* of Cammius Maximus and T. Attius Tutor 77, 81
Solway Plain 41, 136
Solway Firth 52
Sotera, wife of Julius Senecianus 107
South Shields, fort at 24, 94, 108, 122
Spain (see also Cordova), unit raised in 70; *origo* in 85
Stainmore Pass 44, 45
Stanegate, Trajanic *limes* 22, 136
Stanwick 44
Stanwix, fort at 17, 24, 145
Statius, author of *Silvae* 43
Stockstadt (Germany) 94, 98
stonemasons, see sculptors
stone-robbing 53, 55-7, 58, 59, 60, 61, 62, 99
Strageath, fort at 47
Stratfield, Mr, artist 148
streets (see also roads) 29, 31
strip buildings 29, 30, 62, 64

Stukeley, William 29, 58, 61, 62, 132, 133
Swarthy Hill, milefortlet 21, 26, 139, *Fig. 1.5*

Tacitus (see also *Agricola*) 42, 47-8
Tancorix, at Old Carlisle 108
Tara (Ireland), Lia Fáil at 122
Taunus *limes* (Germany) 19
temples, see Maryport, temples
temporary camps, see marching camps
terra nigra pottery 46
Thompson, J., brother-in-law of Humphrey Senhouse (1706-1770) 154
Thynne, Captain William 149
Titianus, Ulpius 68, 81, 97-8, *Fig. 6.3*
tombstone 27, 41, 83, 107-8, 110, 121, 123-4, 127, *Fig. 8.16-17*
toolmarks, tools used in sculpture 99, 127
torque 122
towers, on Cumbrian coastal defences 19, 20-21, 23, 26
Toynbee, Jocelyn 12
Trajan, emperor 69, 135
Trajanic, possible foundation-date of Maryport fort 22, 23
tribunal mound (see also Pudding Pie Hill) 70, 93, 94
tribune (*tribunus*), as title of commanding officer 24, 25, 67, 70, 72-3, 76, 77, 82, 83, 84, 95, *Figs. 4.1, 4.6-7, 4.9, 4.13*
Turoe stone (Ireland) 122
Tutor, T. Attius 67, 68, 81, 84, 85, 95-7, 98, *Figs. 4.12, 6.2-3*
Twentieth Legion, see *legio XX*

Ulpius, see Titianus

Vacia 106
Valour, of Emperor, dedication to 107
Vegetus, Caecilius 67, 68, 80
Velva, Julia, at York 108
Venus 110, 117, 125, *Figs. 8.11, 8.18*
Venutius 42, 43, 44, 45
Verianus, L. Antistius Lupus 67, 68, 71, 74, 77, *Figs. 4.4, 4.10a*
Verona 72
Verulamium, King Harry Lane 41
Vespasian, emperor 42
Victory, dedications to 67, 81, 94, *Figs. 4.12, 6.3b*; representation of 109, 112, 114, 125, *Fig. 8.1*
vicus, see Maryport, *vicus*; elsewhere, 105, 106, 107
Vindolanda, see Chesterholm
Vireius Pau..., tombstone of 41
Virtue, of Emperor 108-9
Volantius (*signum*) 81
Vulcan 77, 116, 126, *Fig. 8.6*

Walton-le-Dale 46
water supply 33, 64
Watercrook, fort at 22, 46, 136
Wenham, L. P. 32, 98
Whitehaven 144, 145
Wigglesworth, Mrs, visits George Senhouse 156
William, Rev. M. 144
Winds, representations of 122
Winskell, Cyril, architect 146
Wolfe, General James 153, 156
Workington 145
Wroxeter 45
Wyck, Jan, painter 144

York 44, 45, 46, 91, 108, 122; Minster, George Senhouse at 149

NETHE

Mou

Sea Brows

Pipeherd Hill

Borough Fields

Serpent Stone X
No 55

Roman Road to Carlisle

(1880) X Altar No 30
x Altar No 37
○ ☐ Temple

as Works

X altar
No 32

X No. 60 altar

Roman Fort
○ Well

Pigeon

Pudding Pie Hill

Campus Martius

Barfold

Roman Road to

Ox Close